... DRUG AGENTS:
A THANKLESS JOB . . . AND A
DEADLY ONE

The undercover agents handed over the money to Kow and Wang. The two criminals then nodded at each other and opened fire at point-blank range, hitting Seema and Montoya in the head, killing them instantly, and wounding Martinez, who managed to return fire as his cover closed in. The murderers climbed in the Nissan and tore away. The entire incident had taken about thirty seconds.

Blue lights flashing, sirens wailing, two government vehicles rammed the Nissan in an attempt to prevent flight. No good. Muzzle flashes lit up the sky as both sides shot at each other. A high-speed chase through three communities followed, with the pursuers finally forcing the Nissan off the road. They exchanged heavy gunfire, and when the smoke cleared Kow and the driver were dead and Wang was critically wounded.

The agents recovered a .45, extra magazines of ammo, ski masks and a quantity of heroin. What they could never recover were the lives of Seema and Montoya. . . .

DRUG AGENT
U.S.A.

Richard F. Radford
and
John D. (Jack) Crowley

ST. MARTIN'S PAPERBACKS

To Lynne Radford, my wife and helpmate . . . *de colores*! And to Amy and Richard III, who collaborate as my conscience and sense of humor.

—RFR

To Jane Marie and Janerie

—JDC

DRUG AGENT U.S.A.

Copyright © 1989 by Richard F. Radford and John Crowley.

ISBN: 0-312-92326-0

Printed in the United States of America

St. Martin's Paperbacks edition/January 1991

10 9 8 7 6 5 4 3 2 1

Acknowledgments

We are indebted to the following people for their assistance: Los Angeles attorney Richard H. Borow for his encouragement and suggestions; Bob Sullivan of the Brookline Public Library for his humanity, kindness, and research help; Officer Gerry O'Donnell, BPD; Educator Vincent Hughs for going into the sewer; Pharmacist Robert Pittman for his private research; Tony Flaherty, MHFA; Gerry Trombley for his expertise and unfailing optimism; "Benny" Sullivan for sharing his experience; and all the unsung heroes at Middlesex Street.

We would especially like to salute the following individuals whose help and dedication are second to none:

Matthew "Matty" Seifer
Kathleen A. Shannon
Robert M. Sampson
Walter "Red Eyes" Houghton
Patrick "Sleepwalker" Hunt
Edward "Fast Eddie" Sullivan
Harold "Hurricane Hal" Mosher
Kathi "Little Kas" Sullivan
Janet "Killer" Gardner
Edward "Easy Ed" Harrington
Margaret "O'D" deWeerd
John J.R. "Senator" Cavendish
Maria "Cheshire Cat" DeMasi
Jo Anne "Jammer" Masar
John Amico
Barbara M. Menhart

Contents

Prologue

IT SHOULD HAVE BEEN A ROUTINE BUY—IF there is such a thing as a routine undercover buy. But something went wrong. When the three Los Angeles special agents—George Montoya, Paul Seema and Jose Martinez—traveled out to a wealthy Pasadena neighborhood that early February day, they weren't admiring the fancy houses. They were there to negotiate a $160,000 heroin purchase from Wen Huei Kow, a trusted distributor for a major supplier of heroin from Southeast Asia's Golden Triangle. But Kow had more than a sale on his agenda.

Seema had been working on Kow for four months, holding innumerable telephone conversations with him and meeting him under surveillance several times. He knew that Kow was regularly receiving shipments of Thai heroin through the mail; he knew that Kow was also associated with a number of LA street gangs. And he knew that Kow was ready to deal.

The cautious game of cat and mouse that all high-level dealers play spun itself out during those months as Seema and his associates played it cool and waited for their opportunity. They could not risk appearing too eager. A veteran of the DEA, Seema let his frustrations with the pace of the case disappear when he went home to his family or spent long hours fishing. He knew his time would come. His partner George Montoya was more impatient, a new agent. But

Seema was happy to have him on his side; he handled himself well and was one of the top five shots in his academy class.

Then, on February 2, Seema got a call on the office undercover phone. He was told that Kow would be able to deliver two pounds of high purity heroin to him that week. Kow would call from a hotel on the 5th to set up delivery. The price was five grand an ounce. The agents got ready to close the deal.

The DEA office sent a team of seven special agents to establish prebuy surveillance of Kow's residence in Monterey Park. When Kow called and set up a meet at the nearby Tiny Naylor's restaurant, Seema, Montoya and Agent Jose Martinez proceeded to the location, Martinez in the back seat with the flash money. Though Seema had never observed Kow carrying a piece, the DEA nevertheless assigned an additional twelve surveillance vehicles to cover any eventuality. They would need them.

At the restaurant Martinez flashed the money. Kow said he had the H at a house in Pasadena. The buyers should drive him there, he said, wait out front, and he would bring it to them. Seema had spent fourteen years in Bangkok, so he carried on the discussion with Kow in fluent Thai. He had every reason to believe that he had won Kow's confidence over the four months and that the buy would go down. The night before, DEA agents on surveillance at Kow's house had observed the delivery of a plastic-wrapped package consistent with the size of a two-pound bag of heroin. They also spotted an automatic pistol tucked in Kow's waistband. They could have moved at that point, but the agents needed the buy to confirm. Anything less and they would risk not having enough evidence for a conviction. What Seema didn't know was that Kow had no intention of selling. He was conducting a sting of his own.

They arrived at the Pasadena house, tense but confident. Kow got out of the car and walked across the lawn. The agents felt as secure as they could in such a dangerous situation. Two surveillance vehicles were parked a few yards ahead. They knew all procedures were being followed; they knew there were five other DEA men in direct contact as well as nine other DEA and narc unit officers backing up. They had arranged arrest signals, trouble signals and operational alternatives in a briefing earlier that day. What they didn't know was that the backups had spotted two counter-surveillance cars, a black Mitsubishi and a red Nissan, driven by Kow's associates. The extra vehicles could only mean trouble.

The house was in a secluded area away from heavy traffic. Kow had been relaxed and jovial discussing the buy on the way over. What happened next proved that in the world of undercover drug buys even the most prepared bust is fraught with danger.

As Kow crossed the lawn the red Nissan roared up. William Wang exited the passenger side and walked toward the buy car. At the same time Kow turned, pulling his automatic pistol, and started back toward the car. Backup officers immediately gave the signal to abort surveillance and effect immediate arrests.

Kow and Wang demanded the money as the backup team moved in. The undercover agents handed over the money. Kow and Wang then nodded at each other and opened fire at point-blank range, hitting Seema and Montoya in the head, killing them instantly, and wounding Martinez, who managed to return fire as his cover closed in. The murderers climbed in the Nissan and tore away. The entire incident had taken about thirty seconds.

Blue lights flashing, sirens wailing, two government vehicles rammed the Nissan in an attempt to prevent flight. No good. Muzzle flashes lit up the sky as both sides shot at each other. A high-speed chase through three communities followed, the vehicles reaching speeds of up to 90 miles per hour. The pursuers finally forced the Nissan off the road. They exchanged heavy gunfire, and when the smoke cleared Kow and the driver were dead and Wang was critically wounded.

The agents recovered a .45, extra magazines of ammo, ski

masks and a quantity of heroin. What they could never recover were the lives of Seema and Montoya.

On April 19, 1988, in a service at the White House, President Ronald Reagan honored the men who had given their
lives in the struggle against drugs. At the service Special
Agent Jose Martinez spoke about the men who had accompanied him on that fateful day in February: "Paul Seema
and George Montoya were victims of society's desire for
drugs. Not until people quit using drugs will it become safer
for those of us in law enforcement and the rest of society."

No epitaph would be better at describing what a drug
agent has to keep in mind every day of his working life.

Introduction

I DON'T HAVE TO TELL PEOPLE THAT DRUG abuse has become one of America's biggest problems. Look at any newspaper on any day and you're almost certain to read of a tragedy caused by what is fast turning into America's pastime. The public has become used to seeing the words "heroin," "cocaine," and "marijuana" on a daily basis. The crack epidemic and the problem of drug use in sports has only served to heighten our awareness that what was once a fringe problem has now become mainstream. Battling the distribution and use of illegal drugs has engaged the considerable attention of drug agents throughout the country.

Justifiably, the public has shown tremendous concern about the effects of these drugs on society. But what the public does not realize is that half the reported drug deaths in this country are attributable to overdoses of *prescription* drugs. In order to truly understand the task the drug agent faces in his battle with the problem, we have to view the whole picture. The media understandably give a lot of time and attention to the thousands of tons of drugs flowing into this country from illicit foreign sources. Hardly a day passes that we don't see dramatic pictures of bales of marijuana seized in California or a Miami coke bust. Nightly news shows feature a grisly scene of a kid in an alley in Dallas, dead from an overdose of South American cocaine. But fully

50 percent of drug overdose deaths reported in this country are overdoses of prescription drugs—and the stress here is on "reported." How many OD deaths are covered up, are misdiagnosed or simply go unreported?

As a supervisor for the Drug Enforcement Administration, my first concern is about the sheer size of the problem. From an enforcement point of view, the numbers are staggering. There are approximately 800,000 registrants in the United States—that is, over three-quarters of a million legally registered pharmacies, doctors, manufacturers, distributors and others who handle, somewhere along the line, drugs listed under the Controlled Substances Act. All of these registrants are potential diverters, people who divert legal drugs to an illegal end, so the logistics of tracking down a crooked handler are mind-boggling.

Add to the problem of this number the fact that there are several thousand different drugs listed under the Controlled Substances Act. Those several thousand items factor out to about twenty billion dosage units of drugs that can, as the DEA says, "have a substantial and detrimental effect on the health and welfare of the American people."

Obviously, not all the drugs are ending up where they're supposed to. Of the twenty billion legally produced dosage units, estimates range from a low of 250 million to a high of 650 million dosage units diverted into the illicit market annually. That's a lot of pills.

To get an idea of the enormity of the job facing the DEA and the other drug enforcement agencies, let's forget for the moment all the street stuff that comes in by boat or plane or the stuff being manufactured in garages, and consider for now just the domestic problem of diverted "legal" drugs. In New England, for example, the numbers are heavily stacked against the good guys. Until very recently there were only four federal diversion investigators assigned to the entire six-state region! In Massachusetts alone, a small state in geographic area, there are twenty-one thousand medical practitioners. Disregarding motives of greed or of the power that money can buy, even the most conservative estimators conclude that at least 4 percent of them are impaired due to drug abuse. And a minimum of another 10 percent are suffering from alcoholism. Now, if only 10 percent of that 10 percent are dishonest—or are forced into crime to support their own drug habits—we still have 210 doctors in the state with a high potentiality for writing bogus prescriptions. This doesn't even take into account the retail pharmacies and other outlets for drug diversion.

You can do your own multiplying to come up with an approximation of the problem nationally. By prescribing or ordering drugs for diversion purposes, these supposedly legitimate sources are pushing one hell of a volume of drugs onto the streets of this nation and, combined with foreign sources of illicit drugs, lining up a formidable array of enemies for the soldiers who wage war against them.

Make no mistake—there is a war going on, a war against evil being waged all over the country. But who are the good guys?

How does the DEA do battle with the staggering number of pushers, crooked pharmacists and smugglers on the other side?

Sired by the former Bureau of Narcotics and Dangerous Drugs (BNDD), now in the Department of Justice, the DEA came into existence in 1973 under the Nixon administration. Made up of attorneys, intelligence analysts, chemists and various administrative and support personnel as well as field operatives, the DEA is this country's leading federal force in the drug war. There are roughly three thousand five hundred field operatives, divided between special agents (SA) and diversion investigators (DI).

Special agents attempt to interdict the flow of illicit drugs into this country from Europe, Asia and the Americas, with special emphasis on heroin, cocaine and marijuana. Special agents also attempt to locate and destroy domestic clandestine laboratories. A relatively recent phenomenon, these modern "designer drug" stills illicitly manufacture anything from hallucinogens to common speed, and are constantly inventing dangerous new drug permutations by altering chemical formulae. DEA special agents conduct, then, criminal investigations and prepare for the prosecution of major violators of the Controlled Substances Act.

Empowered to develop and handle informants and generally do anything necessary to carry out their duties under the law, such as conduct surveillance activities and make undercover purchases for evidence, SAs carry firearms and have full arrest powers because their duties are frequently hazardous.

Diversion investigators, on the other hand, monitor the legitimate side of licensed domestic commerce in controlled substances. DIs identify and immobilize diverters. A diverter is anyone who disrupts the flow of drugs in their normal course between legal manufacturer and legitimate customer. DIs do not carry firearms, conduct regular surveillance activities or make physical arrests. Nor do they actually control informants, though they certainly can respond to information received from confidential sources. DIs conduct a full range of investigations involving anything to do with registrants and protect the public against the diversion of harmful controlled substances into the illegal drug market.

Registrants—the retail pharmacies, doctors, hospitals, researchers, wholesalers, distributors and manufacturers noted earlier—are all required to register with the DEA under the Controlled Substances Act. Investigations by DIs may result in civil or administrative actions or lead directly to criminal prosecution. Administrative actions include license revocations, suspensions or denials of permits and other bureaucratic niceties. Seizure of goods and forfeiture of property is a strong weapon.

Recently, the United States enacted the Chemical Diversion and Trafficking Act which has given the DEA new powers for controlling chemical diversion. The DIs' weapons are more cerebral than physical, but aligned with the SAs they make an effective DEA team. Unfortunately, in spite of the effective DEA investigators and the cooperation of the agencies they work with, the odds heavily favor the criminal. Though these odds may seem staggering at times, the DEA and various state agencies are staffed for the most part by highly dedicated and competent professionals. And, as I repeatedly affirm, the cooperation of those people among agencies is a mighty weapon in the drug-fighter's arsenal.

I've worked especially hard to develop working harmony with other law enforcement and regulatory agencies in order to get the job done. Formally called federal/state liaison, for me it simply means being as helpful to and as friendly with the local authorities as I possibly can, keeping the lines of communication open. I work jointly, sharing my information, and hoping for quid pro quo, with state and local police departments, Board of Pharmacy agents and others, hoping to immobilize the registrant criminals. This way I'm able to minimize my weaknesses and maximize my strengths. It works.

Given the human element, and the fact that career ambition is almost always a factor, you can get caught in the stampede when it's time to roll the credits at the successful conclusion of a case. The ironic thing is that the credit gets shared eventually, anyway. Even when the public sees a uniformed trooper, for example, make the physical arrest on TV during a drug bust, we still get plenty of kudos within our own organization for having set it up, and a guarantee of future cooperation from the states for having worked jointly. Cooperative cases require special types of investigators who are seasoned, experienced, knowledgeable and flexible—willing to fill a role. The best investigators know that they can't lead every case, so they simply do what it takes to get the job done. The success of the case has to be the overriding factor.

In the stories that follow, you will read about some of the most dramatic investigations that my colleagues and I have been involved in. Some of them were solo efforts; most required the invaluable help of others, from state and local agencies to informants. But as far as I am concerned only one thing counts—not the brownie points, but seeing the bad guys get locked up. That is the only event that gives me the satisfaction that we are making any headway in the war.

The chapters in this book highlight the kinds of investigations that special agents and diversion investigators regularly conduct—cases involving pharmaceutical controlled substances, heroin, cocaine, marijuana smuggling, clandestine laboratories, undercover operations, reverse undercover "Sting" operations, physician/pharmacy conspiracies, burglaries of pharmaceutical distributors, internal theft of controlled drugs by means of computer fraud, corruption, and undercover "buy" operations gone awry. They will bring you, the reader, into focus with many of the drugs of abuse covered by the Controlled Substances Act, including narcotics, stimulants, depressants, cannabis and hallucinogens; trade names, generic names and other slang names—and, of course, the types of investigations that deal with them. Happy reading!

1 Ye Olde Apothecary Shoppe

A FEW YEARS AGO I WAS SITTING IN THE BOSton office of the Drug Enforcement Administration, going over reports with my colleague Mark Caverly, when one of those calls that convince me of my dumb Irish luck came in. This call ultimately allowed me to help bag two of the slimiest medical practitioners this side of Dr. Frankenstein, though I certainly didn't know it at the time. Thinking it was a crank call, Mark smiled and handed me the phone.

"Jack Crowley," I barked, hoping to cut it short.

The angry young caller identified himself as a doctor at Massachusetts General, one of the world's foremost teaching hospitals.

"What can we do for you, Doc?" I said, resisting the urge to ask "what's up?"

"I'm treating a female patient for abscesses on her arms," he said abruptly.

"Drug injections?"

"Arms like pincushions," he said. "Obvious junkie." It wasn't a crank call after all.

"Sounds like one for the Boston Police, Doc," I said. "Or referral to rehab—not the DEA."

"Except, she's named a registered Massachusetts pharmacist as her pusher."

"She say she got the drugs without prescriptions?"

"That's only half of it."

Alarm bells went off in my head. I threw a pencil at Mark, signaling him to pick up his extension, before I asked:

"Pharmacist's name?"

"Manny Botenkranz."

I thought I'd heard a lot of that name in the past; over the next few months I was going to hear even more.

"Don't let her out of your sight!" I said, moving out.

The Mass General complex is just a stone's throw from DEA Boston headquarters. We practically flew down traffic-congested Cambridge Street. I didn't want to take a chance on the junkie changing her mind and walking out of treatment. I wanted Manny Botenkranz.

Thinking over the circumstances of the phone call, I thought about that dumb Irish luck of mine. Manny was the type of garbage any drug officer would love to dump, and here was what looked like my chance. Out of eight thousand pharmacists and twelve hundred retail pharmacies in Massachusetts, I had stumbled across a potential case against the worst-known reflection on the profession. He was the kind of guy who made you want to change the rules.

The thing I've taken the most pride in since beginning in government service and the DEA is my professional objectivity, especially an ability to maintain that objectivity in the presence of the stench of the rotten human garbage I've had to handle during my career. Objectivity *uber alles*. But this case involving high-volume illicit drugs and Emanuel "Manny" Botenkranz was different, a real challenge. Manny was so rotten that dealing with him just blew my objectivity out of the water.

I had first heard of Manny Botenkranz about ten years previously, when two of my DEA colleagues initiated a diversion case against him. Special Agent Bobby Sampson and Diversion Investigator Walter "Red Eyes" Houghton were the first DEA people to encounter Manny and his whiz-bang feelgood operation out of the Apotheka, his retail pharmacy on West Broadway, in South Boston. The good guys were turned on to the case by Charles Adelsberger, distribution manager for Wyeth Laboratories, a large pharmaceutical company north of Boston. We'll hear more about Wyeth later. Adelsberger had called our office to compare lot numbers on a quantity of controlled drugs he suspected might be from a stolen shipment.

The distributor's suspicions were first aroused because of the quantity; a retail customer wanted to return an unusually large amount of drugs to his company for credit. Adelsberger traced some random lot numbers through us to see if they coincided with any heisted drug shipments. Lo and behold, the drugs being returned for credit from the Apotheka in South Boston, Manny Botenkranz, proprietor, were drugs that had been stolen from Wyeth's Andover lab in the first place! Technically, the drugs hadn't been stolen from the lab, but from the loading docks of P. A. Milan, the shipping company to which they'd been consigned. Sampson and Red Eyes put their heads together with the distribution manager. Further tracking revealed that Botenkranz had made *no* purchases during the period in question of *any* of the drugs he wished to return. The only way Botenkranz could now be in possession of those specific drugs was to have knowingly purchased stolen material or to have stolen them himself.

A further irony was that quantities of two drugs from the stolen shipment—the depressant Equanil and the federally noncontrolled prescription drug Omniprin—were discovered to be among those that had *already* been involved in a botched attempt at return for credit to Wyeth—just the month previous. Apparently greed can overcome even basic common sense.

Pursuant to obtaining an administrative inspection warrant, Red Eyes and Sampson conducted an accountability investigation at Botenkranz's Apotheka. They uncovered numerous violations of drug laws as well as large discrepancies between amounts of drugs purchased and amounts dispensed. According to procedure the results of the investigation were written up and forwarded to the US attorney's office. That was in July.

In October a federal grand jury convened to hear testimony concerning the DEA investigation of activities at the Apotheka in South Boston, a tight-knit working-class neighborhood of three-family homes mixed with heavy industry around Boston harbor. Besides being the operating base of Manny Botenkranz, it is also infamous as one of the old battlegrounds for school busing over segregation. Primarily Irish, its residents tend to be clannish, regardless of background.

Then a kink developed. For some unaccountable reason, David Twomey, the assistant US attorney assigned the Botenkranz case, became noticeably uncooperative with the DEA investigators. Not only was Twomey not volunteering information to colleagues working the case, but our people felt he was even withholding crucial facts. This can occur temporarily in any agency when there are ego clashes or petty jurisdictional disputes, but that didn't seem true in this instance. Whatever his reason, Twomey just wasn't pursuing the Botenkranz case with normal expedience, let alone with fervor. So in mid-November the Boston office of the DEA prepared a formal memorandum requesting a special prosecution from the office of chief counsel (DEA headquarters). They wanted Twomey off the case.

I was just an observer at this point, handling my own caseload, sharing in the office scuttlebutt and listening to the woes of Sampson and Houghton while relaxing after work. The two agents were constantly badmouthing Twomey for noncooperation. When they began to magnify his smallest personal defects, adding those to the pile of his alleged ethical lapses, their carping started to sound like sour grapes to me. I decided I liked Bobby and Red Eyes, but I wouldn't want to have them against me.

When Houghton and Sampson went so far as to speculate that Twomey was bagging the case for Botenkranz because they were fellow South Bostonians, I figured they were simply justifying what had been a poorly prepared case on their part. I figured maybe their egos wouldn't allow them to admit they hadn't put the case in sufficiently prosecutable form and were laying off the blame on the attorney. Shifting

responsibility can be a highly developed skill in a bureaucracy. In any event, the case got lost somewhere in the paper
shuffle and when enough time had passed eventually closed
with the stamp: *No Action*. US Attorney Twomey then
slipped from my mind as we got busy with new problems. It
wasn't until much later that we learned the assistant had for
years been the best soldier the underworld had.

In the busy years that followed, Manny Botenkranz's
name periodically surfaced at the DEA. He always seemed
to be on the fringe of some illegal activity, but it was usually
so peripheral that the authorities hated to target manpower
and investigation time on low priority business. There always seemed something more urgent on the burner than
Botenkranz. Operatives of different agencies might send us
an inquiry regarding Botenkranz, or our own DEA agents
might mention him on the fringe of an investigation they
were conducting on someone else. Or it might be that a
check of a drug company's records showed a suspicious
amount of Dolphine or methadone going to a single pharmacy, or excessive ordering of some synthetic narcotic. Or
there would be a sudden surge of phony prescriptions for
Dilaudid, all filled at the same place—and you guessed the
place. All roads seemed to be leading back to Botenkranz's
Apotheka.

Then we started hearing rumors from several informants.

Talk on the street was that Botenkranz was offering hard
cash for bogus prescriptions. It seemed common knowledge
that he was moving such volume he needed scripts in order
to cover his excessive ordering and selling without prescription and his other diversion activities.

Another allegation that kept popping up, but had remained unproven, was that Manny was into bartering. I
don't mean the generally harmless underground-economy
trading. I mean a lascivious form of bartering in which
Manny exchanged drugs for sexual favors from desperate
young addicts. After the federal case was dropped, we'd
been stymied. We couldn't prosecute with rumor. Nothing
solid ever stuck to the guy!

Now I had a call that said a woman had named him specifically in an illegal drug diversion. Our tires were still smoking in the Mass General parking lot when we entered the woman's room.

The obviously once prettier woman patient needed no prodding to name Manny as the source of both her drugs and her psychic woes. She called herself Angel Fine.

"That Manny bastard—he gave me these abscesses," Angel accused, holding out her punctured arms.

"How so?" Agent Caverly asked, confused.

"If I was too jiggy to hold the syringe, he'd shoot me up. "Swear—a pharmacist—an' he don't even know how to give an injection!"

"A real sport, that Manny," I said. "Always willing to go the extra mile for a patient."

The woman was unusually open in her revelations. She pulled no punches. She was as unsparing of herself as she was of Botenkranz. A former exotic dancer, Angel had a body that was still spectacular, even in the throes of addiction.

Mark and I listened attentively to the former stripper as she related a tale incredible for its sleaze, even in the drug world. Her initial contact with Manny had come years before, when she routinely presented a prescription for Darvon at the Apotheka, knowing it only as a place that didn't ask too many questions.

"He didn't have to be a detective to tell I was a heroin addict," Angel said, tossing her auburn hair. He asked her if she didn't think she needed "something a little stronger" than Darvon. "I was hooked, what the hell . . ."

When Manny Botenkranz suggested a drugs-for-sex arrangement between them, the incredibly endowed informant saw a way to maintain her habit without the risk that stealing involved. She soon learned this was a common arrangement for Botenkranz, and that he had been and was then involved with several other women, supplying them with drugs also. Manny used his knowledge and experience as a pharmacist to approach only the hardest cases.

"He needed us heavily hooked. Otherwise, who'd agree to submit to *his* sexual demands? He's no Cary Grant." He then added an extra fillip of degradation by taking candid Polaroid photos during the sex act.

Manny supplied our subject with heavy-habit quantities of several drugs, including Dilaudid and Dolophine, both morphine-type injectables, and a Tussionex and tincture of opium mixture. The arrangement soon escalated. At his insistence, and to insure he didn't cut her supply off, the ex-stripteaser began selling drugs on the street for Botenkranz. Given the prices and amounts she quoted and what we knew Manny paid for the substances wholesale, we estimated she made well over sixty thousand dollars for him during a seven-month period. Nor was she the only personal pusher Manny supplied out the back door of the Apotheka on Sundays. The girl on the bed in the Mass General claimed she was only one of ten or so others all doing the same thing. Even by conservative estimates, Manny was raking in big bucks.

"What's the hook?" I asked. The information Angel was volunteering seemed too good to be free.

"Whattaya mean?"

"What do you expect from us in return for pulling the plug on Manny?"

"Nothin'—I'm fed up with the scumbag. And I'm sick and tired of bein' sick and tired. You gotta help me get clean, get me in some kinda meth' program . . . somethin.' "

"I'll try," I said. It would surprise me if getting straight remained her only request, but for now it was some measure of the credibility of her information. "To continue . . . so Manny wasn't Mr. Goodwrench. Did he at least supply all your drugs free?"

Angel's expression suggested I might have been born yesterday.

"As long as I was servicing him, it'd cost me fifteen dollars each for a four-milligram tab of Dilaudid," she said scornfully. "Soon's he found someone else he liked better and stopped using me, the same tablet went up to forty bucks!"

"Give us some detail about his operation."

She delineated Manny's pricing system for the hooked.

Morphine cost the same as Dilaudid, about forty dollars, while Dolophine carried a dollar-per-milligram charge. These same drugs, purchased legitimately, cost less than twenty-five *cents* per tablet. Needless to say, none of these controlled substances was obtained by legal prescription. The picture she drew was of a consumingly greedy man who would sell anything to anyone who had the price.

She also gave depth to our suspicions that Manny had to be receiving some official protection—"official" meaning a rotten apple in the barrel. Even someone as consummately avaricious as he couldn't conduct his business so with such foolhardy abandon and remain unafraid of being caught— unless the fix was in, somewhere.

"He's got to have friends in high places," she said. "Everybody on the street knows to go to Manny's. Word is, he's supplying dope not just for several cops, which he is, but also for a certain judge. That's how he operates so open."

Those allegations have yet to be proven, but it stands to reason that Manny's long-term apparent immunity to the law didn't happen because he was beloved as a civic-minded citizen.

Finished for the time being, Caverly and I prepared to leave the hospital room. Angel waited until we were at the door.

"Jack?" The syrup was so thick in her voice I doubted anyone ever refused her anything.

I turned, disappointed, figuring that like every other junkie she was going to try to weasel something from me.

"Yeah?"

Her expression was as demure as a bride's. "Manny took a lot of them Polaroids of me when—"

"If I can find them, you'll get them."

"Thanks," she said, her quick smile an echo of a lost and regretted girlhood.

Thanks to interagency cooperation, we plugged into a parallel investigation being conducted by the Massachusetts State Police, Diversion Investigation Unit. Botenkranz wasn't the primary subject in the separate, concurrent investigation, but by sharing information we were able to draw connecting lines between the two and buttress each other's work.

One anomaly we discovered was that Manny was filling 100 percent of all the Dolophine and Dilaudid prescriptions written by Daniel Zalt, a Brookline MD. It would be extremely rare for a pharmacist to fill all of one doctor's prescriptions even if the two of them were in the same building. There are always bargain hunters who'll go to the discount pharmacy, or somebody else who knows someone in the business. In this instance too, South Boston is miles from Brookline geographically, and light years distant socioeconomically.

We knew we were on to something when we found that Manny's Apotheka was the *only* place Dr. Zalt's prescriptions were being filled. Not only was it somewhat unusual for all of a suburban physician's prescriptions to find their way to South Boston, but by investigating we found it a little odd that these "patients" came from as far away as Cape Ann (fifty miles) to the north and Cape Cod (seventy-five miles) to the south. Either these patients were drug addicts with nowhere else to go, or Manny must be providing exceptional service. And extra green stamps.

Additionally, these itinerant customers were forking over up to five hundred dollars for their "prescriptions" to be filled. From various sources we were able to put together a preliminary picture of the range of Botenkranz's rookery. For these unusual prescriptions, Manny charged a flat five dollars per four-milligram tablet of Dilaudid on a Zalt prescription. Therefore, if Zalt wrote Dilaudid, 4mg.tab., #60, for acute pain, it would cost the patient sixty times the five dollars: three hundred dollars for what should legitimately have cost between twenty and twenty-five dollars.

At this juncture in the investigation it appeared to be a

"got them coming and going" setup between Zalt and Botenkranz.

If this were true, Doctor Feelgood and your friendly neighborhood pharmacist had a pretty good thing going between them. Not too ethical, but extremely profitable.

I don't know if Manny had a similar arrangement with any other physicians, but, as an extension to this exorbitant ripoff, he had another gouge for his patients. On every known illicit prescription he filled, he demanded a 10-to-15 percent kickback from the person he filled it for. If he filled a phony script for 100 Dolophine, say, he'd short the order by ten to fifteen tablets as a surcharge for filling what both parties knew was a bogus prescription. If the poor addict complained, Manny would threaten to shut him off altogether, an effective muzzle for someone needing the drug to survive.

This kickback scheme was one way Manny kept his Accountable Records Inventory presentably straight while at the same time supplying people like Angel who worked for him. This was one time I keenly felt the arrest limitations of a diversion investigator.

The first few personal contacts I had with Botenkranz were difficult. He fulfilled every negative expectation I could have held. I couldn't be around Manny without wanting to slam him behind bars. In addition to being mired in the slime we suspected he was, Botenkranz was for me a personally unlikable individual. He rarely spoke without heavy sarcasm, and he had the overweening arrogance of someone who feels confident that he can't be touched.

I'd decided to work the case through the records, sensing I could find enough discrepancies in his bookkeeping and other recording practices to bring him before a grand jury. I was determined to find some paper slip-up that would lead to proof that Manny was guilty; if not of all the crimes we suspected him of, at least of unlawful distribution of controlled substances under the guise of legitimate medical practice. When slogging through the paper jungle became too tough, I kept reminding myself that Al Capone hadn't been put away for rum-running, murder or a hundred other crimes, but for income tax evasion.

It was a lovely day for me when, aided by several other investigators, I served a federal inspection warrant on Botenkranz. We lacked a traditional search warrant because I couldn't then risk using the stripper's information in an affidavit. Never having provided information before, she didn't have a track record of reliability. Her credibility could jeopardize my credibility when requesting a search warrant from a magistrate. In the absence of her testimony, the AUSA (Assistant US Attorney), Oliver Mitchell, said we didn't have sufficient probable cause to ask for a search warrant.

I did everything allowable under an administrative inspection warrant. At the Apotheka I collected all of Botenkranz's pertinent purchase receipts, prescription records and relevant sales records. We also conducted a closing inventory of selected controlled drugs in order to establish a time frame for our investigation. While this was going on, Manny gave new dimension to the word obnoxious. Loud, profane and arrogant, he calmed only slightly when I seized his pertinent records, finally realizing he might be in a bit of difficulty.

Delighted though I may have been over getting my hooks in Manny, I had to keep a constant eye on him for his own safety and protection. There's a phenomenally high rate of suicide amongst crooked medical professionals when they've been caught with their hands in the cookie jar. Whether they're walking the thin edge of sanity in the first place, I don't know, but I know they tend to chuck it all in when they see the end in sight. I didn't like Botenkranz, but I didn't want happening to him what had happened to another South Boston pharmacist who, during the warrant/arrest/inventory procedure in his establishment, excused himself to use the bathroom of the store across the street.

"I have no toilet here," he'd told the agent in charge. Then he disappeared. When eventually found, his body was horribly burnt almost beyond recognition. He'd gone to the basement of the building across the street and blown his brains out. His body had toppled down beside the heating boiler in full winter blast.

I didn't want *that* to happen to Manny, but I still had all I could do to keep myself from throwing him through the glass front of his pharmacy out into the gutter of West Broadway.

Assistant US Attorney Mitchell had wanted me to arrange for a series of undercover purchases of evidence from both the Brookline doctor and Botenkranz in order to catch them redhanded. I'd weighed his suggestion, but as well as being concerned about the complexities of coordinating the agencies needed to pull off a sting, I was a little tired of all the begging I was already doing at the doors of the staties and other agencies to build the case. Plus, I wanted to stop Manny's illegal pushing—now!

From even a cursory look at Botenkranz's paperwork it was obvious that Daniel Zalt and Manny were the primary sources for several documented drug addicts—I mean users with previous arrest records, self-admitted addicts and so on. I handed Manny a receipt for the records seized and left the Apotheka to begin the real work.

For a field agent, most of the work is undercover. He or she is in the midst of the criminal activity as it's happening. For the diversion investigator the heavy work is after the fact. Solving the paper puzzle can sometimes be like reconstructing a skeleton from bits of bone to see how something might have looked.

We found dozens of recordkeeping violations and purchase and sales discrepancies in Botenkranz's inventory. The biggest handle we had was the significant shortages that appeared on his inventory of controlled substances. We could take this to the US attorney for prosecution.

I remained in constant communication with the State Police Diversion Investigation Unit, which was conducting the ongoing parallel investigation of Doctor Zalt. The staties had some budding problems with the investigation, one of which was the fact that Zalt was prescribing in Norfolk

County while Botenkranz was dispensing from Suffolk. If it ever got that far, that would mean two entirely separate prosecutions—and all the bureaucratic problems that go with a divided and multiple-entity effort. Nonetheless, I combined my efforts with the troopers and their unit. None of us in the trenches particularly cared which county got the case or whether the prosecution took place in federal or state court—just as long as it happened.

First, of course, the legwork had to be done to build a case. Legwork is the grind of first finding the facts, then getting the facts in prosecutable shape. Even if you accomplish that, it doesn't always mean your job is done. Oftentimes you have to keep the prosecuting attorney and his office happy while at the same time assuring your own superiors that the time and effort being spent is justified, weighed against the potential results. Ultimately, we're all accountable to the taxpayer.

The specific investigative tools used vary between agencies and individuals, and from case to case, but some are fairly standard for detection and compilation of facts. One method I often employ to present an overall picture of movements of people and goods is an old workhorse, the time/flow chart.

Often, recognizable patterns aren't discernible until seen plotted on the chart. I had a chart working on the Botenkranz case, but it wasn't nearly full enough for my liking. I also used the standard interviewing and interrogation of witnesses, and the tracking down and proving of data or rumors received, either from informants or from other agencies.

Successful diversion investigations can be more difficult to pull off than a dramatic sting. Most stings and other undercover operations place the goods in the hands of the criminal. You can show up in court with pictures of the stingee holding the bag. A diversion investigation is almost all "proof through paperwork." What we specifically had to prove in this case was that Botenkranz's activities were indeed unlawful and could in no way be construed as legitimate medical practice. Naturally, his defense attorney would be trying to say precisely the opposite.

Basically, what we had to work with were Botenkranz's own records and the testimony of the addicts he was ripping off. If we could get it. My first major task was to attempt to ascertain the names of the addicts Manny was supplying.

I pulled a surprising number of names from the prescription records just by combing through for repeaters, by drug. For example: regardless of how much volume Manny was pushing out of his store without benefit of prescription, he still had to record a percentage of transactions as legitimate sales to make his tax records look good. I just went down the line, sale by sale. If I found the entry: John Doe, Dilaudid, acute pain, twenty different times, odds were pretty fair Mr. Doe was an abuser.

To serve subpoenas on the potential witnesses, we first had to find them. Amazing how many addresses from Manny's files were for vacant lots on Cape Cod or abandoned buildings in Boston's skid row. Conversely, a surprisingly high percentage of the names were real. Identifying the suspect addicts was one thing; getting them to talk was another. They weren't all like the stripper in Mass General.

Working the concurrent investigation with the troopers, I was also chasing down a number of the Brookline doctor's "patients." True to expectations, the interviews were frustrating because so many potential witnesses refused to speak, under advice of counsel. That's okay, because it's our system—and it works. The frustration level has to be prefigured, and the experienced investigator becomes used to speaking to maybe fifty people before he picks up even a tidbit that's eventually usable. The Botenkranz case was running true to form.

For the sake of sanity retention, it was my habit on many nights to take my frustration to our local links to beat on some golf balls. Not that I'm any good at the game, but it works for me as a way both to relieve stress and as a problem-solver because it helps me change rutted thinking patterns. Then, of course, there is the sociability factor.

I was alone near dusk, fishing an errant Titleist out of the brook while puzzling over the vagaries of mankind in general and Manny Botenkranz in particular, when a raspy voice shouting mild obscenities from behind warned me I was about to be joined by my buddy, Eddie B.

"Whatsamatter, Narc—still short of balls?" he said, signaling me to meet him on the fourth tee.

Eddie's another reason I play a lot of twilight golf. He's a six handicap with a knack for spotting the flaws in my swing, but he's also an ex-drug addict and recovered alcoholic who's been clean and sober for several years. He's not bashful about correcting me in either area.

"Hey, Junkie, I got enough left to beat you," I said, joining him. As far as I know, I'm the only one who can call him Junkie and live. Eddie's very tight about who knows he's an ex-user. We'd met on the golf course a few years back when I was just returning to the game after years of neglect. I could still powder the ball out of sight but had no idea what direction it was going in, whereas Eddie was a master of finesse and control. A friendship began that developed into deep trust. Over a period of time Eddie discovered I was with the DEA and eventually, in bits and pieces, shared his past with me. Everything was off the record between us, and I found him invaluable both in terms of insight into the user's side of the drug culture but also whenever I needed a dose of reality. This night he hit his drive short and straight then watched mine slice sideways into the trees.

"That's awful, Jack—your mind on the golf tonight?"

Without divulging any names I sketched in the background and problems of the Botenkranz case.

"Sounds like a guy in Southie I heard of who fills his 'special' customers prescriptions only between the hours of four to six. During which time he packs a Smith and Wesson automatic with a round in the chamber."

"Could be the same guy," I said. Among those witnesses willing to testify, there was almost universal detestation of

Botenkranz for the way he treated them as humans. And they all readily admitted he ripped them off ruthlessly.

"Why do they put up with it, Eddie?" I asked. "Why didn't someone blow the whistle before this or do a number on him if they know he's ripping them off?"

"First of all, an active addict *expects* to be worked over and crapped on. It's the law of the jungle they live in—it's a jungle full of dealers who have the goodies they need, and they'll do anything to get the goodies."

"I have no sympathy for users, but they certainly seem to get taken over the barrel," I said.

"Even if a junkie has a legitimate, legal prescription, he expects to pay more simply because he's been used so often. And he feels so guilty and wrong to begin with that he's like a doormat—anybody can wipe their feet on him. He can't help it. He's operating out of a craving that makes all his choices for him. The addict settles for less and less from himself and accepts being ripped off as part of the price he pays for being allowed to continue living in the wonderful world of drugs."

"What I can't figure is that almost to a person the same addicts being interviewed who knock Botenkranz say good things about Zalt, the doctor who appears to be ripping them off just as badly as the pharmacist."

"Figure it out yourself, Narc—he's their source. They can try to fill a script anywhere, but without him they got no script. Would you knock Santa Claus?"

I took that thought to bed with me that night. And for many nights to come.

2 Doctor Feelgood

THE NEXT TIME I PLAYED GOLF WITH EDDIE B., he didn't leave me any less disconcerted. It was a few weeks since we'd started pulling the Botenkranz investigation together, and I'd spent the first two holes griping about how slowly everything seemed to be moving in the case.

"It's like somebody hit the pause button," I said. "Every action needs a pile of paperwork first, then getting even simple things done . . . It seems to take so much effort to get through the red tape with this case."

"The cops you workin' with straight?" Eddie asked.

"I won't dignify that with an answer."

"How many lawyers working the case?"

"Plenty, why?"

"What's their vig?"

"Come again?"

"Vig—vigorish, remuneration. The lawyers aren't gonna push a case unless the vig is there—publicity, notoriety, whatever. Unless there's something in the case to either boost their careers or stroke their egos, forget speed. Beware of suits bearing briefcases, chum."

"You don't care for lawyers."

"Don't take offense, Jack, I know you wear a suit on the job. I mean suits-suits; you know, legalitarians wearing suits. A lot of guys and dolls that are PDs or public prosecutors just seem to work extremely fast when the case they're working is on the front page. These guys are out to either build a practice or land a cushy job in a big firm. To do that they need to get known. They ain't gonna get known prosecuting small-timers like Botenkranz."

"Hmm."

"Get them a case involving a Kennedy, say, then watch the wheels turn."

The longer we worked on the Botenkranz case, the stronger grew the consensus among us that the Brookline doctor was as culpable as Manny, and that these were two individuals who deserved time in jail.

I've been accused of being a tad gung ho on the job. I admit to being a bulldog sometimes. But because it's my end of the business, no one is more acutely aware than I that fully half of the drug ODs that get reported in this country derive from prescription drugs. That's not to say they've all been negligently prescribed: there are as many methods of illegal diversion as there are criminals. Drugs get stolen, prescriptions get forged, some people deliberately overdose. But the overdose deaths caused by prescribed drugs seem to hurt the most because we entrust ourselves to the care of professionals who are sworn to the service of mankind. Here were two supposed guardians of the public welfare who, if they were doing all they were suspected of, could set medical public relations back twenty years.

As the evidence mounted we were in a hurry to protect the public from the Doctors Feelgood. Unfortunately, unusual little glitches seemed to be happening around this case that gummed up the works and forestalled the fulfillment of our wishes. To begin with, there was a rather sudden decision to decline to prosecute on the part of the Norfolk County assistant DA, Peter Agnes.

Agnes's reason for dropping the ball, he stated to the rest of the prosecution team, was that because of "perceived difficulties" he expected to encounter along the way, he would not go ahead with the Zalt prosecution. None of the team could believe there were any even imagined "difficulties" in what was then generally seen as a strong case. But because there were several other avenues open to us at that time nobody lingered long over Agnes's strange exercise of prerogative. Agnes, it seemed, was gearing himself up to help out the campaign of a local politician. It may have seemed different from the lawyer's angle, but from my personal view it looked like Eddie B. was right: the lawyer had balanced the amount of work against the possible gain, as well as potential for losing the case, and made a career decision.

On the federal level I was proceeding with all possible haste with my part of the investigation. Except I was having my own problems with the assistant US attorney, Oliver Mitchell. Mitchell wasn't doing anything obvious like outright foot-dragging, but I was picking up vibes around him, little telltale sensations that Mitchell's heart wasn't 100 percent behind this prosecution. Despite these obstacles we didn't slow down the investigation. We field people were especially eager to prosecute the South Boston pharmacist and the Brookline doctor.

It was a frigid November day when I rolled to a stop in front of Doctor Zalt's brick Georgian townhouse on the tree-lined lane in the exclusive Brookline neighborhood. The doctor had prepared well for my arrival. His attorney was present for the interview but contented himself with an advisory position. The doctor opened with a statement that in itself, because of the points it tried to cover, showed he knew well what was up. After some prefatory remarks about training and education, he said he'd recently been the Town Physician for Brookline, as if that were a status position. It is, part-time; but it isn't usually a doctor's primary practice. His job there had mainly been to do routine physicals of town employees and evaluations for industrial-accident, workman's-compensation type cases. Zalt stated his severance from that position was due to Proposition 2 1/2 (a tax cutback similar to California's Proposition 13). Closer to the truth was that the tax cut was the perfect excuse to let him go.

Zalt stated his present practice was limited to treating only patients with "chronic pain" (a nice gray area). His "specialty practice" had expanded to where he was now treating fifty patients on a weekly basis.

"What do you mean, 'chronic pain' patients?" I asked. I wanted to hear his definition, though sensing in advance it would be vague enough to cover prescribing megadoses of addictive drugs.

Zalt repeated that he treated for chronic pain. "Both benign or nonmalignant pain," he said, "such as backaches, headaches, stiff necks, etcetera, versus chronic malignant pain, like that associated with cancer."

At this point Zalt began sounding more like a lawyer than a doctor, playing word games and occasionally getting caught in them. He suggested that his patients were people who formerly had their street sources for narcotics to either maintain a habit or to supplement legal prescriptions. He admitted that fully one half his patients were "medically dependent." In English, that means they were pure addicts.

Since the passage of the Harrison Narcotic Act in 1914, it has been illegal in this country to write prescriptions for addicts solely to alleviate craving, with no hope of a cure. There was considerable early case law on this. The actual statutory law came into effect in 1974 in the Narcotic Addict Treatment and Control Act, now incorporated into the CSA. If a doctor wishes to treat an addict either through controlled maintenance or detoxification treatment, he or she has to obtain registration from both the DEA and the Food and Drug Administration. Strict control is enforced in this area to prevent addicts from "doctor shopping"; that is, traveling around until they find the doctor most liberal in dispensing drugs or most lax in monitoring them or in some cases, outright criminal—and willing to supply anything for a price.

Dr. Zalt had never bothered to register his patients under the Controlled Substances Act. He felt his clientele and their unique problems justified the prescription of heavy narcotics.

"When you're talking pain," he said, "you're talking narcotics."

I agreed that there are no easy solutions. He said that as a doctor dealing with chronic pain he was faced with "a lifetime situation," and that his task was difficult because he must deal with the "addictive personality." "It seems strange to me," I opined, "for a doctor situated less than three miles from the Boston Common to have patients coming fifty and a hundred miles away, from Gloucester and Cape Cod, week after week to be treated by you. How do you explain that uncommon loyalty?"

"My specialty," he answered, straightfaced. "As far as I know, I'm the only private physician treating such patients."

I'd already interviewed and observed many of his private chronic pain patients. Most were in their twenties and thirties, and from my observation of their physical dexterity, none seemed hampered by any debilitating pain.

"You've stated that at least half of your patient load are documented drug addicts. If they are addicted, how do you justify prescribing such potent narcotic analgesics as Dilaudid and Dolophine to these people—often at the same time?"

Dilaudid is normally used in the treatment of severe pain such as encountered in terminal illness. Dolophine is used for maintenance treatment of severe pain.

Zalt stated that he prescribed Dolophine for "chronic" pain, but that occasionally a patient would have "acute" pain.

I interrupted. "Acute?"

"For example, from a fall downstairs. This, superimposed atop his chronic pain . . ." In those instances, Dr. Zalt said he wrote one Dilaudid Rx for the acute pain and another Rx for Dolophine for the chronic pain.

From my perusal of Rx records there must have been an incredibly high incidence of stair-falls among Zalt's patients. No doctor in his right mind would allow a patient to leave his office with such a ticking bomb in his pocket; it's also highly illegal. My facial expression must have hinted at my incredulity.

"Then there are always 'rescue' situations," Zalt offered.

"Meaning?"

"Medication gets lost, or stolen. Or accidently falls into the toilet . . ." He explained he'd rescue the drug-dependent patient by writing another prescription.

I shook my head. The way Zalt described himself, he was a combination crook, frustrated social worker and a quack.

"How do you determine what dosage of Dolophine to prescribe for a *new* patient?" I asked.

Zalt replied he *guessed* what dose would cover the patient's dependency needs. Then he'd "add a little more to cover the chronic pain."

He was tacitly admitting his patients were addicts and that he was using chronic pain to cover it up as a legitimate medical condition.

"Do you refer your patients to Manny Botenkranz's Apotheka?"

He answered he hardly had any control over where people took their prescriptions, though he realized they all did "happen" to be going there. "It's the fault of the state police!" he claimed.

According to Zalt, the reason his patients went only to Botenkranz was that the state Diversion Investigation Unit and Lieutenant Bill Sutherland had "badmouthed" him all over the greater Boston area. He claimed that their intervention made most other pharmacists afraid to get involved and thereby get the DIU on their case. Zalt said he'd heard the word on the street was that Manny was the only pharmacist *brave* enough to risk the displeasure of the authorities. Sure.

"Are you aware of Botenkranz's exorbitant prices?"

His answer was that he assumed they were due to the high insurance premium for someone at such high risk for burglaries.

A known filler of many narcotic Rx's would have to maintain an invitingly high inventory of drugs. He said he didn't particularly agree with the high fees, but that it was perhaps the only alternative to street prices of thirty to forty dollars per tablet.

When I asked for a profile of a typical chronic pain patient, he picked one from his files, apologizing first that the case he'd chosen wasn't quite typical or the best example he could have chosen. The example was a twenty-four-year-old clammer from Gloucester. Bearing a low IQ, the clammer worked only sporadically. He became hooked after drug treatment for a neck injury incurred playing football a number of years prior. He'd first come to Zalt about a year and a half ago. The doctor described the clammer as a drug addict who suffered from a stiff neck that periodically required a Thomas collar. Zalt repeated his disclaimer: "You're dealing with the addictive personality here."

I had him there. The patient he spoke of was an informant for the Gloucester Police enrolled in the Veterans Administration methadone program, and he and his girlfriend were known to be two of the biggest drug abusers on the North Shore. He had no history of chronic pain, or recorded currently known medical problems other than those associated with his addiction.

Most of Zalt's fifty patients had similar medical records, very sketchy around the area of chronic pain. From what I could ascertain from the records, most of his patients were as heavy or even heavier drug users *after* beginning a course of treatment with Zalt than they had been before coming to him. Their addictions may not have been helped, but his pocketbook was.

Grateful to be outside after the interview I took a deep breath of clean fresh air.

Back downtown, I subpoenaed twenty-five of Zalt's "patients," preinterviewing as many as possible, to appear before the federal grand jury. I was rolling. Then we got hit with another glitch.

At the end of those interview sessions, Attorney Mitchell suddenly announced he'd become "disenchanted" with the case. My immediate negative premonitions were borne out later when Mitchell stated there was "no doubt in his mind these guys are guilty," but that he would decline to prosecute from the criminal side. Although Zalt and Botenkranz appeared to be guilty of unlawful distribution of controlled substances and conspiracy, Mitchell reasoned, we would have some difficulty in proving it and therefore were in danger of losing the case. My pal Eddie was right, dammit. I had been naively idealistic about lawyers. I didn't know that some attorneys only took the cases they could win.

The state police DIU unit was furious that Mitchell refused to go after the two. I kicked and screamed a bit and was generally unpleasant to be around at home for a few days, but I soon got going on some other available options. If I couldn't get the brothers Grim on one charge, I'd get them on another.

The first action I took was to file complaints against Zalt before the Massachusetts Board of Registration in Medicine, and against Botenkranz before the Pharmacy Board. At the same time, I requested show cause proceedings against both in order to revoke their DEA registrations "in the public interest." Show cause hearings are formal adjudicatory hearings and can be held at either the state or federal level.

Before going ahead with the show cause hearing, Zalt and his attorney reached an agreement with the DEA attorneys to surrender his DEA license for eighteen months.

In Zalt's case before the Board of Medicine, three full days of testimony about unlawful prescription practices were heard. Sometimes the mills grind slowly. But the Board eventually revoked his medical license and he became a taxi driver!

For Angel, the stripper/informant whose crucial initial testimony turned us on to Botenkranz in the first place, her only monetary gain was a fifteen-dollar witness fee. But I was able to help her get almost immediate entrance into a successful narcotic treatment program for which there's normally a months-long waiting list. I'm happy to say she got clean and has remained so. We were never able to retrieve the Polaroids Manny had taken of her.

The next step was to try to convict Botenkranz.

Although we in law enforcement sometimes lose sight of the fact, the most important, the overriding ethical concern with people like Zalt and Botenkranz isn't that they be successfully prosecuted, (although that's not only ego-gratifying, it's quantifiable by a bureaucracy)—it's that the criminal be immobilized, stopped, put out of business. That of course is the spirit of the law. Nice if they can be criminally convicted too, but the victims don't especially care about your personal conviction statistics, they want to stop the scum from spreading their slime.

Technically, a professional board hearing is a disciplinary hearing and differs from a criminal trial to the extent that, unlike trials where the prosecution must prove guilt "beyond reasonable doubt," at a hearing all that need be proven is that the defendant has indeed committed gross misconduct of his profession. A prime example of misconduct for pharmacists would be misuse of controlled substances.

State Trooper Francis M. O'Brien and I were the two main witnesses and complainants against Emanuel Botenkranz and Coolie Drugs, Inc., also known as the Apotheka, 384 1/2 East Broadway, South Boston. The Massachusetts Board of Registration in Pharmacy meets only every other Tuesday, so scheduling can be a problem if your case requires more than one sitting. From May through August, O'Brien and I appeared three times before the eight-member board.

I assume that were I in a similar position, trying to convince a board they should allow me to keep my license to dispense drugs, I'd be polite and act in a professional manner. Botenkranz seemed bent on alienating everyone. He was loud, arrogant and abusive throughout. During one break in the proceedings he even challenged Trooper O'Brien to a fight in the hallway.

"Hey, O'Brien—how'd your nose get so brown?" Botenkranz snarled. "From being up Sutherland's ass?" He was referring to Lieutenant Bill Sutherland, DIU commander.

Botenkranz was no midget at six-foot-two, 220 pounds. But inciting O'Brien was dangerous policy; he was giving away at least an inch and several pounds, not to mention an age and physical conditioning differential. O'Brien ignored

Botenkranz, suggesting to his attorney that he take charge of his client. I thought O'Brien showed remarkable restraint by not putting out Manny's lights with a shot from one of his hamlike fists.

Apparently Botenkranz was trying to intimidate the people involved in the case, but his outbursts and behavior were having the opposite effect. At one point he called the entire state police force "stupid," then began screaming to the board about me.

"Crowley's lying through his teeth!" His misguided vituperation got me laughing so hard I had to leave the hearing room.

Manny Botenkranz appeared three times before the Pharmacy Board. The board revoked the store's license and permit to operate. The DEA revoked his federal permit. Some months later the board finally issued the order revoking Botenkranz's personal license as well, meaning he could no longer legally operate as a pharmacist in Massachusetts. Additionally, they ordered Manny to liquidate his interest in Coolie Drugs, Inc., forthwith, or face revocation of all permits issued to the pharmacy. Remember, state boards license pharmacists personally and individually, and separately license the establishments. Then the DEA registers them.

The operative concept here, as with the Rackets Bill, is hitting the criminal where he hurts the most, in the pocketbook. If the state revoked all permits issued to the pharmacy, that meant that not only could Botenkranz not work as a pharmacist, he couldn't operate or sell the business as a pharmacy, either.

On a subsequent Friday afternoon, Charles Monahan, executive secretary of the Pharmacy Board, informed me by phone that Botenkranz had just surrendered his personal license.

"Great, Charlie. Better get someone over to the Apotheka right away." I advised them to immediately secure his premises so that nothing untoward would befall the narcotics inventory. Similar experiences had taught me the high coincidence rate of theft in stores about to be shut down. "Get a formal state inventory before the narcotics mysteriously disappear," I warned.

"Like to, John, but my pharmacy agents are dispersed all over this Commonwealth. Nobody's anywhere near South Boston. You know what it's like on a Friday afternoon . . ."

This was one prophecy I didn't want to see come true. But my hands were tied; this was now a state action. The date Botenkranz surrendered his personal license to the board was December 14.

The day after next, December 16, District 6 Boston Police, South Boston division, received a report from one Emanuel Botenkranz, victim of an alleged armed robbery at the Apotheka on East Broadway. Manny Botenkranz had been relieved of money and all of his narcotics.

Manny couldn't give an exact accounting of how much of which substances he'd had on hand in inventory. Only that "all narcotics were taken." No witnesses. All his money and narcotics were stolen from his two safes. Perpetrators unapprehended, unknown. Botenkranz claimed I was the only person who knew he had two safes.

A few weeks after that, a conference was held before the Pharmacy Board regarding compliance with its order that Botenkranz divest himself of interest in the store. They also asked about his filing DEA form 106, in accordance with regulations requiring such any time there's a reported loss or theft of controlled substances, and the armed robbery.

Richard Dudley, board president, pointed out to Botenkranz the apparent discrepancies of his reporting in one place that all his narcotics were stolen on December 16, then certifying another report of an inventory taken by him and the new Apotheka manager of record, Max Hessman, two days later, that included various schedule II controlled substances. This made Manny's earlier statement that he was robbed of "every single schedule II pill" somewhat questionable.

Botenkranz had an elaborate story about the holdup. "I

was putting rubbish in the dumpster out behind the store—there were three of them!" He vehemently insisted that three gunmen accosted him. One stayed behind a truck in the rear lot while the two others, holding a gun to his head, ordered him back into the store, where they cleaned him out.

"Like a grocery store. They cleaned out both safes and a buncha shelf items, like Valium. We presently have nothing," Botenkranz said. "The only people who knew I had two safes are right here in this room!"

He went on to name the board members, stenographers, Trooper O'Brien and me. He was insistent it happened the way he said, despite the conflicting evidence of the official reports and his own previous statements. The board confirmed its order that Botenkranz divest.

His attorney, Henry Cashman, filed an appeal to the Supreme Judicial Court to set aside the board's order and filed a direct appeal to the board for a six-month stay of their order to allow Botenkranz time to liquidate his interest in the Apotheka.

The board eventually denied the request, stipulating they had until the end of the month to liquidate. Attorney Cashman again appealed, this time to Justice Paul Liacos of the Massachusetts Supreme Judicial Court. Liacos also denied their request, stating he didn't think Botenkranz was taking the board's action seriously. He gave them until the end of *that* month to comply and said that he'd personally revoke the store permits if they did not do so. In the process, the defendants gained another month's stall.

Manny's troubles seemed to be just starting. In midmonth, he was arrested for drunk driving. By itself, OUIL is a very serious offense in the Commonwealth. Metro Police Sergeant Richard Cashin stated that at the time of his arrest, Botenkranz was carrying a fully loaded Smith and Wesson .22 with a round in the chamber. He was also carrying Percocet and Dolophine tablets (both schedule II narcotics) in an unlabeled container.

Staying in character, Botenkranz had been extremely abusive to the arresting Metro officers. Sergeant Cashin asked

Brookline police chief George Simard, issuing officer, why a person like this had a weapons permit for "protection of life and property." Botenkranz had been a resident of the town at the date of issuance but no longer lived there.

Chief Simard summarily revoked Botenkranz's firearm license, sending a follow-up letter to Frank J. Trabucco, Commissioner of Public Safety, and his licensing section to insure that Botenkranz will never again legally carry a firearm in Massachusetts.

Fran O'Brien and I had worked many "professional practice" investigations together, and we were only semisatisfied with this one. We had taken it as far as we could and stopped the diversion of controlled substances into the illicit drug market. By stripping Zalt and Botenkranz of their professional licenses, we insured that if there ever were a next time, a traditional criminal prosecution would result.

Sometime later I was on the putting green of the Putterham Meadows Golf Course, getting ready to play in what the inner club members call the "Big Roundo," when Eddie B. came sauntering over.

"You gonna lose money again today, Jack?"

"As long as it's not to you, I won't mind. Besides, I'm here to enjoy the hell out of myself—not to live or die over a putt."

"By the way, whatever became of the sweat hog pharmacist?"

Several of the better golfers at the club are practitioners and pharmacists and vaguely interested in what I do for a living, so some of them were awaiting my answer while killing time before teeing off. I said, "You'll love this epilogue, Eddie, but first let me give you a little background."

Having become supervisor of our diversion group in Boston covering five of the six New England states, I was constantly searching for better ways to combat the bad professionals. With the encouragement of special agent in charge John J. Coleman and also from my direct boss, George C. Festa, I forged a new relationship with one of our enforcement groups. Group II had a good blend of senior special agents and young and eager SAs. We decided that whenever possible we would concentrate on asset removals (especially the seizure/forfeiture of real estate). Special agents Joe Coons, Jack Fencer, Al Lively and Bobby Sampson each pledged his support.

Working as part of our Intelligence Group was Boston Police detective Frank Dewan, one of the finest I had ever met. In January, Frank began reaching out to me, explaining that my expertise would be needed at some time in the future, but he was very secretive about the details. Since he was such a pro, I naturally understood and accepted it.

About the same time, Coleman received a phone call from Leonard J. "Lenny" Henson, assistant district attorney and chief of the Organized Crime Division for Suffolk County, who requested the DEA's technical assistance in setting up a wire tap of a major target. Coleman is committed to helping all who seek his assistance and quickly dispatched personnel to set up the equipment and provide on-site assistance. Since this was, of course, a court-ordered wiretap, disclosure of information was strictly prohibited unless authorized by the judge.

The Suffolk County OCD was staffed by Boston Police detectives and two Metropolitan Police detectives. This squad had been staking out an old-time Boston crook named Bill Murtaugh from the Brighton section. Bill was sixty years old and had moved into the illicit drug business as he became too old to continue hijacking trucks. The detectives referred to him as a "tailgater," very dangerous in his day, who once sprang his infamous friend Elmer "Trigger" Burke from the Charles Street Jail at gunpoint back in the fifties.

Detective Ken Beers provided the bulk of the surveillance work on Murtaugh as he frequented the Rock Cafe in Brighton. Ken also realized that Murtaugh was in partnership of some kind with none other than a guy named Botenkranz, who seemed to be the money man. The surveillance activity was conducted periodically over a six-month period. Frank Dewan knew I had a case on Botenkranz and had passed that information along to the squad. The other assistant DA, Mike Gafney, got permission from the judge to brief me on the wiretap so we could compare notes on our man.

Boston detective Jim Carr visited me in my office in early February, and we exchanged information. I was not surprised to learn that Manny was the main target of the Suffolk County OCD Squad, and as we talked I came to admire Carr for his professionalism.

Since I had been inside Manny's former pharmacy several times and had knowledge of the location of his safes and the general layout of all the rooms in the basement, Carr invited me to participate in their upcoming search warrants of that location. I was excited and genuinely curious. On February 12, at seven in the morning, I attended the initial briefing at the Boston office of the squad.

The briefing was controlled by Boston Police sergeant Steve Murphy and was attended by approximately twenty police detectives, including detectives form the Boston Police Drug Control Unit, Brookline PD and Watertown PD.

Murphy gave a rundown of the case and targets and specifically gave instructions *not to arrest* anyone during the serving of the search warrant. The primary targets were Botenkranz and Murtaugh. Murphy broke the detectives down into four teams, which were instructed to go to several different addresses. I was assigned to assist Murphy and Jim Carr at the West Broadway location along with detectives Brendan Craven, Jack Pierce and Jake Bird. Since I had this new alliance with Group II, I invited Joe Coons to accompany me and assist the squad.

Manny arrived at the store and we moved in under Murphy's direction. Immediately we asked Botenkranz for any weapons he had, and we eventually secured four loaded handguns and a shotgun. Next Jimmy Carr asked Manny for the keys to the basement. He lied and said all his keys were at his home. Carr and I searched the rear storage room of the pharmacy and Carr found a ring of keys hanging on the wall.

There was no direct access to the basement from the for-

mer pharmacy, so we had to go out the front door, up to the
second floor and eventually make our way to the back stair-
case and down. (There were at least ten separate storage
rooms in the basement.) Murphy, Craven, John McReyn-
olds and Coons remained upstairs searching the old pharmacy prescription area and Botenkranz's office, while Carr
and I went to work downstairs. Carr began trying keys
(about twenty-five on the ring), and he eventually found one
that unlocked the first door, which opened into a hallway
with rooms on the left and right. We turned the corner and
there was Murtaugh coming out of the back room. (I didn't
know who he was at that point but sensed he was part of the
action.) I said in my Boston accent, "Howaya, Bucko?"
Carr moved right in and informed Murtaugh that he was
being detained and that Carr was going to search his pockets.

We immediately found an eighth of an ounce of cocaine
and fifty Valium tablets in his pockets. We took him back to
the back room and began our search. Carr immediately
found a kilo of cocaine in a cabinet in the corner, while I
noticed all the paraphernalia associated with cocaine distribution and pill distribution, including an OHAUS Scale,
glassine bags, spoons, a Kirby Lester tablet counter, razor
blades and the diluents lactose and Inositol. Next I found a
bag with approximately a thousand Valium pills while Carr
found six one-pound bags of processed marijuana and fifty-
five one-ounce retail plastic bags of processed marijuana. At
this point we realized several things—that we would be on
location for most of the day completing our search and inventory and photographing; and that we were going to find
more drug evidence before we were through. We hadn't even
done the heavy searching yet.

We were in no hurry, and Carr called in reinforcements.
Meanwhile I opened a drawer and found six portable radios
and a portable charger, which we learned later were stolen
from a construction site. During the next several hours we
continued our search and systematically entered all of the
other rooms. At one point I heard Jimmy Carr laughing and

rushed to join him in another room. I was dumbfounded. There before my eyes, in urban South Boston where not too many tomatoes grow, were almost one hundred marijuana plants in cultivation, along with special lighting, a copy of *Indoor Marijuana Horticulture* and assorted gardening tools and hoses.

Now my alliance with Group II and Joe Coons was going to pay off. Among many other areas, Joe was an expert in marijuana cultivation and property seizure. Joe had a quick meeting with Murphy and informed him that we would seize the property and that DEA would eventually share most of the proceeds with the Suffolk County OCD Squad. Simply stated, we had the statutory authority to seize real property used for the illegal distribution of controlled drugs.

We went on to find five large bags containing approximately sixty thousand blue Diazepam tablets. Next we found what appeared to be the beginnings of an operating methamphetamine lab, including the chemicals Methylamine, Benzene, formic acid and a burner. We also found such interesting items as burglary tools, a genuine police detective's badge and handcuffs.

Wrapping up my story I said, "You know, Eddie, a funny thing happened to me on my way back to the office that day. I became involved in a traffic altercation and I was so wound up I told the driver of the other car that he deserved a punch in the face. The guy jumps out of his car and screams at me, 'I'll cut you lengthways, sidewise and repeatedly. I'll cut you so fast the last place I cut you will bleed first!' Needless to say, I apologized for my rudeness and got the hell out of there. Since then our group has utilized that expression quite often when targeting registrant crooks—as in the objective of this case is to get him lengthways, sidewise and repeatedly."

And that's exactly what we did to Botenkranz and Zalt, proving that obstacles can be overcome through liaison, co-operation among agencies and working in harmony. Botenkranz was indicted by a Suffolk County grand jury. With the help of Assistant US Attorney Fred Dashiel, we seized property currently valued at $1,600,000. When this case is finally completed, the Suffolk County OCD will get at least 60 percent of the proceeds from the sale of the property. Oh, and by the way, Botenkrantz and his friends received stiff prison sentences, the former pharmacist himself drawing the Big Ten (years). Howaya, Manny?

3 California Sting

PROBLEMS WITH PRESCRIPTION DRUGS ARE certainly not confined to the Northeast. Little pills make big business all over the country. In the state of California alone, illicit prescription drugs are a billion-dollar-a-year business, and the DEA has its hands full just keeping up with the statistics.

Around the same time as my East Coast operation against the Doctors Feelgood, an unusual California sting was coming down to the wire. I was on a trip to Washington, D.C., when I first heard about the sting from Jim Smith, an undercover agent intimate with the details. Unlike the druggist involved in my Boston operation, the California pharmacist was on our side.

Like many things Californian, the West Coast sting was unorthodox and trend-setting. Hoping to get the real scoop, I met agent Smith in the hotel bar for some after-hours suds. The way he did Miller Lites, I figured California had a drought.

"Not only is our man a civilian, and a registered pharmacist," the husky undercover agent enthused, "but he's a *volunteer* undercover CI, at that; *he* came to *us!*"

The bogus script trade was flourishing—especially in southern California. Authorities were salivating for a way to make examples of some unscrupulous dealers and phony doctors. Enforcement people knew what was happening, but they weren't sure exactly who was doing it so they could put some brakes on it.

"Thank God for informants," I concurred. "The reason I'm in Washington now is to confer on an operation I was turned on to by an ex-stripper."

"We were batting under .200 in southern California—until Rex came along. Rex is our code name for the pharmacist, get it, Rx—Rex?"

"Mmm," I said, sipping. I've never been in our monument-strewn capital without thinking what this country needs is a good sense of humor.

At the time of the Washington meeting I didn't know Rex's real name was David Hall, nor did I know most of the actual locations the sting unfolded in. That information became public much later when the case went to trial.

As staff writer Allan Jalon reported in his article on Operation Rx in the Sunday June 8, 1986, edition of the *Los Angeles Times* magazine:

David Wheaton Hall was a small-town druggist. He came to Los Angeles in search of adventure and a new life. He found both in a pharmacy on Slauson Avenue, where he stumbled into a seedy world of corrupt doctors, fake prescriptions and huge profits. Hall turned government informant in an undercover investigation that took him . . . Inside the Pill Trade.

"Multiforms," the agent said, putting down his glass. "Bloody paperwork got us going. You guys use multiforms?"

I shook my head, no.

California is one of only nine states with multiple-form prescription programs and computerized systems used to follow the paths of prescriptions for the most potent drugs, which also happen to be the most abused and the most diverted for profit. Several other states are now considering the multiple prescription program. There is no doubt it's a helpful mechanism in the closed-distribution system for controlled drugs, but there is an ongoing debate concerning the economics of the expensive system.

"I'm a traditionalist," I opined. "Myself, I'd rather see the few bucks most state budgets have available spent on training good agents and keeping them in the field."

"I agree. You can't beat an agent who knows his turf and the people in it," Jim said, smiling. "But this is one time we probably wouldn't have spotted the pattern without the forms and the computers."

I have to admit that the states using the system seem satisfied. It is a cost-effective way of targeting your resources. And the system certainly helped in Operation Rx.

"Dilaudid, Doriden, Preludin and Ritalin; those were the drugs the system red-flagged for us," Agent Smith explained.

For these and any other specifically listed, extremely potent drugs, the state issues books of registered triplicate prescription forms. The doctor keeps one copy of the numbered form, the pharmacist keeps another, and the third gets mailed to the Bureau of Narcotic Enforcement in Sacramento. The forms create a closed system. Anyone who obtains these drugs by means other than the forms is either willfully breaking the law or participating in direct criminal activity.

"The only other way to get those drugs, Jack, is to steal them. The doctors have to use those special forms for the potent drugs. They're a nuisance, but the pharmacists who are legit know they're necessary."

"But how often are those drugs prescribed?" I asked sarcastically. "Even in lotus-land?"

"These drugs are so potent that they are hardly ever prescribed in regular practice—even in sunny Cal. The average doctor wouldn't use a book of a hundred forms in his whole career."

Signaling for more beer, Smith told me how the California Narcotics Bureau had established parameters for the number of prescription books requested each year. They can adjust to cover population expansion and other variables, but there are limits. When in the months preceding Operation

Rx, requests for triplicate forms began pouring into the board, they began to take notice.

The first thing they noted was that the majority of requests was coming from the Los Angeles area. They narrowed the critical area down to south-central Los Angeles, and then to a handful of pharmacies in that area. They had the geography targeted. Now they needed to get someone in there from our side.

David Wheaton Hall had come to Los Angeles looking for a job after a failed marriage and a series of less-than-enriching business experiences. He answered a newspaper classified ad for a pharmacist to work in a store on Slauson Avenue, in south-central L.A., the heart of the neighborhood initiating all the requests to the narcotics bureau.

"That's how Rex got into the picture—a new job. Though he had some misgivings about the neighborhood where the pharmacy was located . . ."

"Slauson Avenue isn't exactly Beverly Hills I take it."

"Rodeo Drive it ain't. But that wasn't what really bothered him. What did rattle his chain almost immediately after starting the job was coming across files and records showing the small store had been filling between five hundred and a thousand scripts per week—and that most of them were for the same drug." The store records showed that almost all the pharmacy's drug business was in the stimulant Preludin and a few other commonly abused codeine-based substances. It also seemed that the pharmacy's prices were grossly inflated. David Hall found slips and receipts showing the allegedly legitimate pharmacy selling prescription drugs at prices equaling those of a street pusher!

"That was only the first thing he noticed," Smith went on. "Added to that was a stream of phone calls unlike any the guy had ever had when running his own business. These callers asked weird questions, talking in hip street lingo."

"Not, 'What's the price of Ex-Lax?' "

"More like: 'How many scrips can you bust today, man?' "

"A definite tipoff," I said. "A Clousseau special. What'd his boss say?"

It was later proven that Hall mentioned these concerns to his new employers several times, but they consistently brushed him off.

"That meant a lot of wrong numbers. Rex was no babe in the woods, but he was a conscientious citizen and an ethical practitioner. Whatever was going on at his new location, it didn't appear to operate like Ye Olde Apothecary Shoppe. Things just didn't add up."

After repeated rebuffs by his employers he decided to share his misgivings with the state pharmacy board. Phone calls to the agency didn't work. He could never catch an inspector in his office. They had always "just gone out." After several fruitless attempts David Hall/Rex went in person to the board's office, determined to settle whether his imagination was working overtime or there was something illegal going on at Slauson Avenue. He liked the land of palm trees and string bikinis and was hoping to settle in.

Hall thought his luck was changing when he managed to find not just an inspector, but a supervisor of inspectors, *in* his office. Unfortunately, the supervisor shuffled him out of the office, suggesting to the former suburban pharmacist that inner-city L. A. might not be his kind of place.

Angry now, as well as growing in curiosity, Hall moved up the bureaucracy ladder a rung, contacting the Los Angeles office, DEA. As luck would have it, the agent to field Hall's call was John Uncapher, a veteran of over a dozen years in the prescription wars.

After prolonged questioning Uncapher and his officemates sensed David Hall was telling a believable story. His information was their first peek at a crack in the wall of silence around the goings-on in south-central L. A. It seemed almost too good to be true to have this guy just walk in off the street. The DEA people were eager to have a man on the inside but nonetheless tested him out thoroughly when he volunteered to help. A volunteer in a situation like this is so rare, he is automatically somewhat suspect. He could be an outright flake, or he could be one of the enemy sent to infiltrate, sort of a reverse undercover.

Along with a strenuous background check, they gave Hall gradually increasing responsibility, starting with orders to write down everything suspicious that he witnessed at the pharmacy.

"Sounds dangerous to me," I said. "I'd rather have no informant than one who didn't know what he was doing."

"They gave him some impromptu training. He was enthusiastic, eager as hell. Being a pharmacist he had the natural cover going for him, but he was a diamond in the rough. If we were going to use him undercover, it meant starting from scratch. He was ready to help but, naturally, untrained as a drug cop. He had to learn the rules of evidence, what constitutes entrapment, and all the other legal intricacies you need to have in order to convict."

Hall took his orders—to write down whatever appeared suspicious—seriously. During his initiation period he noticed and wrote so much he began burying his new compatriots under an avalanche of paper.

"Besides script numbers and doctors' names, he was also writing down car descriptions and license-plate numbers of suspect customers. He recorded scraps of conversations he overheard between the owners and any shady-looking repeat customers," Smith said. "Judging from the volume, I'd say everyone looked suspicious to Rex. He put everything but his own lunch order on paper."

The agent said the authorities were intrigued with their volunteer pharmacist because, though much of the information Hall initially turned over was irrelevant or inconsequential, the mass of intelligence pointed to some kind of hanky-panky on Slauson Avenue. They kept him at it.

Then he came up with something they could get their teeth into: Hall reported one of the owners had come to him hinting at seeking kickbacks from Los Angeles area doctors for filling "certain prescriptions."

After his tryout period and a polygraph test, Hall officially became Rex, an authorized CI (confidential informant) for the Drug Enforcement Administration. He agreed to work without pay and to even turn over to the DEA any monies he received while working undercover—which turned out to be considerable. In court, it's a relatively simple and common tactic for a defense attorney to impugn a witness as a paid informant, casting at least a shade of doubt on the moral reliability of someone who obtains and passes information for profit. Credibility is the issue. Disregarding whether the informant may have risked his life during the undercover operation, the lawyer and the jury look askance if the informant has been paid.

"The beauty part of this case was that Hall couldn't be impugned, because he wasn't taking a nickel," Smith said, hitting on a bowl of pretzels.

During the course of the sting the owner of the pharmacy paid Rex, in addition to a thousand-dollar weekly salary, another thirty-eight thousand dollars in illegal doctors' kickbacks. All of which he turned over to the government, which helped make his eventual testimony virtually unimpeachable.

It didn't take long before Rex himself was convinced his new job wasn't the standard, legitimate pharmacy operation he'd been used to in Hicksville. From some people he got friendly with in the neighborhood, he learned that prior to his coming to work at the small store there had often been prescription waiting lines right out the door. Lines so long they looked like movie premieres from Hollywood's heyday. For prescriptions?

"Getting the undercover operation into gear, Rex did some testing of his own," Smith told me. "He chose some of his more suspicious-looking customers to begin with. He charged them outrageous prices—sometimes doubling the price on the same script from one day to the next. Any legitimate consumer would've raised the roof. But, Rex said, 'Nobody . . . ever questioned our prices.' "

"Another tipoff," I interjected.

"Shady clinics in the L. A. area even began sending patients in groups! All with scripts for the same drugs. Like Talwin—"

"A convenient painkiller," I interrupted. "Convenient because junkies can boil it down and inject it. More bounce to the ounce. Sending people in groups . . . The clinics *must* be in on the juice."

My California compatriot had taken my interruption as an opportunity to destroy another Lite. He came back smiling.

"The transporters tie the bad clinics up," he nodded.

"Even own one or two themselves. Contract to use them to siphon script drugs at tidy profits; drop a bit on the clinic clients to keep them happy. Dealers also use unemployed street people as runners to fill and retrieve the phony scripts for them. Lotsa times the runners are strung-out addicts themselves, working to support a habit. Dealers who tie up this type of pipeline operation from doctor to addict, and grease all the skids in between, are known as transporters."

As Operation Rex proved, the transporters had several doctors and at least a few pharmacists on the payroll. In this case the doctors were doing the most damage. Less than two dozen of them, centered around L. A., were writing 10 percent of all the triplicate-form prescriptions in the entire state! A detailed examination of the scripts turned up an inordinate number written for patients named James K. Polk, Millard Fillmore and J. F. Kennedy.

Rex took to his undercover role like a duck to water. He learned to detect and shake a tail, to record conversations clandestinely, and to maneuver suspects in front of hidden cameras. Rex loved the spy act. These were all skills he used during the term of the sting. Skills that saved his life.

The DEA managed to get the Slauson Avenue pharmacy phone bugged, hoping for tapes to back up Rex's eventual testimony. As Rex branched out, wheeling and dealing outside the pharmacy and drawing more people into his net, they set him up in a specially equipped apartment, with bugs and two-way mirrors. Here Rex secretly filmed deals reminiscent of the tapes showing Delorean's alleged cocaine deal. Authorities feared for his life several times. The people Rex was rubbing elbows with in the drug world were very suspicious, the type that shoot first and ask questions later. Fortunately, his cover held.

As Rex became known and accepted by the local underworld, doctors from area clinics began to call him directly, sounding him out for their high-volume drug needs.

"How many 'ludes can you do for me today?" was a common phone request. The doctors who dealt with him directly often sounded like junkies themselves. They'd ask his limit on certain drugs for that day. Then they would send runners with as many prescriptions as Rex had told them he could fill.

The West Coast agent signaled for our check. "You talk about public spirit," he said. "This Rex has put his ass on the line more than once and never asked for a cent. Despite several close calls—and I mean *close*—Rex hung in there. He helped build solid cases against twenty area doctors and numerous pushers, transporters and dealers. I hope you're as lucky with your CI, big guy."

Leaving Washington, I thought about Agent Smith and the California sting often in the hard times during my own investigations of the Doctors Feelgood. Agent Uncapher and his associates knew as well as I the difficulties and frustrations of building tight cases for prosecution, particularly against the abusers in the professions. That's one reason someone like Rex is so invaluable as a source of solid, prosecutable intelligence and testimony. And when you're on a roll it can be tough to let go.

Operation Rex died of its own success. It had to come to an end if only because of the sheer volume of the drugs going out across the counter. Our primary job, even if we can't convict, is to stop the flow of junk from going out onto the street. We could justify the Slauson Avenue flow for only so long once we had a handle on how it worked. If we missed a diverter or two by shutting down, so be it. The drug flow was stopped from the source. Local enforcement agencies were understandably upset when the decision was made to end the operation, but the longer it went on, the more dangerous it also became for Rex.

Just before the operation was shut down, Rex and California state narcotics agent Dale Ferranto made a hurried midnight raid on the pharmacy. Despite the pending shutdown, they weren't ready for the owner or any of the bad guys to know their plans. Rex's life was in serious jeopardy if there were any premature leaks. Rex and Ferranto snuck up to the darkened store from the rear. They hoped to spirit away records of the thousands of prescriptions filled and disengage their planted telephone bug.

It seemed like a Three Stooges rerun for a while. The two undercover men had what they'd come for. Loaded with evidence they were just sneaking back out the rear door when searchlights flooded the area. When Rex jumped back in to the store, the door slammed shut. Agent Ferranto was locked outside the store in the pitch-black alley, arms full, just when a heavily-armed L. A. police department chopper, looking for B-and-E suspects, was lighting up the high-crime neighborhood with searchlights.

Luckily, they were passed over. Cops or not, they would have had a hard time explaining their presence in that neighborhood, in an alley, arms full.

Things were tight right up to the end for David Wheaton Hall. In addition to the people arrested on his testimony, many others, though unindicted, had profitable businesses short-circuited. There was never any doubt that some drug kingpin, or just an underling angry at getting caught, would try to nail him for his undercover work and subsequent testimony. The government had to work overtime to keep him alive.

Pressure on Rex lifted when word came that the underworld believed Rex dead, victim of a gangland revenge hit. Our ruse had worked. Rex's apartment was tossed. The Toyota pickup registered to Rex was abandoned—where else in California but in a mall? Rex's truck was set up to look as if he had been the victim of a professional hit. The newspaper photos showed it, complete with bullet holes and fake blood.

Rex was flown out of the L. A. area and is now a part of the government witness protection program.

4 Drug Buy Gone Awry

STEVE MURPHY WAS ONLY TWENTY-FOUR years old. He had been working for the DEA less than two years when he was chosen to work an undercover assignment with the Boston PD. He was a young man in a dangerous job, but the assignment should have been a routine undercover drug buy. Unfortunately the buy went awry. The suspects tried to turn the tables but got caught when the tables tipped over on them.

A lot of jobs involve danger. Construction worker, soldier, firefighter—all have some level of risk, as does a law enforcement worker. But regardless of the level of peril in these occupations, we tend to spend the time in between crises forgetting the last action that caused the adrenaline to flow—until the next one comes along. I guess that's what makes the high-risk professions bearable.

The drug business seems to attract more than its share of violent types. I suppose it's the enormous profit margin involved, as well as the general instability of users, the street folk that agents most often deal with. The potential for danger is in every phase of drug work. Three DEA men were shot in the month of January 1987 alone.

Because I've been in the business so long, usually as "Mr. Inside," and because most of my direct work is in intervention or after the fact, I tend to forget the omnipresence of danger—at least until some young whippersnapper like

Murphy walks into the middle of my routine day and, whitefaced, announces, "I just killed a guy."

Death, as the poet says, diminishes us all. When we confront the death of any person, friend or enemy, we glimpse our own mortality. When we have caused that death, regardless of the circumstances, we can't help but second-guess our actions. We ask ourselves a thousand times: Could there have been another way?

The case began when Boston DEA office group supervisor Larry Lusardi teamed babyfaced Steve Murphy with veterans Jim Sullivan and Al Keaney and sent the three of them on temporary assignment to the Boston Police Department Drug Control Unit.

Steve took a lot of ribbing because of his age. "Hey Murphy, you wanna look good? Have the cat lick your whiskers off before going over there." This and other comments sent him on his way. At Boston Police HQ our men got together with Boston detectives Tom Maher, Tom Matheson, Walter "Mitty" Robinson and Jack Parlon and their key and trusted informant, Spelt. Trustworthy informants are crucial to police work, both for reliable inside information and as an entree into the enemy camp. CIs provide information to the authorities for any number of reasons—including money, the need to stay in the good graces of the cops or, in certain instances, the desire to get a bargaining chip for leniency or consideration in some crime they've been nailed for. People's lives often ride on the reliability of intelligence received from an informant. That's only textbook stuff unless it's your ass on the line.

In this instance it proved to be Murphy's life that was in the balance. Spelt had worked for Boston PD before. He insisted he had a good line on two busy (meaning high-volume) Hub cocaine dealers. He seemed to know what he was talking about. The Boston PD did not call us just because they needed our professional expertise. They needed the bodies, extra manpower for proper backup. They also wanted some fresh faces, faces unknown on the local drug scene. And, most importantly, they needed the up-front money to make the undercover purchase.

As the detectives briefed our guys on the background, it unfolded that Spelt had recently made contact with two narcotics traffickers who claimed to have ounce quantities of cocaine for sale. It would logically follow that if they were dealing ounces, they had pounds in inventory—which made this a tempting bust.

"Nothin' to it, man. Ferbush and Gander, two laid-back dudes," Spelt assured them. "Cool and easy bust. Get all that shit off the streets."

At this point in the operation, much remained unknown —price, potency, quantity. Any street-drug price is volatile, depending on supply and demand and how much heat is in the dealer's territory. Purity and potency are strictly sometime things with street drugs. That's one reason why diverted legal drugs are so popular; people know what they're getting.

Inconsistent potency is definitely the main danger with analog or designer drugs; school-age kids are particularly prone to these home laboratory concoctions because of high supply and low price. Other drugs such as acid and angel dust, wherever manufactured, are also dangerously fickle in potency. Single sample hits of crack have been known to kill.

Despite variances, street-strength cocaine powder usually sold for roughly two grand per ounce of perhaps 12 percent purity in those days. Though the details had yet to be proved, Spelt alleged that these dudes were selling 20-percent potency cocaine at fifteen hundred bucks an ounce. A steal.

Being the newest and youngest, the least apt to be recognized or otherwise arouse suspicion, Murphy was chosen as the front man to meet the dealers, Ferbush and Gander. He definitely looked the least like a cop, a babe in the woods.

They agreed upon a procedure plan, divided assignments, and sent the informant ahead to set up a meet and buy for the next day. Then they obtained official advance funds, as the money used to purchase evidence is called, from our DEA cashier.

Spelt returned after setting up a meet with the coke dealers at Park Square, not far from BPD headquarters. The veterans reminded Murphy to stay in visual contact with the backup team at all times. His safety, they told him, depended in large measure on the cover crew being able to spot trouble before it started. They went over the details of the plan one more time. Murphy took the OAF money and, accompanied by Spelt, proceeded to the designated meet area in Park Square.

It is common among those involved in drug deals to arrange an initial meeting to see if the dealer trusts the setup. Even if the purchaser has been vouched for, the dealer will usually want to feel him out. The talk is always vague, avoiding specifics so that if the buyer does turn out to be heat or is wearing a wire, the dealer can deny everything in court—or claim he was talking about selling furniture or some other merchandise.

Here is yet another reason why CIs are so invaluable to law enforcement people: they are generally known by the dealer—or at least recognized as part of the underworld scene—or they have been vouched for by another denizen. If the potential buyer passes whatever minimums the dealer has, then often there is another meet to set up the terms and location of the deal. Sometimes, usually depending on the quantity of drugs and cash involved, the buy is set for a distant and removed location, with varying degrees of security. On a minimal street buy, however, the participants usually just step around the corner and make a swap. Drugs for money.

This time, having already spoken for Murphy, the CI was bringing Steve and the sellers together, our side hoping to negotiate and consummate the deal on the spot. The spot was the sidewalk in front of the Playboy Club, chosen so that Murphy would remain in full view of the backup team.

Teetering between the encroaching edge of urban renewal and the backwash of the infamous moral sewer known as the Combat Zone, the Park Square area of downtown Boston was primarily an area of fading glory: old office buildings, former chic retailers, an old hotel, a bus station, a bar or two frequented by workers and locals, and a few of the inevitable tourist-trap bars. And the Playboy Club.

The agents got backup coverage finally in place ten minutes before the scheduled meet for the buy. The meet was set for the public sidewalk at one in the afternoon. Murphy and Spelt were there on time, waiting, trying to look inconspicuous.

The backup team is crucial in any law enforcement work, but especially so in drug work, where the financial stakes are so high and the potential sentences so severe. The risks to bodily health are also high; most of the people drug agents confront are apt to be unstable from using the substances they are dealing. Add to that the fact that we are taking away their means of quick and easy big bucks, and you can see why it's such a violent subculture.

Detective Matheson waited at the window of a tavern at the intersection. Detective Parlon waited on the mall of the old monument in front of the bus terminal. Maher pretended to be buying tickets in the glass-fronted airline office on the street-level floor of the formerly grand hotel. Two DEA agents, Sullivan and Keaney, were parked in a drab brown Plymouth sedan in front of local radio station WEZE. No one was more than a hundred yards away.

Shortly after 1:15 p.m., two black males in their mid-to-late twenties approached from the direction of Boston Common.

The backups identified them as Ferbush and Gander as they sauntered through the parking lot. The suspects stopped at the end of the building, looking furtively around. Even if they had not been suspects, the agents would have suspected them anyway because of their behavior. The dealers called Spelt over and had a brief conversation with him. They did not even acknowledge Steven Murphy's presence.

Murphy saw that the suspect called Ferbush looked the part in waist-length red leather jacket, plaid slacks and a powder blue baseball cap. His partner, Gander, wore a sweater and dungarees. He knew that both suspects had lengthy police records. Watching them, Murphy wondered what amount of greed or desperation drove men to deal or use such a deadly drug.

His philosophical speculation ended abruptly when he remembered his skin was on the line. The two suspects and the informant were just beyond earshot, but they were gesticulating wildly in his direction, obviously in disagreement over something.

They were trying to set up a deal, testing each other out and talking ounces, grams and eightballs. An ounce of cocaine runs between 25 and 28.35 grams, depending on how the measuring is done and who does it. An eightball is an eighth of an ounce (just over three grams) and used to go for three hundred bucks. A gram today sells for anywhere from 80 to 250 dollars, depending on what the traffic will bear. A gram yields about ten lines for a snorter, and most coke users go through that pretty quickly. Don't forget, we're talking street cocaine here. Pharmaceutical strength cocaine is 100 percent pure, so if someone steals a pharmaceutical ounce, multiply everything by at least five. Even taking into account wide variances in price and purity, that's extremely big bucks—enough to kill over, as we were to discover.

Despite Murphy's relative newness, he could tell Ferbush and Gander were being cautious, perhaps beyond even normal street wariness. What he didn't know then was that Gander, of the sweater and jeans, had just completed a four-year prison term at Danbury Federal Correctional Institute on a narcotics charge.

He'd tried to sell to the wrong person.

For a while it looked like the deal wouldn't go down.

"I promised, in prison," Gander said, loudly repeating his vow that he'd never again sell cocaine to any living white person.

"He's allfuckinright man, he's straight!" Spelt assured the two nervous dealers.

Ferbush finally came over to Murphy. They began cautious negotiations. Things seemed to go smoothly until the question of where the deal would go down came up. Murphy didn't want to move.

"Here, right here, man—what's wrong with right here in front of the Playboy Club?" Needless to say, Murphy liked having his formidable backup team in place, and nearby. His life might depend on it.

Ferbush and Gander kept pushing for a move to a location of their choice. "No man, let's go to Hammond Street!" they insisted. Hammond was deep in the city's heavily ethnic Roxbury section where the white backups would stick out like sore thumbs. Whoever they were, Ferbush and Gander revealed they had some experience in these matters.

Murphy held out. "Should go down right here."

"Our place," Ferbush and Gander repeated.

They had reached an impasse. The negotiations went nowhere for about an hour, and the detectives and agents in hiding grew apprehensive.

"Knew I shouldna tried to sell to a honky," Gander complained, stalking the sidewalk angrily. Apparently he was mad at himself for even thinking about breaking his self-imposed prison rule. He said he wanted to call the whole thing off, not sell to Murphy.

Ferbush repeated his marketing plan. A couple of other totally unsuitable locations were offered. Murphy held firm, but he was getting worried about losing the suspects altogether. No arrest was any good until they'd tried to pass the actual drugs. We needed that for evidence.

Gander finally decided to make an exception in the case of Murphy. Of course, greed and stupidity are powerful negaters of caution. Eventually, both sides agreed to meet in front of the YMCA on Huntington Avenue. Though offered by the suspects, it was more desirable than the Roxbury location for Murphy, and more maneuverable and racially camouflaged for his cover.

Ferbush went with Spelt and Murphy. They got into Spelt's car, Murphy taking the wheel.

"I'll go to Hammond Street," Gander said, "meet another individual and get the powder."

Leaving the Park Square district, they agreed they would all meet in front of the Y in fifteen minutes.

Alerted, the backup team began to mobilize for relocation. None of the veteran drug men liked the way things were developing, but they hung in there, reluctant to abort the case at this late stage.

According to a contingency plan, DEA agents Sullivan and Keaney were to follow Murphy, Ferbush and Spelt to the Huntington Avenue area, then radio back to the Boston DCU detectives, who would move up and disperse themselves strategically. Matheson took his initial surveillance position in the window of a pizza shop near the Huntington Hotel. Maher remained behind the wheel of an unmarked car near the intersection.

Murphy could only get more apprehensive as time passed. The longer a deal goes on, the more room there is for error, the longer the suspect has to find you out. He and Spelt and Ferbush waited parked near the Y several eternities before Gander finally reappeared, approaching from the rear of the car. He jumped in the back, sitting directly behind Murphy, who was in the very vulnerable driver's seat.

Murphy got doubly jiggy when Gander jumped in the seat behind him. Gander said that "his man," meaning the man he'd gone to Hammond Street to meet, the man with the cocaine, was waiting in a cab nearby. He added that the man wanted Murphy to go to a different location with him, in the cab.

"We'll pull down some side street, finish this deal," he said.

Needless to say, Murphy balked. He didn't want to get out of sight of his backups for more than a few seconds—not if he could help it. He suspected Gander of being up to no good while he was away. He could have done anything or gone anywhere.

Later Murphy found out Gander's movements during the time he was gone. He had hailed a cab at the Combat Zone intersection of Washington and Essex Streets, then ordered the cab, driven by a Haitian immigrant, Jean Rouge, to Schuyler Street where they picked up another man; then they drove to the previously mentioned Hammond Street address—where the new arrival picked up a sawed-off shotgun!

In the car, things were getting a little heated with Gander wanting Murphy to go elsewhere with "his man." Murphy refused, even when Gander pointed to the cab parked nearby on the corner of Gainsboro and St. Botolph. Gander was too anxious to have him travel.

"The farthest I'd go would be a block, and that's walking," Steve said. "No rides."

"My man's right in the cab."

Murphy pointed out the street next to the New England Conservatory of Music. That was as far as he was going. He parked the car in the nearest spot to the corner.

"This car and this money don't move again. You bring the coke to me, you want to make a deal. Bring it here. I'll test it right here in the car and we can do it that way," Steve said firmly, hoping this would mean the end of negotiations.

Now Ferbush demanded to see the money.

"Good idea, man," Gander agreed.

Glad for the chance to move from the front seat, even for a moment, Murphy got out, opened the trunk and displayed the $1,500. Seeming satisfied, Ferbush and Gander agreed he could lock it back in the trunk.

Gander then walked up the street to the cab and conferred with the third man we now know as John Dressing, another black male. Dressing stepped out of the cab. He sported a light-colored broad-brimmed hat. He was holding a silver boutique-type plastic shopping bag that presumably contained the cocaine. Seeing Dressing and the bag, Steve thought, "Thank God, it's finally going to go down."

After conferring briefly, Dressing and Gander turned and waved him up the street. Spelt waited by his car. Murphy met Dressing and Gander about halfway between the informant's car and the taxi.

"Show me the coke," Steve said.

"This street's too open, man," Dressing complained. "But we could do the deal just up the street."

He indicated the pedestrian bridge that spanned the railroad tracks. This vantage point would be the urban equivalent of meeting in an open field. Dressing could observe anyone approaching, from a distance. Like cover.

Murphy hemmed and hawed but didn't really figure he could balk too much at this point over Dressing's desire for secrecy without souring the deal. Of course he didn't know then that it wasn't cocaine in the bag, but an automatic shotgun. The whole deal had been planned by them as a straight ripoff right from the get-go.

He finally relented. Gander returned to wait at the cab.

We never proved any collusion on the part of Rouge, the cabdriver, but he has to be suspected, especially since he and Dressing lived on the same street. Even if he were terminally ignorant and didn't speak a word of the language, he'd have to figure something was up and that these dudes bouncing around the city with the meter running weren't collecting cookies from grandma's kitchen.

Ferbush and Murphy followed Dressing toward Arena Street and the railroad footbridge. Spelt remained at his car.

The surveillance team started to close in the perimeter, cautiously. Murphy was apprehensive about all the delay and switching, but what he didn't know at the time was that the instincts of the older, more experienced cops were telling all of them that, like food left out too long, this thing was going bad. Unfortunately it was probably just as dangerous for Murphy to abort at this point as to go ahead.

Reaching the footbridge, they went up a couple of steps, then Dressing stopped to let a few pedestrians pass and go on their way. The neighborhood this side of the bridge, though low on the socioeconomic scale, was bustling and lively with people and traffic. The other side was an urban wasteland, desolate and deserted, a place for hidden deeds. Murphy's instincts told him he didn't want to go over there.

"Far enough," he said. "Let's see the coke."

Dressing reached into his silver shopping bag. He came out with a murderous looking sawed-off shotgun.

"Don't move or I'll kill you right here," he said, jamming the gun into Murphy's midsection.

Steve wasn't *about* to move.

"Gimme the money or I'll kill you right here," he repeated, needlessly.

"Don't shoot! I left the money in the car," he said, looking to Ferbush. "I don't have anything on me."

Ferbush stepped in. "Gimme the keys." he said. He probably felt stupid for not making sure Murphy had brought the cash from the trunk.

Steve complied, carefully reaching for the keys. "Take the car too, if you want. Just don't shoot," he said, trying to play it light. It didn't seem to go over with Dressing. He kept the shotgun buried in his gut.

Steve heard Ferbush move off. Dressing's glance alternated, darting between his accomplice and Murphy. When Steve couldn't hear Ferbush's shuffling step any more Dressing pointed higher up the bridge stairway.

"Come with me," he said, using the barrels of the blunt gun to push back his wide-brimmed hat. "I'm going to kill you." Murphy believed he meant that.

Steve's cover was that he was supposed to be a simple John Doe out to make a drug purchase. Though the gunman hadn't responded to his attempt at humor about the car, Steve sensed he might favor a subservient, wimpy demeanor that posed him no threat. He was willing to try anything that would keep the man from pulling the trigger.

"I can't make it up those stairs," he said. "Don't shoot; Christ, I feel like I'm going to faint!"

He was trying to make it look as if he was so frightened by the threat of death that he might have heart failure any second. It wasn't far from the truth.

Dressing moved to his side, prodding him with the shotgun. They walked up the rest of the stairs. At the top he took the gun out of his gut and draped the boutique bag over it. With the shotgun now hidden from casual sight by the bag in case pedestrians happened along, he motioned Murphy across the span over the tracks.

"Move with me, or I'll do it right here," he warned. Steve went. Dressing moved ahead of him, walking sideways with the menacing shotgun trained on him through the bag at all times. Murphy's mind seemed to be frozen numb but racing at the same time, scrambling for ways out of this spot. He felt Dressing had already chosen the other side of the tracks as his execution ground.

Reaching the end of the bridge and the stairs at the far end, Steve felt time was running out. Dressing now had a feral look in his eyes. He took a few steps down, momentarily taking his eyes off Murphy. He glanced down the stairwell to see if anyone was coming, then back at Steve, ordering him down.

"Move it!"

Murphy stalled. In the split-second Dressing had taken his eyes off him, Steve had snaked his hand onto the butt of his gun tucked into his trouser waistband. Dressing now turned full face toward him, lips tight and twitching.

"I'll just have to do it right here!" he said, raising the abbreviated barrel. Enough.

Murphy whipped out his gun, pointing. "I'm a cop—drop it!" Dressing jabbed his weapon toward him, leveling, finger tightening on the trigger.

Steve jerked off a round, jumping behind the steel girder on his right and dropping to the prone position, all in the same movement. As he dropped he observed Dressing tumbling down the stairs, gun still in his hands.

Had that wild shot hit him?

No. Hitting the ground, Dressing aimed the shotgun up at him from a crouched position. Shit. Murphy ducked then got up and let go another quick round. The shot missed again but forced Dressing to scramble for cover behind a Buick parked close by.

At ground level the nearest backups, DEA agents Sullivan and Keaney, vaulted the railroad fence. They did a scrambling broken-field run across the tracks, zeroing in on

Dressing. Sullivan closed from the right, Keaney from the left, guns drawn.

Hearing the shots back at Huntington Avenue, Detective Matheson, assisted by Maher, immediately moved in on Ferbush and Gander at Spelt's car where they'd gone for the money, and on the Haitian, Rouge, still waiting at the cab.

The combatants, meanwhile, were cat and mouse. Dressing popped his head up, shotgun resting on the fender of the Buick to shoot at Murphy. Steve let fly another missing round. Same scene again, seconds later. Another round flew. Duck and shoot. Then, the fifth round Murphy fired struck Dressing in the side of the head. He was dead instantly.

Sullivan and Keaney secured the area as Steve sat on the bridge in shock, stunned at the enormity and finality of killing another human being. They scooped up Dressing's weapon, and, per procedure, relieved Murphy of his service weapon for ballistics tests in the Internal Affairs investigation. Dressing's gun was an Italian Excelsior 12. gauge, overall length twenty-two inches. Live round still in the chamber. Agent Murphy's pistol was a .9mm Smith and Wesson model 39 semiautomatic. Five rounds of Luger Super Vel fired.

As at any accident or tragedy, the area's inhabitants gathered around, gawking. Except this time, suspecting police brutality against a black, things quickly took an ugly twist.

All the neighbors knew was that they'd heard shots: now they saw a dead black man. The yet uninformed, angry residents started threatening our agents, yelling racial epithets and in general hassling them. The situation was barely defused when the men identified themselves as federal agents and the neighborhood people became involved in helping. An ambulance was summoned. Detectives Maher and Walter Robinson assisted Matheson in recovering the money back at the car and holding Rouge, Gander and Ferbush for the uniforms.

An Internal Affairs investigation, a procedure followed in every case a weapon is fired, was held immediately to determine if Murphy was justified in firing his weapon. In addition to all the media interviews, Murphy was officially questioned, first by officers of the BPD ballistics office, later by Lieutenant Eddie Connolly, head of the DCU, and officers of District 4, and finally by Detectives Arthur Kelley and William Smith of the homicide unit. The investigation eventually cleared him. The report stated he had justifiable cause for discharging his weapon, in that Dressing was clearly trying to punch his ticket. It ruled he had fired to protect his life.

None of it may have happened if the informant had had any smarts, or hadn't been so anxious for a payoff. He should have a better handle on the situation. The BPD never again trusted him in any sensitive situation. Murphy and everyone involved with the ripoff attempt wanted to penalize Spelt for endangering lives, but they were satisfied he hadn't knowingly led Murphy into a trap. And how can you prosecute someone for stupidity?

In Suffolk Superior Court Gander and Ferbush both received sentences of twenty to thirty years for armed robbery and conspiracy to commit. The federal court judge, knowing the stiffness of their local fines, sentenced them only to an additional two years probation for assault on an officer and attempted theft of funds. They each served twelve at the state prison.

Steve Murphy went on with his career and continues to be a hell of an agent. Older, but wiser.

5 The Big Payoff

THE RECOVERY OF EIGHT MILLION DOLLARS' worth of drugs from the Wyeth Labs break-in is the best example I know of how undramatic doggedness in diversion investigation can pay off in dramatic results.

I was hardly through the office door that September morning when the call came from Frank Ferraresi, distribution manager of Wyeth Labs. Hadn't even had my morning coffee.

But his frantic tone commanded urgency.

"Cleaned us out," he lamented. "Broke into our vault—took every last injectable narcotic."

At this point, neither the labs nor we knew exactly what quantity of drugs had been taken, except that Wyeth had been cleaned out. With a distributor the size of Wyeth, that can be an alarmingly large amount of drugs. A division of American Home Products Corp., Wyeth distributes many prescription drugs and sundries as well as controlled substances to wholesalers, hospitals and medical practitioners.

"We're on the way," I assured Ferraresi.

The company maintains warehouses in key locations throughout the United States. The distribution center that Ferraresi managed lies near the New Hampshire border in the historic town of Andover, Massachusetts.

At the scene, Red Eyes Houghton and I quickly ascertained that the job wasn't done by amateurs. This was a very professional operation. The perpetrators had compromised the firm's entire electronic security system, completing the job sometime between 5:30 Friday evening and the time when the loss was discovered early this Monday morning. The burglars had severed the telephone cables, disrupting the "McCullough loop" that constitutes a party-line setup with other security subscribers hooked into 3M Alarm Service headquarters in Boston. Though it had picked up the signal disruption, 3M had simply noted "circuit line difficulties" and done nothing beyond notifying the phone company.

"They were in no rush," Red Eyes surmised. Reconstructing the crime in our minds, Red Eyes and I figured that, after cutting the phone cables, the thieves waited outside awhile in the weekend quiet of the industrial park before committing themselves. Once it was obvious no response from the security company or local police was forthcoming, they went inside and used an acetylene torch to burn off the lock of the Mosler vault door. They helped themselves to over a half-million dosage units of codeine, meperidine, hydromorphone and morphine. Street value in the neighborhood of eight million dollars!

Knowing we'd need help, we enlisted the aid of Special Agent Bobby Sampson, a veteran drug agent and registered pharmacist on assigned duty to the State Police Diversion Investigation Unit. DIU detective Tom Jackson, a Metro cop also on assigned duty, joined us as well.

The first action I took, once we were sure of what had been stolen, was to send out a teletype to all DEA domestic offices, along with hundreds of other law enforcement agencies, notifying them of the break-in and including a detailed inventory. You never expect much specific help from so general a broadcast, but it always makes me feel better to know I'm hooked into a network of like-minded officers who might spot something relative to a case I'm on. In the bulletin I included the national drug code numbers on all the drugs, as well as product descriptions, lot numbers, package quantities and size and number of dosage units. There's al-

ways a shot that if another agency comes across those specific numbers in a raid they'll notify us. That teletype turned
out to be the smartest thing I did in the entire investigation,
though I didn't know it at the time. I did it because it was
procedure.

Initially, I thought the job was of local origin. It's well
known in law enforcement circles that the Boston-Provi-
dence area is the major concentration point for burglar
alarm experts. Unauthorized experts. The clustering may be
due to the large number of electronics-related industries in
the area or the presence of the Patriarca Mafia family. I
don't know why, but certain types of criminals are known to
exist in specific parts of the country: hit men from Detroit;
drugs, Miami; arsonists, New Jersey; burglar alarm special-
ists, Boston/Providence.

That teletype eventually led to direct and substantial input from Massachusetts, Vermont and Rhode Island state
police; DIU and Crime Prevention and Control Units; attorneys general of several states; the Jefferson County, Kentucky, Narcotics Unit; the Metropolitan Nashville,
Tennessee Vice Squad; and, of course, the Federal Bureau of
Investigation. There was also major input from DEA offices
in Hartford, Boston and Louisville among others.

We began our investigation by having Bobby Sampson
and Tom Jackson develop suspects from the burglary angle.
Red Eyes Houghton and I concentrated on the drugs, hoping for subsequent recovery. We also hoped that chasing the
drugs would lead us to the drug lifters. When we established
that the burglary hadn't been an inside job, the security
company was greatly relieved. They may not have been too
swift, but they weren't guilty of covering for anyone.

Nothing of any great import happened for several days of
laborious drudgery. I had the going-through-the-motions
feeling you get when you know the odds are stacked against
you. Then, the end of the first week in October, we got our
first break. Corporal George Strong, a trooper in Sharon,
Vermont, recovered materials from a highway rest area that
were identified as being from the Wyeth break-in. Non-nar-

cotic and of relatively negligible resale value to the thieves, they had been discarded.

This roadside find may not sound like much, but it was at least something tangible and gave me the needed inspiration to go on. It was also a clue that I was on the right track with the blanket coverage. I doubled my efforts on the phone, calling various parts of the country once again.

The case had extensive geographical reach, that's for sure. About the time of the Vermont retrieval, Sampson and Jackson were working the street, gathering information about some Rhode Island residents and other southern New Englanders who were rumored to be involved in the burglary. Meanwhile, I was following up on leads south of the Mason-Dixon line. Though the main trail seemed to be leading south, I was calling investigators all around the country, constantly hounding them for information and keeping my case, if not uppermost, at least fresh in their minds. Then I got a surprise call from Louisville. One of our DEA people, Paul Johnstone, told me that undercover officers of the Jefferson County PD were onto something that might interest me.

"Guy name of Bud Farmer led some of the good ole boys on an undercover operation—bought some drugs," Johnstone said.

"You think they're from my Wyeth job?"

"According to the numbers they are."

"Yahoo!" I yelped. My officemates are inured to my outbursts. "Make an arrest?"

"Not yet—I'll keep in touch."

Sleep didn't come easy that night as I anticipated a major turning point in the case. My wife, Jane, knows I don't usually bring the job home, but there are times when it's hard to contain the excitement. Or, sometimes, the anxiety.

These were days when I couldn't wait to get into work in the morning. Although the street agents were out there doing their thing more glamorously, I seemed to be getting the information that would eventually crack the case. That it was coming from far-flung venues meant I was getting the data a little late, but getting it at all gave me credibility in my own office and encouraged others to stay on the case.

The detail work was beginning to pay off. If I hadn't sent the original teletype, followed up on it and maintained good relations with the Jefferson County boys for a while, we'd have none of this. The small boring stuff was putting some heat into the case.

The very next day Johnstone reported arrests, by the Jefferson County PD, of Frank DeWayne Calvert and his paramour, Doris Wallace. Calvert had sold drugs to the Kentucky undercover agents that were traceable to the now month-old burglary on the New Hampshire border. Calvert refused to tell where he got the drugs or where the rest of the stash from the Wyeth heist was hidden. Time for the calabozo.

The case had begun to bubble. We had people contributing information from Vermont to Louisville, which was super, though there was often a frustrating communication time gap. In mid-December Paul Johnstone called to bring me up to date on their case. His case information had strings attached to the investigative work that was being done back in the Northeast. Agent Bobby Sampson, on our end, and Resident Agent in Charge Harold Brown of Louisville had already begun developing some of this connecting data. Frank Dewayne Calvert had spent the intervening month in jail before posting fifteen thousand dollars cash bail. Five days later he was picked up, with his girlfriend again, on a federal warrant charging both of them with violations of the Controlled Substances Act. Two days after Calvert's rearrest, a Rhode Island resident, Angelo W. Frigosi, Jr., of Coventry, flew into Louisville with a woman identified as his wife and a companion eventually identified as Allen Vesco, aka David Wagner, originally of Springfield, Massachusetts. Vesco had changed his name to Wagner in Milwaukee in 1970 after picking up a criminal record in the Air Force.

"They rented a U-Haul van," Johnstone reported. "A twenty-footer. Our people saw them with the van at a farmhouse in Butler, Kentucky. It was being loaded with 138 plastic garbage bags."

"Garbage bags."

"A farmer close to the place tipped off the Butler police, who contacted the Newport police. The farmer said he couldn't tell what was in the bags."

"What made him suspicious?"

"Two other guys standing guard with loaded shotguns, that's what. He figured it wasn't garbage in them there bags."

"Sounds logical to me."

"RAC Brown says this Wagner/Vesco is linked with William Osteritter; Osteritter has a company in Louisville called Antec that is suspected of selling burglary tools to bank robbers and safe men in this area."

"Burglary tools . . . cutting torches?"

"Yep, magnesium burn bars, various and sundry other equipment necessary to the nefarious trade. Get a lot of orders from up your way, Boston and Rhode Island."

"I believe it," I said, staring at my chart, trying to tie everyone together in my head.

A general broadcast bulletin went out to every PD in the nation requesting information on the U-Haul truck and Frigosi. Frigosi was next reported seen in Pennsylvania. Though the rental truck was missing, he was undeniably moving north with what we were now pretty sure was the Wyeth haul.

North could only mean the drugs were on the way back to Rhode Island! Now I was able to give Sampson and Jackson something concrete to confirm their suspicion that Rhode Island people were involved with the Wyeth theft. They stepped up their efforts with the Rhode Island state police. Nearing Christmas we were busier than we'd been the entire year.

We were temporarily sidetracked when Sampson, acting on a tip, led a big armed raid on a house in the mountains of western Massachusetts. In retrospect, there are always clear and cogent reasons for an operational foul-up. When you're in the midst of it happening, you can't always see it. Or stop it if you can see.

I now see that three things were working against us on the barn raid in the Berkshires. First, there must be some sort of physical law that events, once started, pick up a momentum of their own. Second, so many suspects are developed and profiled during an investigation of this sort, and so many leads chased, that the agents begin to get a little anxious. When what seems like a sure thing comes along, they become like kids waiting for the candy store to open. Third, plain bad luck: what seems obviously white is black; immutable facts like two and two add up to five. Call that one bad luck if you were counting on the total coming out four.

It was Christmas week. The foul-up started when we got excited looking for the truck. Frigosi had been seen in Pennsylvania, though without the rented U-Haul. We figured it was heading north with the drugs, regardless of who was driving. We figured the destination was Rhode Island.

The next development had three Massachusetts state troopers reporting the sudden appearance of two Kentucky-registered automobiles around the South Deerfield, Massachusetts, home of Vesco's mother—the same Vesco/Wagner who'd accompanied Frigosi south to Louisville, the same Vesco/Wagner who was seen with the purveyor of burglary articles similar to those used in the Andover job. You can imagine our excitement at this news. Could it be just coincidence that Kentucky-registered vehicles appeared just about the estimated time of arrival from down south?

Next we learned that when the troopers did a cursory, drive-by inspection (all that's allowed by law, unless you have a warrant or permission from the owner) they noted a large barn and garage on the property. The troopers could see inside the barn "some kind of truck." Our van?

Deerfield wasn't Rhode Island, as we'd predicted, but it was definitely north. Sampson and Detective Tom Jackson, the Metropolitan District Commission man assigned to the DIU, figured it had to be the Wyeth drugs, coming home to roost in rural western Massachusetts!

Things started picking up a speed of their own about this point. Sampson sent for a warrant and requested my services to help in the recovery from my boss, Matthew Seifer. Known as the oldest narc in the world, Matty got a whiff of gunpowder. He also saw success just around the bend. He called our Hartford office requesting back-up assistance.

"Send all available personnel—now!" Seifer ordered. The Hartford office was a little slow catching the fire of Matty Seifer's enthusiasm. It was just before Christmas and he had caught them in mid-party. They diplomatically suggested a delay. Matty insisted that they meet us at the Northampton, Massachusetts, state police barracks—and that they arrive armed with shotguns! Matty was expecting a heavy-duty shootout. Can you see a little malevolent momentum building here?

The excitement was contagious. Despite the proximity to Christmas, when most people are looking for an excuse to duck work, Red Eyes Houghton thought we were closing the net and jumped aboard. We loaded a couple of DEA cars with men and weapons and headed out west on the Massachusetts Turnpike.

We rendezvoused in the frigid Berkshires just before dark. Our crew hooked up with state troopers Eddie Branscombe and Carlton "Harry the Net" Stillings. Right behind us, Edward Noone arrived with several still-disgruntled, shotgun-toting agents from Hartford. It wasn't the best time for swapping pleasantries with associates.

Not only did they resent leaving their party, they weren't happy with Seifer's rather peremptory summons either. There was also the unspoken chance that one or more of us could be leaving widows at home.

There were places I would rather have been that night also, but at least I was intimate with the case and looked forward to recovering the drugs. During the time we'd been gathering from around the compass, the three troopers had kept the area staked out. Vesco was detained as he left his mother's house and taken to the barracks for questioning by

Trooper Randy Stevens, while the other two troopers remained on surveillance at the farmhouse.

Vesco/Wagner insisted he was just on a Christmas visit to his dear mother. He denied all knowledge of any break-in, drugs or even knowing people like Frigosi. Meanwhile, back at the Vesco corral, we had the joint surrounded. About twenty of us were armed to the teeth and eager to battle the elusive burglars and drug thieves.

As soon as the search warrants for the garage and barn arrived we moved in. Hours before Christmas and visions of sugarplums, promotions and eight million dollars in stolen drugs danced in our heads. We must have looked like the charge of the light brigade; twenty weapons-brandishing agents in gray flannel suits, eight o'clock on a clear December evening, closing the dragnet.

The dreaded words came floating back from the first man in: "It's a truck—but it's not a U-Haul."

We scoured the truck that was there, and the rest of the barn and garage.

"Nada," the reports came back. We knew we were close and we knew Vesco was no altar boy, but we had come up empty.

If you think the boys from the Hartford office party were unhappy when they arrived, you should have seen them depart!

About ten o'clock, before heading back to the Boston area and our families and warm beds, six of us Indians from Massachusetts (the three feds, Jackson of the MDC and two troopers, Stillings and Branscombe) were lucky enough to find a ma-and-pa diner open in a nearby town. It looked like they were getting ready to clean up and close when we arrived, noisily cursing our luck and trying to forget our failure.

We had some bacon burgers and more than a few beers as we commiserated over the case and talked about how tough it is being in law enforcement around the holidays.

The owners and their daughter eyed us somewhat skeptically. I couldn't blame them, given the hour, the proximity to Christmas and the fact that we'd brought our artillery in with us rather than leave all the guns unattended in the cars. One of the troopers explained we were on "official business."

"Being a public servant isn't all it's cracked up to be," I announced to no one in particular.

"Tell that to the boys from Hartford."

We kidded back and forth while we ate filling stomachs left empty from missing lunch and dinner in quest of glory.

Later we learned that our Rhode Islander, Frigosi, had turned the van in at Bob's Texaco on the Bristol Pike in Andalusia, Pennsylvania, and departed on foot, walking north on Route 13. That the South Deerfield raid turned out to be a big flop didn't deflect our conviction that we were getting close.

As often happens after a drought of information, we were suddenly hit with a storm of data. Agent Joe Coons of the Hartford DEA received word from an informant he'd been developing and came up with a very probable sounding Rhode Island location for the remainder of the Wyeth drugs. Coincidentally, Trooper Gilbert Johansen, the independently working Massachusetts state police officer attached to the attorney general's office Organized Crime Section, arrived at the same conclusion almost simultaneously. According to investigative discovery now confirmed by virtually unimpeachable inside information, they knew the drugs, about eight million dollars street value, were being secreted in a garage on Andersen Avenue in Coventry, Rhode Island.

Sampson, meanwhile, was a study in frustration. He regretted the last roundup at Deerfield corral but chalked it up to experience and had new hope from another direction. He'd received valuable leads and assistance from Massachusetts State Police, which hooked him to the Rhode Island force and its investigation into suspected buyers of stolen merchandise. This in turn led full circle back to some Boston-area criminals suspected of having been involved in the Wyeth burglary, and back again to his Rhode Island suspects. His frustration sprang from his impatience to cap the case.

Sampson felt vindicated that other agencies were finally recognizing that his Rhode Island suspects were indeed deeply involved in the Wyeth case, as he'd been asserting for a long time. But since the drugs arrived back from down south, he hadn't had time to tie his lead suspects to the drugs "beyond the reasonable doubt" needed for criminal prosecution.

After consultation among all interested agencies, the decision was finally made not to risk losing the drugs again. They'd recover them now at the risk of not prosecuting Frigosi and the others then try later to build a case from there.

The Wyeth case was a textbook example of interagency cooperation from start to finish. On Monday, January 17, Sampson and Troopers John Curtin and Johansen met with Rhode Island State Police Officers Donald Bodington and Richard Sullivan. Along with Captain Leon Blanchette and Detective Mike Urso, they would coordinate all new incoming information in the case.

The garage in Coventry was attached to a house on Andersen Avenue owned by "Bubba" Kowalsky. The fifty-year-old Kowalsky had a criminal record dating back over fifteen years. His constant companion was Barbara Ann Strombota, a petite, brown-eyed, voluptuous beauty of Portuguese descent. Barbie doll lived at the house on Andersen Avenue to which the drug garage was attached. Both Kowalsky and Strombota were under constant surveillance once the drugs were known to be there.

We'd learned from the Rhode Island staties that Kowalsky and Strombota were reliably considered high-level members of a large organization primarily engaged in the sale of stolen property as well as the distribution of pornography and illegal fireworks. On January 19 a search warrant was finally secured from the Warwick, Rhode Island, district court, and Sampson and the composite police force moved. Recovered intact were nearly a half-million dosage units of the drugs originally stolen from Wyeth Labs back in September. Also confiscated in the raid was an incredible quantity of pornography and fireworks, all of which I personally had to inventory at the National Guard armory.

All the above-mentioned units took part, as well as men from the Hartford and Boston offices of the DEA.

While this was going on in little old Rhode Island, DEA agents and members of the Nashville vice squad were making a series of raids on local individuals who held the small remainder of Wyeth break-in drugs that hadn't traveled back north.

Kowalsky was held in lieu of posting a one-million-dollar surety bond, and Babs was released on seventeen thousand dollars personal recognizance. Bubba Kowalsky was eventually released pending trial when five couples posted a $130,000 property bond with the court. I make no judgement on the IQ level of the average criminal, but sometimes it almost seems he wants to draw attention to himself when he claims to desire anonymity. Intelligence sources stated that one of the people posting bond was Satch Bonnello, an inmate of a Rhode Island state prison at the time, and Gerald Ouillette, a fellow resident of the penal institution. Both were reputed organized crime members.

After his release, Kowalsky just couldn't seem to stay out of trouble. He kept getting arrested with fireworks, of all things. Judge Francis J. Fazzano finally ruled him in violation of his bond and had him report to state prison to be held until his trial without bail.

I questioned Kowalsky time and again, hoping to get info on some of the others involved. By this time we had profiles on over thirty individuals we figured played some part in the Wyeth case. Kowalsky refused even to identify who he had received the drugs from.

"All you can do is send me to jail for a few years. They can kill me!"

A strange legal footnote here. The break-in was in September, the raid the following January, just about four months from commission to conclusion. Kowalsky was sentenced to five years but released pending appeal. His attorney challenged the validity of the search warrant utilized by the law enforcement personnel in the raid on his garage. It took almost four years before the Rhode Island Supreme Court upheld the validity of the warrant and Kowalsky began serving his sentence!

He never talked—and later was murdered after his release from prison.

The Rhode Island Attorney General's office never asked for an indictment against Barbie Strombota because of insufficient evidence (we could prove she rented the house from Kowalsky but not that she had actual knowledge of what it contained, and she had no legal control over how the garage was used) and because she testified before the grand jury and would have testified at a jury trial if necessary. It wasn't. Kowalsky waived trial.

Agent Bobby Sampson and MDC detective Tom Jackson each received monetary rewards under a federal incentive program. Red Eyes Houghton and I received a two-sentence letter of appreciation from the DEA Administrator. And some sour grapes.

6 Undercover: Accept No Substitutes

UNDERCOVER WORK IS NO PICNIC ON A GREEN lawn. Most buy or sell drug situations are so volatile that anything can happen, anytime—even with the best support systems and backups in place. Agent Jimmy Sullivan found out the hard way—as did the heroin pusher who tried for an easy $7,500 and got instead his liver, lungs and heart perforated by five steel-jacketed slugs from Sullivan's .38 caliber Smith and Wesson Chief's Special.

Heroin traffic in the suburbs north of Boston, especially Revere, Chelsea and Lynn, was at an all-time high when Jimmy Sullivan entered into a joint investigation with drug cops from the Chelsea force. He had a sit-down with three detectives from the Chelsea force involved in a long-term investigation.

"We're being buried in this brown shit all of a sudden. Mexican heroin.

"Out of New York, we're pretty sure. Our informant led us to put heavy surveillance on the Chelsea Hotel. There's enough going on there to keep us all busy. A lot of the dealers and users we know already. But the influx of brown seems to coincide with the arrival of this guy, Junior, from New York. Real name, Tino La Quenton Labelli Gonzalez. We think. Supposed to be in default on seventy-five thousand dollars bail back in the Big Apple."

"What do you want me to do?" asked Sullivan, a veteran

of Vietnam and Northeastern University's School of Criminal Justice.

"There's just too much local traffic on this one," the detectives said. "We'd be spotted immediately. You've got access to some big front money to set up a score, plus no one knows you. You can get in there, see what's happening. We'll do all the backup and protect your ass, plus we can identify all the locals and locate their stash pads. We already got an information source in close. Maybe you can pull another one out of your hat."

Lean, curly-haired Sullivan was known as a good street agent. He had the reputation of having the most and best informants of all drug enforcement workers.

DEA group supervisor Lawrence Lusardi agreed on the joint endeavor for our office. It was determined that the informant would arrange an introduction to Junior. Agent Sullivan would be presented as a sizable buyer. Alert signals were arranged and agreed upon at that first meeting. His own experience—and that of some recently deceased drug agents—had taught Sullivan the wisdom of a quick bailout if an undercover operation was going sour.

A day in March was set up for the attempted takedown. Agent Sullivan showed up in his street uniform: beard, jeans and leather jacket. He conferred with the locals and members of his own team to be certain everything was in place. They planned the surveillance team locations carefully, trying to insure Sullivan would be covered at all times. Sullivan would activate his car emergency flashers as a visible panic button if he felt the undercover operation was turning strange.

After shaking down the confidential informant for weapons and contraband, Jimmy drove him to the dingy Chelsea Hotel in an official government vehicle, in this case a gold Cadillac, befitting Sullivan's cover as a heavy drug buyer.

"Bring Junior to Riley's Roast Beef," he instructed the informant. "Convince him I'm reliable. Tell him I just inherited a pile of dough from an insurance claim, that I want to invest it in heroin."

Sullivan went to wait in front of the sandwich franchise.

Cops of all kinds learn patience or grow ulcers. A lot of their time is spent waiting, especially on stakeouts. Waiting, Sullivan pondered the blackened curbside humps—stubborn, ugly remainders of February's urban snow. He prayed the outcome of the investigation would be brighter than his present surroundings. This time he was lucky. He wasn't waiting long before a medium-sized Hispanic approached from the direction of the Chelsea Hotel.

Junior Gonzalez must have thought things were cool. He smiled his approval of Sullivan's gaudy transportation when he and the informant arrived at Riley's Roast Beef. Getting in the gold Caddy, he went through a brief routine of feeling Sullivan out before the real negotiations began. Some dealers do it for security; some do it to live up to their cool image.

"I got six ounces, man. You can have it for ten thousand."

"I'll buy four ounces," Sullivan rebutted. He opened a paper bag and showed Junior his money. Government advance funds, $7,500. Junior's eyes lit up.

"No sweat," Junior said. "Jus' lemme have the money for a few minutes for front to the man, you got yourself a deal."

"Front my money? If I was as stupid as I look, Junior, I wouldn't live long, fuchrissake."

Negotiations stalled. Exasperated, Junior left, allegedly to confer with his partner, Michael. Sullivan and the informant also left the meeting locale once Junior agreed to meet Sullivan again at three.

Junior arrived for the three o'clock meeting, shaking his head. "Me and Michael talked it over, man. Four ounces is too much to be selling right away to someone we don't even know. We'll start you with an eighth of an ounce, see how that goes." You mean test me with the small amount to see if I'm a cop, thought Sullivan.

"Nah, too little," Sullivan countered. "Stay in touch, but I'm gonna try somewheres else."

Driving away, Jimmy Sullivan met with his surveillance team—a DEA agent and the three Chelsea detectives. The drug cops took it as a positive sign that Junior had come back. Regardless of what he said, it showed he was eager to move some stuff. They all agreed that Sullivan should break contact for now, but that the informant should go back to the hotel to get a feel for how the deal was going and to see what could be learned about Michael.

The informant called in his report to Sullivan at six o'clock.

"There's a shitload! *Pounds* of the brown heroin stashed at the hotel. Small buyers are coming and going out of there like ants at a picnic. Michael has direct access to it. Junior and Michael want to deal with you—they really do, I heard them. All you gotta do is buy the eightball ounce for $250 tonight, they'll sell you four ounces tomorrow. It's like some kind of test."

The kicker came when Sullivan asked: "Did you recognize this Michael?"

"Careful—Michael is Loco Strallago."

Spanish for "crazy," Loco was aptly named. Pedro Martina Chevez-Strallago was street tough and well known in the Hispanic community for running true to his name. Teamed with the New Yorker, Junior, he would fill out a dangerous pair. Although the details were unknown to our intelligence at the time, Chevez-Strallago was known as a ripoff artist who preyed on anyone smaller, weaker or dumber. He was a terror—especially with naive teens who would come looking to make a drug score, only to get picked clean by twenty-three-year-old Loco from Maya-guez, Puerto Rico.

It was said his favorite ploy was to sell drugs to a shaking addict for an exorbitant price, then follow the junkie until he was alone, hold him up, steal whatever money he had left and get his drugs back for resale.

"Set me up for a meeting with Michael," Sullivan told the informant. "I'll be there in half an hour."

Sullivan was beginning to feel he should pay for parking at Riley's. Loco was on time.

"Freakin' Junior was right—a freakin' gold Caddy!" Loco seemed impressed.

Sullivan played it cool. He acted as though he'd just been testing Junior and was pleased to be doing business with a man of the stature of "Michael." He agreed now to buy the introductory eighth of an ounce after he'd negotiated the price down to $230. Accepting a price too quickly can be a dead giveaway of an inexperienced narc. In return, Loco handed Sullivan a small plastic bag completely wrapped in Scotch tape. It was impossible to tell what was inside. Sullivan bridled inwardly, but held, sensing something was up. The dealer got out of the car.

"Wait here a few minutes," Loco said, enigmatically. "I gotta make a drop to a customer in the Melody Lounge."

Sullivan stuck fast. He left the tape-obscured packet unopened. Loco was back in five minutes. Leaning in through the passenger-door window, he handed Sullivan a clear plastic baggie.

"Gimme the other one back," he said.

Sullivan made the swap. "What the fuck?" Sullivan acted surprised. Able to see through the new clear plastic baggie, he could see what appeared to be brown rock heroin. The first bag must have been a plant.

"Just a test—see if you were a cop," Loco said, grinning coldly.

He had given Agent Sullivan a bag containing flour the first time. It was a clever lure designed to snag narcs. If Sullivan had blown the whistle, revealing himself as a cop at that apparent conclusion of a buy, he'd be arresting Loco for trying to sell flour. Once again, patience had paid off. Loco congratulated Sullivan. "There's seven ounces waitin' for you tomorrow, man. You passed."

"I'll still take the four," Sullivan said angrily. "No more fuckin' around." The stage was set for the next day.

Sullivan met again with his surveillance team. They quickly field-tested the brown substance in the baggie. It tested positive for heroin. A formal lab test later determined the buy bag was cut so much it was primarily lactose and barely 5 percent heroin. The meet the next day was set for 3:30. The behind-the-scenes work started early. Sullivan had agent Pat Doherty cruising the area on foot. In addition to his initial backup team they'd added several other officers in unmarked vehicles.

Sullivan arrived for the meet in the gold Cadillac. Staying in character, he negotiated for a favorable price. Loco, in white socks, gray loafers and sweatshirt, was volubly and visibly upset at what he considered Sullivan's insufficient respect for his position as a dealer. Like Junior, Loco tried to get Sullivan to front the purchase money.

"Show me your fuckin' money, man. I'm pissed. Forget it —you ain't getting this shit at no price!"

Sullivan read him to be bluffing and played him along, negotiating for a better price per ounce whenever Loco stopped for breath. The seesaw bargaining went on for almost an hour before the price was firmed back at the original bid; four ounces for $7,500.

Loco then got in the car, instructing agent Sullivan to drive around the block to the hotel. He did so. Loco got out. "Gotta check with my man," he said. Loco was making a point, stressing that he didn't own the source, that he was a middleman between Sullivan and the supplier. "Meet you back at Riley's."

Loco returned at four o'clock. They again drove to the corner of Cross Street and Broadway.

"Lemme see the money again," Loco ordered.

Sullivan took the stack of government advance funds out of the paper bag on the floor and counted it out in front of the practically salivating Loco.

"Seventy-five hundred," Sullivan said, finishing. He stuffed the bills back in the paper bag.

"Okay, gimme," Loco said, gesturing impatiently.

"Give me the heroin first," Sullivan insisted.

This new back-and-forth exchange was repeated childishly about twenty times, each time more heatedly, until Loco left the car and stomped away. To get the dope, Sullivan hoped.

He waited.

Loco returned in fifteen minutes. "I need the money to

front the deal," he said, shrugging as if it were out of his hands.

"No way," Sullivan scoffed. "No H, no deal."

"You think I'd *steal* the dough? Never! I'd never rip you off—why lose a good customer?" Loco protested innocently.

Sullivan seemed to be considering. He *was,* in a sense, because he felt he could be at the point where Loco *might* be telling the truth about needing the front, and would go no further without it. "I could never do it without checking with my people . . ." Sullivan said.

"I'll wait at Riley's," Loco said.

Realizing Loco was clever enough and patient enough to have set up another test, the agent was extra careful of a tail. Sullivan drove aimlessly for a few blocks before backtracking to confer secretly with his backup team and supervisor Larry Lusardi. Permission was withheld; no front money. Agent Sullivan agreed to try one more time to get the drugs without the front.

Back at Riley's, Loco got in the gold Cadillac and the bargaining began again. Loco asked for the money in advance. When Sullivan firmly reiterated his position of no front, Loco began to show how he got his nickname. He went crazy. For five echoing minutes Loco hurled obscene curses at the cosmic fates and the world at large. Then he honed in on Sullivan personally.

"No-money-motherfucker! You won't front the money? A lousy $7,500?" Loco was bouncing on the front passenger seat, gesturing wildly with his hands. He lapsed into several rapid-fire sentences in garbled Spanish. His accusatory rage was escalating. "Probably figuring on stealing the stuff. I bet you got a gun and plan to steal my heroin! You got a gun?"

Prepared for such an eventuality, Sullivan opened his jacket, fanning it out from his right side to show he had no weapon.

Seeing Sullivan was unarmed seemed to be permission for the bully to really go out of control. Loco slid a quick hand to the small of his back, whipping out a six inch double-edged pigsticker. Loco suddenly grabbed Sullivan by the throat, flashing the terrible hunting knife in front of his eyes.

"Gotcha, motherfucker," he screamed. "I'm *takin'* the money!"

Sullivan managed to raise an arm and shove Loco off. "Take the friggin' money," he said. "Just don't use the knife."

Loco wasn't to be placated. He slashed with the blade, cutting Sullivan on the face and one arm as the agent tried to ward off the blows.

Enough!

Sullivan identified himself. "Policia! Policia!" he yelled in Spanish, warning Loco. Loco kept slashing.

Sullivan held off his attacker with his right hand while with the other he reached for his own weapon, concealed in his *left* jacket pocket. He thought the sight of the Smith and Wesson would be enough to subdue the crazed drug dealer. He brandished the weapon at Loco. "Stop!"

The sight of the gun didn't even slow him down. Loco slashed again. Now he seemed to go completely berserk. Ignoring Sullivan's warnings he lunged again and again at Sullivan's face, neck and chest.

The agent managed to kick Loco away on the seat for a split second. He reached, activating the emergency signal to his backups. The surveillance team started to close immediately.

But Loco lunged again, stabbing at Jimmy Sullivan's heart. Deflected, his knife arm went behind Agent Sullivan. They locked in a death embrace. Sullivan knew his end was near. He felt the breath of doom. He fired his weapon.

"Motherfucker!" Loco screamed. "Motherfucker—" Loco's attack continued unabated. The shots didn't slow him. Wrestling on the seat, he tried again to stab Sullivan.

In the seconds it took for the backups to close, Sullivan fired again. Loco kept attacking, struggling to swing the knife at close quarters. Sullivan fired again. His assailant finally stopped all slashing movement just as the backups flung open the Cadillac door.

It had taken five rounds to stop Loco. Stopped him dead. The attention from this case and the ensuing crackdown and arrests around heroin distribution left a gap. The law of supply and demand was re-enacted. And the old physical law of push and shove, action and reaction had to come in to play again. The marketplace demanded heroin. The heroin had dried up. The addicts went looking for a substitute.

Some of the faces changed, but the dealers were there to meet the demand with a product. Unfortunately, the substitute was even more deadly than heroin.

7 Pac Man

THE LAW IN PHYSICS SAYS: "FOR EVERY ACTION there is a corresponding reaction." That law holds in the drug business.

As mentioned before, if the heroin supply dries up, the users look for a substitute. Like pacs.

Kids love pacs.

It could be a jingle for breakfast cereal. Kids love pacs.

Except pacs are a deadly combination of highly addictive substances that produce a heroin-like rush. Pacs are especially attractive to young people and teenagers because they are available, easily hidden and inexpensive. And pacs pack a lot of bounce to the ounce.

Eddie B. says about them: "Mostly the bounce is into an early grave. *Sane* junkies don't use crap like that . . . not if they have a choice."

But choice is a commodity most drug users surrendered long ago. Addiction takes it away. Heroin users *have* to have their fix. If heroin is taken off the streets, they look for the next best thing. Pacs.

Pacs are especially lethal among young people. The primary ingredient of pacs, Glutethimide, is extremely addictive. Glutethimide short-circuits the central nervous system, so there's no way to tell beforehand what the next jolt of the drug will do to the brain or nerves. Especially in developing young bodies and brains. If pacs are followed by alcohol, as young people are wont to do, forget it. Not far to the vegetable farm or cemetery.

The current East Coast street price for pacs ranges from forty-five to seventy dollars. The price varies only slightly, nationally. Sounds expensive, but not compared to hash or coke. Resembling packs of lifesavers, the foil-wrapped, eleven-pill packages contain Doriden, or Glutethimide, a schedule III depressant, combined with generic aspirin, codeine tablets or Tylenol 4. Also known as "4s and Dors," "Ds and Ts" or "loads," they are usually wrapped three Doriden/Glutethimide tabs to eight of the generic aspirin and codeine, or Tylenol and codeine.

As police have become more aware of pacs and on the lookout for the foil packages, the kids have begun to carry them loose in a pocket for quick ingestion or destruction of evidence if they think they are about to get caught. The most common method of usage is to liquify the tabs, then shoot the pac drugs into a vein. Drug abusers go for the pacs because of the heroin-like euphoria.

"Getting off on pacs is it, man," a user told me. "It's like no-name brand heroin." Unfortunately, it hooks like heroin, too. And it doesn't let go.

Conceding the underground chemist's ability to combine, alter or recombine chemical compounds, and the insatiable, unquestioning high-seeking of America's young, there will always be a new product coming down the road to entice them and promise the ultimate high. This week it's pacs, next week it's crack, or bazuko—five, ten years ago it was smack. Whatever chemical is chic or hot or publicized gets the most attention—for a while—but the basic problem of abuse remains the same.

We have to help kids make right choices.

Pacs emerged nationally in the early eighties and came to my attention over the winter of 1983–84, when as many as twenty deaths in the Chelsea/Revere/Lynn area north of Boston were traced to pac drugs. The deaths were because of the unpredictable effects of Glutethimide on the central nervous system. The user doesn't know, one fix to the next, what the drug will do to him; but he knows he *has* to have it.

The price of a heroin-type rush was getting very high. Good enforcement work had taken much of the heroin off the local streets. Now our job was to get at the source of the pacs and cut down on the slaughter.

A pac task force was set up, including personnel from the state police DIU, DEA, district attorney's offices from two counties, the state pharmacy board and officers from the Boston, Revere, Chelsea, Peabody and Danvers Police Departments, the most severely affected North Shore areas. State trooper William "Beeper" McGreal, representing the DIU, began checking out the local pharmacies as possible ingredient leak or sales sites for the pacs. Beeper is so-named because he was the first trooper to employ the electronic paging system on the job. It was suspected by less than totally charitable associates that Beeper was headed for the golf course every time he said, "Call me."

The Boston Police Drug Control Unit (DCU) contingent was headed up by detective Joe Mugnano. Five-ten, dark-haired Joe had a surveillance going on an East Boston paint and wallpaper store and had already arrested several people for possession of pacs. Mugnano knew from his surveillance, coupled with informant leads, that the paint store was a distribution center for the illegal drugs. He obtained a warrant and engineered a raid, but his search of the premises had come up empty, except to seize a small-caliber handgun. The only thing Mugnano's people found relating to drugs were several paint cans half-filled with sand where the drugs had been hidden. The store had to have been tipped off.

Mugnano wasn't happy to have been foiled but was so eager to get at the primary source of the drugs that he could stand some disappointments with the lower echelon mules and distributors. During the next few months he arrested six other pac distributors and identified or arrested at least ten additional individuals involved. His progress seemed to lead him in an ever-tightening spiral.

The people he'd arrested, though none was admitting it

yet, all appeared to be supplied from one source. It seemed to the investigators that virtually all the pacs action emanated from one super-broker or dealer. Though the structure of this drug ring was typically pyramidal, with the guy at the top sitting on all the layers of protection, the Boston detective felt upbeat about his chances.

"My intuition tells me it won't be long before we positively identify this dirtball. Whoever the pac ringleader is, he'll be ours," Mugnano said optimistically. But for now, he was frustrated and running out of leads.

Finally, a lucky break. During a meeting with a subject it was revealed to Mugnano and Detective Mike Fiandaca that the source of all but a trickle of the pac drugs in the targeted area was a pharmacy on Bennington Street in East Boston owned by one Angelo Baratto. Mugnano and Beeper McGreal came to the DEA Boston for permission to review our files relevant to Baratto and see if we had any other cross-references to him or the pharmacy.

The files did contain references to a 1976 case, a burglary of Pentagon Laboratories in Montreal, involving over half a million dosage units of Dilaudid. Two Massachusetts men, Gerard Pono and Rocky Canolli, had been arrested in East Boston with a quantity of Dilaudid traceable to the Montreal burglary.

These arrests had led to the establishment of a confidential informant from the DEA Boston. Working deep undercover, the CI learned from a reliable source that most of the illegal Dilaudid in the East Boston neighborhood was being purchased from a local firefighter, Joseph Urbi. Urbi's alleged partner in the Dilaudid business was our suspected pac pharmacist, Angelo Baratto.

The informant's cover had been solidly established, and there was no way Baratto could suspect him. When, however, the informant attempted to make an evidentiary undercover purchase from Baratto, he was told: "Too much heat. You and me don't transact any business until things cool down." Baratto's reluctance intimated another tipoff, or at least uncommon caution.

Urbi the fireman eventually pled guilty to one of two counts of an indictment returned by a federal grand jury in Boston for conspiracy to manufacture controlled substances. He was sentenced to four years in a federal pen and two years special parole, though these charges were unrelated to the Dilaudid business. Urbi would pop up again in a clandestine lab scam. Baratto was not prosecuted at that time.

A second file reference to Baratto was found in another investigation focusing on cocaine traffic in the same locale north of Boston. Enough information was culled from our files to give Beeper McGreal his probable cause for warrants to investigate Baratto. With Fast Eddie Sullivan and myself representing the DEA, we agreed that Beeper and his task force people would handle the undercover and street end of the case and our agency would attempt to determine where the legal drugs originated.

"We'll get to the crust of this matter," was Fast Eddie's typically well meant but slightly off articulation. "If it is Baratto, we'll expedite *!&#•/½ the mothuh!"

We also agreed that when the case against Baratto was nailed down, at the time of arrest our office would take charge of the physical premises and conduct the accountability audit.

I should mention here that unlike novels, real life is a little less neatly ordered. It would seem from the way these cases unfold sequentially that we work case A, finish that, and start case B. Not so. More often a diversion agent is working many cases simultaneously, all at varying stages of development. The good agent gets used to juggling many investigations at once, bringing his strongest attention to bear on the one most hot at the moment.

At the time the pacs investigation started, I was already deep into a computer fraud investigation, a drugs-for-sex case and concurrently chasing a bogus script ring that took me to Cape Cod and the islands of Nantucket and Martha's Vineyard. I also had one eye on a smuggling case originating in Lebanon that an officemate was shepherding. Added to that, there were always court or board appearances to be made on cases pending. I'm not complaining—I like the variety of the work even if it does sometimes get hectic.

The computer fraud case was heartbreaking because the owners of the drug distribution company involved were decent, honest people trying their best, but who were raked over the coals. In the end, disillusionment and cynicism forced them to sell the family business they dearly loved.

The general manager of the P. Fraley Co., Inc., had tipped off Bill Sutherland of the state DIU, and later myself, that he suspected a part-timer, a seventeen-year-old kid, of stealing some drugs from the warehouse. He was reluctant to blow the whistle because the youngster was the son of a longtime trusted employee. Lieutenant Sutherland caught the kid in the act and managed to retrieve ten bottles of Valium, five-hundred tablets each, which the kid had hidden by the railroad tracks near his home for eventual resale. He wanted to buy a dirtbike.

The theft had been easily accomplished. The drugs were literally scooped from the firm's security cage after closing time. Previously overlooked, there was a gap of six inches between the bottom of the #10 gauge wire cage access doors and the floor. The kid simply knocked the drugs to the floor from the outside of the cage then fished them out with a broom handle. Simple. End of story. Only that, under questioning, the kid implicated "others" in the firm as also stealing.

"I'm not the only one rippin' them off!"

From the kid's statements it appeared the firm might be losing a lot more than just the few bottles of Valium he had purloined. At this point Sutherland called me in to work the case jointly with his DIU. I was still paired with Fast Eddie Sullivan.

Fast Eddie is six foot two, 235 pounds, and good at his job. But he is prone to verbal gaffes, and given his brainpower it's hard to believe he isn't scrambling *some* words on purpose. But how can you tell?

Fast Eddie wants an apartment that has "all the annuities." He assures prosecutors that "the suspect ceased to

stop at that time," but he'll keep them "appalled" of the
situation. And he's "bilivious" to mistakes when he says,
"Doug Flutie will make an excellent TV common-terrier."
Or he knows "a guy in the landscapin' business who'll give
you a 400 percent discount. His thinkin' has come around,
he's made a 365-degree circle." I'm so used to Fast Eddie
that I don't even notice half of them.

To build a case, the state Diversion Investigation Unit
first had to prove that drugs were missing, and how many of
which kind. We needed proof. The kid hadn't gone much
beyond implicating "others." Sutherland assigned Troopers
Bishop and Curtin, two of his DIU men, to work with Fast
Eddie and me on the firm's internal control systems, while
he went after suspects. It was quickly perceived that the
kid's theft was probably just the tip of the iceberg.

We established a five-month period as a control check for
our accountability audit, which gave us an idea of what was
going out. A physical inventory showed that twenty-three
different controlled drug substances could be swept under
the security gap, but Valium was the drug of choice. Our
quick check revealed alarming shortages. In that short period alone, almost a quarter million dosage units had gone
out.

"This could be a president-setting case," Fast Eddie
opined. Company officials, proud of their family business
and eager to plug the leak, cooperated fully. They even paid
for industry consultants to come in for an overall evaluation
of their plant operation. A new, expanded audit now
brought us up to half a million units missing. It seemed
impossible for someone in the company not to have noticed
such a shortage. Someone had stolen 850 bottles of Valium,
each bottle containing 500 capsules.

I was somewhat embarrassed for the company, as well as
being in a bit of a moral bind. I liked them and could see the
principals ran the company honorably, a rare enough occur-
rence nowadays. But technically they *were* negligent in their
control and record-keeping of controlled substances—and
that is punishable under the law. I knew my boss wouldn't

be at all understanding. He'd go for their throat, theft or no
theft. All security is the responsibility of the company. Fraley was facing heavy expense, perhaps a half-million dollars
in civil fines, plus possible suits.

The DIU were developing suspects and polygraphing everyone in sight, while I was trying to figure out how so
much product could get by. The flaw wasn't easy to find.
Overall, the record-keeping system seemed to be adequate.
Until I discovered there was no reconciliation system to
crosscheck physical inventory counts against computer-gen-
erated inventory figures.

The firm's stock status/buyer's guide also seemed to present a weak link. As an item leaves inventory it's marked
down and eventually keyed into the computer. This com-
puter-controlled inventory sheet is supposed to reflect current supplies on hand so that the buyer, noticing dwindling
amounts of a given product, will reorder for the firm before
they run out. One problem I saw was the big lag between the
time the merchandise moved from the shelf and the time
when it became a data entry into their computer system.
There were other potential problem areas, not the least of
which was that the company had always relied on the
DEA's periodic unannounced audits as their main double-
checking system!

Centering on the firm's adjustment procedure, I discovered that if the proper Fraley Co. product code number was
known for a certain item, it could be entered anonymously
through any computer terminal in the company. An in-
depth internal investigation then revealed the unauthorized
Valium inventory adjustments. Whoever was doing the
stealing simply ordered more whenever they or the company
were running low! They'd been ordering it up by computer,
then sweeping the Valium out under the cage.

The perpetrator had to be somewhat familiar with the
company's buying cycle so as not to be too far out of line
when ordering. Every other Thursday seemed to be the right
time to reorder Valium. The key to entering the orders undetected eluded me for a while. But I had other things to

worry about. At the same time we were also moving on the pacs investigation.

The concurrent drugs-for-sex case was all over the media because the doctor was a closet homosexual. I was working that case with Bill Sutherland too, and Sergeant Jim Jajuga, the Polish Prince. It looked like the doctor had killed his alcoholic, drug-addict lover with an overdose of an exotic mixture of synthetic narcotics. A local TV spotlight team, always alert for the sensational, was following me around as I tracked down scripts written for the deceased. We'd discovered that many of the dead man's drugs had been prescribed by an unregistered doctor recently on the staff of a major Southern medical school.

The doctor denied writing the scripts, but Elizabeth McCarthy, a Boston handwriting expert, testified he did write over a hundred scripts for the deceased, as many as a dozen in one day. We were having some trouble proving this one because the body had been cremated, giving us no opportunity to exhume and find traces of the drugs. With all the media attention added to the workload of the other cases and the mushrooming body count from pacs overdoses, it was a busy time.

In the pacs investigation, after our agreement to cooperate, Beeper and Mugnano went back to the street, working their way toward the pharmacist, Baratto. The quarry was no slouch. More than once Baratto, smelling a rat, rebuffed the efforts of undercover agents attempting illicit buys at his pharmacy.

"Don't got none," he said, when the bogus scripts were presented. The DEA was monitoring the telephone activity of the suspected drug trafficker. Beeper also utilized toll analysis of the suspect phones and managed to have pen registers installed in some vital phones. A pen register attaches to the phone and records all numbers pulsed, or dialed, from that phone. For incoming calls it can only determine length of time off the hook. It is a valuable investigative tool because there's no telltale interruption of service or signal, no weird sounds on the line to tip off the suspect he is being recorded.

Much of the phone activity originated from the Baratto pharmacy on Bennington Street and from a sun-tanning studio and suspected prostitution clearing house on the same street. Both phones were registered to Baratto. We found that Baratto actually owned two pharmacies in East Boston, both under the same name. None of this was definitive proof that Baratto was dealing, but at the very least he had fallen in with evil companions.

During the latter course of the overall investigation it became apparent that there were at least two separate illegal pac distribution rings operating in the greater Boston area, and that though unrelated, in both cases the drugs were emanating from retail pharmacies. Beeper McGreal, coordinating us and the task force, had soon narrowed the trail down to Baratto's place and to John Kipden and Sons Pharmacy, another retail outlet in Salem, Massachusetts, home of the infamous witchcraft trials. McGreal and other task force members arrested four prominent members of the Salem distribution ring, and then nabbed Kipden himself in his store following an illegal drug transaction. Salem Police Detective Sergeant James Gauthier had this to say about criminal arrogance: "We were taking Kipden to the Salem station for processing. The guy, he's lookin' for sympathy. You know what he says? 'The big chain drug stores were causing a drop in business'—that's his rationale for dealing drugs! Chain-store competition. Can you believe it?"

Kipden was estimated to have sold, without prescription, *one quarter of a million dosage units* in a one-year period. Medi-Mart must have done quite a number on him.

Coordinating the flow of information from the task force, Beeper McGreal made sure we at DEA and Charles Monahan at the Pharmacy Board had the information on the arrests and charges. Kipden and Sons Pharmacy was closed under the provisions of MGL chapter 94c, Mass General Law section 14—imminent danger to public health, safety and welfare. We'll hear more about that provision later.

One of the suspects nabbed in drug raids related to the pacs case unequivocally named Baratto and his pharmacy as the source of the drugs. Meetings with various reliable informants in and around Boston were confirming street gossip and hard evidence—all pointing to Baratto. Beeper McGreal and the task force were close to putting a lid on it. Meanwhile, I was trying to find the commercial suppliers of the pacs, to establish whether or not there were any irregularities from the distribution angle, and to shut off the source.

Going the long way around, we found there are about sixty legitimate suppliers of Glutethimide in the country.

Transactions involving the substance aren't computerized on the DEA ARCOS system, so identifying suppliers for one account can be extremely exhausting detail work. Fast Eddie Sullivan and I were able to obtain through the ARCOS computer system all the legal suppliers of the schedule II and III pacs component narcotic drugs like codeine and Tylenol, but Glutethimide doesn't fall into those categories. For that we had to do it the old-fashioned way—by telephone and personal contacts around the country.

"I'm gonna stay on this until I'm completely saturated," Eddie said. "Or until I need a brain marrow transplant." Finally, I was able to identify four different suppliers of Glutethimide to Kipden in Salem. This preliminary screening process also revealed that Baratto was making his purchases of pac components from not one, but eight suppliers up and down the Atlantic coast. A later, more exhaustive study revealed a total of fourteen suppliers of pac components to Baratto. Fourteen separate suppliers, all for the same product, tends to give you a clue about shady dealings. Baratto was also estimated to have diverted another quarter-million units to the street.

By this time, Baratto was definitely noticing the heat from the investigation and its subsidiary arrests. Some of his customers were laying low. Dealers and mules who bought from him and sold on the street weren't coming for reorders because their addicts were shying away. Local law enforcement efforts had the kids temporarily holding back. Distribution was slowing to a trickle. Things were really tight. Remember, it was the pressure on heroin traffic that brought pacs to prominence in the first place.

Word came back from reliable sources (later confirmed by phone recordings) that Baratto was worried. He'd supposedly overextended himself financially with a ski chalet in the White Mountains and a new Cadillac. Relying on the immense profits from his pacs business, he'd also bought his daughter a sailboat to match his own speedboat. And then there was his stable of thoroughbred horses to maintain at Suffolk Downs Racetrack.

"Things are so tough, I don't get the pacs business going good again fast, I'll have to burn the store down for the insurance," Baratto was heard to complain.

The idea of arson went beyond mere contemplation. Street word had it that Baratto was willing to pay three thousand cash and a carload of pacs for a torch job. A fire would be an alibi for not having any drug records as well as a source of money from the insurance.

Fast Eddie Sullivan and I were salivating to get Baratto's records because we knew there'd be definite proof of diversion. Given the hundreds of thousands of dosage units he'd ordered—just from legal sources—there was no way he could account for all their sales. Unfortunately, the threat of arson forced Beeper McGreal's hand. He moved too fast.

Sullivan and I were out west when Beeper applied for an immediate and secret search warrant. His speedy action bypassed us and the local force, demanded by protocol at least, and hinted at insufficient forethought and preparation.

Our first knowledge of the raid (which we were supposed to be in on for an accountability audit) was when Fast Eddie and I saw the raid on the six o'clock news from our motel room. Unfortunately, the raid failed to arrest Baratto, the source pharmacist, on the premises. In fact, the TV cameras showed him driving away in his late-model Cadillac! I was pissed at the foul-up and unhappy for a while at McGreal's undue haste, but we managed to get Baratto through the records as I'd figured—through administrative action. It was a good twelve months after the pharmacy raid, but we got him.

In the computer fraud case, we finally saw how the fraud was being done. False inventory adjustment sheets were given to the keypunch operators. Subsequent to adjustment of the computer printout of stock on hand, the person or persons creating the false sheets then removed the sheets from the keypunch area so no one could inadvertently make a comparison and catch the discrepancies. The computer printout available to the buyer then reflected the actual stock on hand and disguised the losses that were occurring. When the extra new stock arrived at the cage it was ultimately stolen. A couple of people from the warehouse have been arrested, a computer programmer fired, and a vice president has resigned. The company's key executives, all family, decided to sell out. The heart was gone out of the business for them.

We stayed after the pacs. We managed to close Baratto's pharmacy during that year and used disciplinary board action and licensing tactics to block him while McGreal went after a grand jury indictment. Baratto was sentenced to do nine to fifteen years at a maximum security prison. He's eligible for parole after three years.

Pacs continued to be a problem in the Greater Boston area, especially when the heroin supply on the illicit drug market was low. We learned from our Baratto investigation and were ready whenever we became aware of new sources of supply.

The latest cooperative effort resulted in the closing of a retail pharmacy in Saugus, Massachusetts recently. We acted within days of receiving our information on that particular situation.

On a separate case initiated a year earlier, Fast Eddie Sullivan targeted the illegal activities of pharmacist Joe Brackenopoulos in nearby West Roxbury. We knew that the pharmacist was running an illicit "pills for profit" operation from his store and we also knew that he was dealing in the deadly combination of pacs.

During our initial strategy session, I instructed Sullivan to enlist the assistance of the Massachusetts State Police, DIU and the Massachusetts Board of Pharmacy. I also instructed Fast Eddie to find out whether or not Brackenopoulos owned the real estate housing the West Pharmacy. Not only did the businessman own the real estate—he owned the entire block.

Fast Eddie directed the investigation aggressively, having made the decision to go after Brackenopoulos "lengthways, sidewise and repeatedly." Utilizing surveillance techniques, accountability audit procedures, search warrants, interview/interrogation sessions, handwriting analysis, verification of records, legwork and phone calls, we were able to catch Brackenopoulos red-handed. Sullivan ran the case superbly from the federal side, while Sergeant Bill Brown of the DIU directed the undercover operation. Working in harmony, we arrested Brackenopoulos and several associates and simultaneously seized the entire block of real estate owned by him under the federal forfeiture laws. If that wasn't enough, agents Bernie Fitzgerald and Sid Pransky of the Board of Pharmacy ordered the pharmacy closed under the provisions of Massachusetts General Laws, Chapter 94C, Section 14 (Imminent danger to the public health and safety).

"So what's the big deal?" I can always count on Eddie B. to cut me down to size.

"I found this case to be particularly exciting, that's why! And I'll tell you, I enjoyed how we 'arrested' the entire city block more than the main guy himself." The burden of proof then shifted to Brackenopoulos to try to get his real estate back—and we knew he couldn't do it—primarily because we had Assistant US Attorney Jeffrey Robbins working for us.

The strip of commercial real estate was eventually forfeited to the United States under the Controlled Substances Act. Brackenopoulos was prosecuted and found guilty of drug trafficking. He was forced by the Board of Pharmacy action to sell his store at below market value. The new owner was awarded a twenty year lease by the US Marshals, custodians for the property.

The property was then auctioned off by the US Marshals for over a million dollars. The DEA in turn, shared those proceeds, under our Asset Sharing Program, with the Massachusetts State Police, Suffolk County District Attorney's Office and the Board of Pharmacy.

Sure enough, Fast Eddie reached his objective in this case by smashing another pacs ring and getting pharmacist Brackenopoulos "lengthways, sidewise and repeatedly."

8 Lead Us Not Into Temptation

IT HAS BEEN SAID MANY TIMES, AND IN THE drug business it is a truism: The love of money is the root of all evil.

There's so much money to be made in drugs that the surprise is not that some law enforcement people are crooked, but that any remain straight. It is an incredible testimony to the upbringing, training and personal morality of the average drug agent that he doesn't sell out. That basic, ground-level honesty is what this country expects from its soldiers in the drug wars. From neighborhood busts to international deals, the success of the good guys depends on the incorruptibility of the agents.

The diplomatic implications of the international drug trade are so intricate and so interwoven in political intrigue they are mind-boggling. The role governments play in the drug trade can be significant, as became apparent in the inside story of CENTAC and its attack on huge underground drug conglomerates.

A creation of the DEA, the unfortunately short-lived Central Tactical Unit (CENTAC) arose from the bullet philosophy—going directly to the top of a drug distribution network. The practical idea was to destroy the leadership, cutting out the pumping heart of the business either politically, economically or judicially. An operation that has had its head cut off is less likely to reopen for business. In princi-

ple it made a lot more sense than worrying about interdict-
ing a few bales of marijuana on a beach near Tacoma. And
it worked. The DEA had agents deep inside some of the
biggest drug rings in the world, from Hong Kong to Marseille. CENTAC was extremely successful.

CENTAC doesn't exist any more.

While it lasted, it seemed like something out of Frederick
Forsythe by way of Robert Ludlum. CENTAC director
Dennis Dayle shepherded a crackerjack staff of individual-
ists and idealists who went after international narcotics
kingpins. Though giants in the sleaze trade, the CENTAC
targets were still punks, albeit punks with megadollar push.

One such punk was Lu Hu-shui, a Chinese man head-
quartered in Bangkok who is believed to be the largest importer into the United States of Southeast Asian heroin.
And you have to go quite a way to be the largest in a business where practically everybody west of Catalina Island
aspires to be a heroin exporter. Another bogus entrepreneur
whose operation was infiltrated by CENTAC was Donald
Steinberg, a barefoot boy with cheek from Illinois operating
out of Fort Lauderdale, Florida. Steinberg reportedly was
importing up to eighty million dollars' worth of marijuana
per day. Perhaps the most dramatic figure CENTAC ever
went after was Alberto Sicilia-Falcon, a Cuban homosexual
and killer working out of Mexico. Sicilia-Falcon planned to
use the multimillions of his cocadollar drug profits to buy
himself his own country.

The whole CENTAC story is well told in *The Underground Empire: Where Crime and Governments Embrace,*
by James Mills. Among other stories, Mills tells of
CENTAC's pursuit of those three international darlings. I
can't recommend the book highly enough to anyone interested in studying the minutiae of international dealing.

CENTAC was bureaucratically shuffled off to Buffalo
when, in President Reagan's celebrated war on drugs, the
FBI was given concurrent responsibility for federal drug law
enforcement.

Not being a natural child of the FBI, CENTAC wasn't

adopted either. The FBI wasn't the only non-cheerleader for CENTAC.

They were already in opposition to the CIA and its covert purposes in certain parts of the world.

Hypothetical example: CENTAC is in, say, a small Central American country and discovers a percentage of its political leaders to be tied into the cocaine trade, sending drugs to the US. The tactical unit reports the profiteers to our government, asking for diplomatic leverage to be brought to bear. Reaching the power base in Washington, this information is either sidetracked or sacrificed to political expediency. The CIA argues the Bigger Picture; the evil these men do in the drug business is outweighed by the good they do for our government's purposes, etcetera, etcetera. End of hypothetical example. CENTAC was allowed to die a bureaucratic death.

Megamoney means more power to corrupt. I think it's a big deal when my agency, the DEA, spends fifty thousand dollars to float a Goodyear blimp above the Texas Gulf Coast on drug patrol for US Customs. But then, my agency is only the government. To an international drug operator dealing in hundreds of millions of cocadollars, to men who can afford to abandon ships and planes after one deal, a million-dollar bribe is no big deal.

But something that huge and globally involved doesn't hit home to me the way I can relate to something more personal and human. Now consider the all too common conscience-wrenching moral dilemma facing men and women in law enforcement all over the world. How about a career cop in a small lake town in Ohio who's making nineteen grand a year working two jobs plus side deals. He's doing his night patrols with half his mind on what the hell he can do to raise money for his two kids nearing college age. He's approached with the following proposal:

"Sixty thousand dollars will be deposited in an account anywhere you name. No strings. All you have to do is not patrol the south cove on your rounds tonight."

It certainly makes one think.

Or it could be as seemingly innocuous as a sheriff in Iowa who has a new car and a wife on vacation in Florida while his kids are getting their tuition paid—all on a salary that used to just get them by. He's not actively *doing* anything wrong—just his tacit ignorance of a few acres of marijuana growing in the midst of some local farmer's hundreds of acres of far-flung cornfields.

Lead us not into temptation.

The following conversation with two average cops working in a city of about fifty thousand people is typical of the allurement the locals are facing. I'd known these men a long time and knew they weren't pulling my leg.

"How's this, Jack," the older cop says, shaking his head in wonderment at his own recent behavior. "We're working plainclothes, following a line in a drug case. We pop into the room at the Motor Hotel and there's our two guys with a suitcase open on the bed between them. Jeezuz! There's $180,000 in cash crammed in the suitcase."

"They'd been working a drug deal—this is definitely drug proceeds, illegal, untraceable," the younger cop said. "No way these guys are gonna tell anyone if we boff it."

"They're Cubans, they don't even speak English."

"Right. It's ours for the taking. Not like we gotta dust them. We just have to pick up the money and walk out of there. That's what they expected us to do. I know a cop in New York saw it happen just like that."

"No one would ever know. A hundred eighty thou," the older cop said again, still shaking his head. "More cash than I ever saw."

"No one woulda known," his partner repeated.

"But you didn't, obviously," I said. "Christ, the temptation must have been unbearable, knowing up front there was no way you could get caught for it . . . How did you resist?"

"We didn't," the older one said.

"But we only took the wrinkled bills," his young partner said, joining in his smile.

"Seriously," I said, wanting to know, hoping they could

articulate a rationale for my own morality. "How can you walk away from something like that?"

"Just lucky I guess," the young guy shrugged.

"Just Irish I guess," the other cop said, smiling again. "Too stupid. Plus all that built-in guilt."

"A friend of mine says that too," I said. "He maintains that the FBI, DEA, CIA and other security branches all have a specific hiring policy. Says they go after the Irish-Catholics."

"The moral family upbringing—or intellectual superiority?" the younger officer joked.

"Tight-assed," his Irish partner growled, standing. "The acute guilt."

Whatever it was, the nonaction of these two cops represents the typical righteous response of most United States law enforcement people in general, despite the endless enticements.

Then there's the flip side.

The local security guard who turns his head for a few hundred is as guilty as the big-time bad cop or other officer of the law selling out for hundreds of thousands. There are, of course, bad apples at every level of law enforcement. Just as the crooked doctor or pharmacist rankles worst because of the trust deposited in them, so too do corrupt officers of the law. That rankling seems to double when the bad apple is an attorney. I believe that's so because as an officer of the court, the attorney represents an extension of the protective power of the police, and what is the ultimate haven of justice in our society. If we can't trust the legal system to protect us . . .

In Houston, 1983, federal prosecutor and assistant US attorney Frank Robin was convicted of trying to sell information relative to various investigations to the bad guys. Money was his motive. Not the only bad apple, certainly. But his defection from rectitude has a stunning impact because he was a *federal* prosecutor. American morality dictates that the higher one goes, the cleaner one should be.

Closer to my experience was the selling out of federal

prosecutor David Twomey, who had crossed my path when he failed to prosecute Manny Botenkranz with sufficient zeal. Twomey's crime had a ripple effect beyond the act per se. Officials knew there was a leak of vital investigatory information. Due to the nature and timing of the information, it could only come from someone inside. Twomey's crime was particularly insidious because his dealings with the other side of the law gave the criminals a leg up—but they also resulted in widespread suspicion among some of the good guys, which poisoned relationships at least temporarily. It's hard to press on efficiently when you feel you might be the one under suspicion or you suspect a coworker. One sellout threatened the reputations of several honest agents and rendered futile the work of many good officers. But after Twomey sold his soul to the devil, the devil eventually turned around and sold Twomey out.

All for the love of money.

The Boston Organized Crime Strike Force had been commissioned to go after the syndicate, especially drug dealers. They had some successes. They'd discovered a lot of smuggling activity to be emanating from the South Shore and, good police work had finally brought them close to nailing Frank Lepere, a well-known South Shore businessman and suspected major smuggler of marijuana. A combination of undercover and standard investigative work had brought the task force this far with Lepere. Looking to put the finishing touches on their case, they had even planted a bug in Lepere's girlfriend's phone, a phone on which they knew Lepere conducted a lot of his drug business.

Owning a fish business, Frank Lepere had originally begun his life of nautical crime as a smuggler of mercury-tainted swordfish. Moving up to drugs, he seemed to lead a charmed life—always one step ahead of investigators. Agents remarked it was almost as if he had information on when the strike force was going to move, and against whom, and where. They figured now they had the bug, the mystery should be solved. Except Lepere stopped using the phone. Suddenly. Too suddenly. Was he tipped off?

Alarmed when called in by his superiors (who were routinely questioning everyone connected with the investigation), prosecutor David Twomey drew what he thought was suspicion away from himself by accusing agent Jack Kelly. Nothing was found to suspect Kelly of, beyond Twomey's accusation. Without being charged, Kelly was taken off the strike force. Just to be on the safe side. The investigation continued. Then, just as agents were preparing to close in to arrest him, Lepere suddenly disappeared. The task force wasn't the most pleasant place to work during those days; everyone was sure there was a leak but no one knew where.

Frank Lepere remained free, his whereabouts undiscovered for the next three years, conducting his drug business on an even grander scale. We didn't know it then, but Lepere always had precise knowledge of where the authorities weren't. If he knew they were looking for him off Long Island, he could plan a drop on the shores of Lake Michigan. Lepere made an estimated twenty-five million dollars overall in the drug business, and the biggest part of it was made *after* he was forced to go on the lam! He must have had great information.

Twomey's house of cards began to fall when Lepere came in from the cold. In May of 1985, under the terms of a deal with the feds, Lepere gave sworn testimony about who had supplied him with the inside dope. Former chief prosecutor David Twomey. Agents Houghton and Sampson could now see a possible reason for Twomey's lack of zeal when prosecuting their old case against Botenkranz.

Twomey's price had been approximately $200,000 and a cigarette boat, a superfast speedboat of the type familiar to viewers of "Miami Vice," used for drug smuggling. (Ironically, some former marijuana kingpins, now government witnesses, have said that Twomey sold himself short.) He laundered his money through a number of banks and variously named accounts. By never depositing or withdrawing more than ten thousand dollars at a time, the cutoff point for banks reporting transactions to the IRS, he avoided detection. This is a favored tactic with the Mafia and others moving large amounts of cash around and wishing to remain unnoticed. Now doing time in the federal pen at Fort Worth, Texas, Twomey had once been the government's very man responsible for narcotics cases and going after Mafia dealers.

Why Twomey? Even those who knew him best can't explain it. As firemen have "sparkies," policemen have blue groupies, people who seem to derive more than the ordinary amount of vicarious thrill from being around cops. Though the pieces were never put together until too late, Twomey was a cop groupie who even jeopardized cases he was supposed to be prosecuting by being too intimate with the investigative procedure. The average cop isn't going to buck the wishes of a federal prosecutor. Twomey's obsessive zeal to be one of the boys in blue had him going on raids, carrying a gun, even doing aerial surveillance. He loved every minute of it. Though excessive, none of that was particularly unhealthy unless you count that it could have gotten a case or two thrown out of court.

At some point Twomey slipped from being a cop groupie to being a criminal groupie. The desire to be with the boys became a need to imitate the flashy lifestyle of the likes of Lepere.

At that time, Lepere was the number-one target of drug enforcement people in all of New England. He remained number one for three years after his elusion of the task force and remained virtually untouchable because of the data being passed to him by Twomey. Twomey left the task force for private practice during that time, but his well of information didn't dry up. He was still privy to inside gossip and the odd bit of hard knowledge due to established friendships, the old boy network and occasional consultant work for the task force.

Twomey seemed to want to emulate everything about Lepere.

He appeared to be particularly attracted to the tough, silent, macho image sported by the criminal. But even though Lepere became Twomey's hero because the Marshfield boat skipper was known as an extraordinarily closed mouth, a stand up guy amongst his underworld compatriots, when Lepere wanted to surrender after being a fugitive in New York for those years, the government wouldn't make a deal with him unless he named the leak. With fitting irony Lepere's groupie, Twomey, the man who sailed his former cigarette boat and even bought a Cadillac Eldorado just like his, was the *only* person Lepere ever ratted on. Other than giving testimony about Twomey, Lepere lived up to his *omerta* reputation. Silence.

Turning government witness, Lepere forfeited a home in the Catskills worth at least a million and a half, and another million and a half in cash. But he *was* allowed to keep another million-dollar house in Florida and will spend, maybe, a year and a half in jail. Unless his conviction is overturned on appeal, Twomey won't be eligible for parole for eight years.

Yielding to temptation is never a good idea.

9 Beacon Hill Caper

IF YOU LOOKED FOR THIS CASE IN OFFICIAL departmental records you wouldn't find it. Officially, it was a case I had nothing to do with, because I never wrote it up. I think it will be easier to understand why after I reconstruct these recent events, as I did for Eddie B.

We met downtown before the basketball game. The Celtics were playing the Los Angeles Lakers and Eddie had won a pair of tickets in a golf bet.

"Thanks for the invitation, Eddie," I said, paying for the coffee. "And the free ticket."

"Had to invite you. I was afraid my cashmere sweater would stretch if you shed any more tears on it," he smirked.

"Please, I wasn't that immature."

"No, you didn't cry all that much. But the begging was a trifle unmanly. You looked a little silly, on your knees to me there on the clubhouse dining room floor, interrupting the Ladies Annual Awards Banquet."

We fell in with the crowd heading toward North Station and the grimy Garden, home of the Celtics. Unlike most Bostonians, Eddie placed his crumpled cup in the litter receptacle.

"What's the big grin for," Eddie asked. "You anticipating a Celtics blowout?"

"That, yes—but also I'm thinking that this case I've been on lately may *never* get written up."

"We need more people in the government with your intelligent disregard of paperwork. But why *this* case?"

"I had some illegal drugs delivered to the lieutenant governor's office," I said.

Eddie pulled me from the path of a licensed Boston kamikaze pilot in a yellow cab. "You better start at the beginning on this one, Crowls," he said.

"Once upon a time . . ." I quipped.

Eddie held out the ticket. "You still want this?"

"Okay," I relented. "Walk a little slower. Plenty of time before the tipoff. I'll call this the Beacon Hill Caper."

We stopped, letting the crowd flow around us on Canal Street like water around rocks in a mountain stream, until Eddie headed us down a little-used side street that would bring us to the Garden unscathed. I began at the beginning . . .

"It was nice to get out of the office, but it was nicer to pull a local assignment for a change. As you know, the field assignments I've pulled lately have been kinda far-flung."

"Wait, let me get my violin."

"Anyway, you remember the famous novel, *Joy Street?*"

"Title only. Long before my time. Fannie Hurst?"

"Mmm. Well, that's the center of what action there is in this job, Joy Street on Beacon Hill."

"Next to the State House. Classy."

"Always a very patrician neighborhood."

"Patrician," Eddie said. "You're getting there."

I ignored him.

"Like a lot of information that comes our way, this started because of a resentment. We got a call from a woman, a lady pharmacist working at the Woodard Drugstore on Joy Street. Says she wants to file a complaint against her boss."

"Hell hath no fury . . ."

"Something like that. Don't keep interrupting or we'll be late."

The story I was relating to Eddie had begun several weeks earlier in perfectly routine fashion. I was laughing, but it hadn't ended so hilariously for the criminals involved nor, while it was happening, did it look so funny to me.

Quite coincidentally, I'd had official contact with the principals in the case a short while earlier, before the state Diversion Investigation Unit actually had it as a case. The famed Mass General Hospital was phasing out its outpatient pharmacy. They had set up a Proposal Reviewing Committee to search for alternatives and to assist and service their patients upon discharge. Common sense would dictate that a sensible alternative would be a pharmacy close by, near public transportation and with maximum parking. No mean feat in Boston.

The Woodard's managing pharmacist, Marylin Green, had sent a letter of application for consideration of the establishment she managed. In the letter she stated her impeccable qualifications and the nature of the store, which had been doing business at the same Beacon Hill location since 1840, despite many changes in the economy and ownership. She stated that the present owner, Christopher Munk, wanted to provide "optimal service and health care to the community" and, she hoped, to the larger community, meaning the Mass General Hospital area.

Munk's business was not seriously considered because Joy Street is at the top of Beacon Hill, a climb so steep as to be impossible except for the healthiest ambulatory patients from the hospital side. Plus, no parking. And no public transportation, except by taxi. Woodard Drugs was going under from the competition with CVS, Rix and other efficient and cheaper chain operations, as well as shifts in population. Anyone knowing demographics and business dynamics, especially pharmacy operation, could see this store was a dead horse as a pharmacy today, and would not soon be a live one. Mass General was not going to be its bailout.

A few months later, instead of another proposal from Marylin Green, we got a complaint—and it was against the same owner whom she'd praised in the proposal. The complaint stated that Christopher Munk was up to his eyeballs in illegal diversion activity.

My ears perked up at that: it's often a short hop from a downward trend in business to arson or drug diversion or interesting combinations thereof. This one seemed especially potent for skullduggery because, in addition to things being slow, we'd learned the owner was not a registered pharmacist himself, meaning he had to pay for professional coverage a minimum of sixty hours per week. The store just wasn't generating sufficient legal cash flow to justify paying a full-time manager/pharmacist and part-time relief pharmacist.

The DIU unit got the job to check out Marylin Green's story. Big John Curtin and Chester Bishop, DIU troopers we'd worked with before, were the first to interview her. She told them about Munk not being a registered pharmacist.

"You told me once you don't *have* to be a pharmacist to own a drugstore," Eddie interrupted.

"Right, shut up. But you do have to be a pharmacist to fill prescriptions—which the Green woman claims her boss is doing, among other things."

"Is she a woman scorned?"

"If you mean, were she and the boss lovers and she got dumped, apparently not. But I'll get to the love sidelight later. Here's where it gets interesting. She told Bishop and Curtin that besides illegally filling prescriptions on a regular basis, the guy was part of a large organization of drug smugglers, as well as being the primary narcotics conduit for some of the internationally famous families of Beacon Hill—including the families of some powerfully connected in national politics and the entertainment industry. This is where I come into the act, myself and Pharmacy Board agent Lou Pacifico."

"Natty Lou, three-piece suits?"

"Right—very effective agent because included in his qualifications is he's a registered pharmacist himself."

I had been on the phone several times with Trooper John Curtin and offered my help in the investigation because of my prior familiarity with the store, its proximity to my office, and the fact that I needed a break and wanted out of the office. Big John Curtin, an Irish-Lithuanian ex-boxer with hands like meat hooks, was the lead DIU investigator. A charter member of the unit when it was first formed in 1974, he had been assigned elsewhere often the last several years. Though fearsome physically he was no slouch intellectually either and was considered a good investigator by his peers. Because he was newly reassigned, he was feeling his way around and was moving with extreme caution, a caution which I misinterpreted and which figured largely in the conduct of the case. But all that only became evident later.

When the guys met with the Green woman she announced she wanted to cooperate.

"I'll be your agent," she said.

Her accounts of the owner's activities, if true, painted an incredible picture. In addition to repeating her allegations of him dealing to underage socialites, she insisted Munk was involved in smuggling large quantities of marijuana into the New England area.

By now some background information had come in on Christopher Edward Munk, co-owner with Alexis Fields of the Munkfeld Corporation and the Woodard Drugstore. It seemed our complainant had some factual basis for her wild claims. In prior encounters with law enforcement people the drugstore owner had listed his occupation as a plumber. I wondered if it was the Watergate type. Munk had already been before a federal grand jury in Oklahoma for import and export of marijuana and was the suspected pilot in a Wichita, Kansas, plane crash involving tons of the weed. He was a suspect in too many other high-volume dope deals to mention here. His record certainly made him a prime suspect for the dealings Marylin Green described. I, for one, would be delighted to put away anyone dealing to minors.

A loosely knit, informal task force came together to brainstorm on Green's allegations. The group met practically next door to the pharmacy, in the Massachusetts State

House. We crowded into the office of Chief Beaulieu of the Capitol Police to set up a strategy, hoping to catch Christopher Munk in any of the activities described by his manager. The irony of our choice of the Capitol Police office would only become apparent at the conclusion of the case.

John Curtin and his aide, Trooper Chet Bishop, were there, as well as Lou Pacifico and I. As the lengthy planning session drew on, I grew impatient. We didn't seem to be going anywhere. I began doodling and outlining what-if strategies on some blank Mass General prescription pads taken from my pocket.

"Isn't that illegal?" Eddie B. asked. "To have blank prescription pads?"

"I interpret it as zany," I said.

"Someone more tight-assed might call it against regulations."

"No, only passing phonies is illegal."

Looking back at the whole investigation and that meeting in the State House, I can see that my impatience and Curtin's caution were bound to clash. When I suggested a plan he didn't like, he let it be known in a way that could be taken as a put-down that he was used to working with *special* agents, not diversion investigators.

"I reminded everyone that all we had to do, because Christopher Munk was not a registered pharmacist, was to catch him filling a prescription for *anything*— it didn't even have to be narcotics. I further suggested, holding up the blank Rx pad, that we get the hell on with it. Curtin gives me the fish-eye."

"Wonder why?" Eddie B. said, crossing Chauncey Street to the Garden.

"I say, 'Let's really clinch the case fast. Write out a few scripts for narcotics and give them to Christopher Munk to fill.'"

"Which diplomacy I'm sure endeared you to the leader," Eddie observed.

At this point I was trying to overcome Curtin's reticence and pushing for *someone* to make a buy. It must be remembered that under the restricted provisions of my job I'm technically not allowed to do any undercover work. Making a buy is definitely undercover. It looked to me as if no one was going to move without a push. I convinced myself that this one time, for intelligence purposes, I could make the buy. Besides, somebody had to; Curtin wasn't going to *order* anyone to. John Curtin accepted my volunteerism. Right about then, he probably hoped I went down in flames.

Once I'd compromised my professional ethics a tad, I thought "what the hell" and went all the way. I made out the prescription addresses to Room 107, upstairs in the State House. If I was going to get into trouble with my boss, Dennis Johnson, I wanted to go out laughing. I got artistic with the bogus prescription request. Simply because I liked the sound of it, I gave myself the name Cyril Keniry.

Marylin Green had informed us that Christopher Munk's pattern was to fill in the day shift himself if she was out, leaving the night work for Carol Bowie, his relief pharmacist. We had instructed her to call in sick, hoping to increase our chances of Munk being on the premises.

Off I marched to Woodard Drugstore. Sure enough, the six-foot-two-inch, 180-pound clerk matched the description for Munk, and he was alone in the store. Testing his brazenness, I had written a few scripts for Percodan and given them all the Room 107 address, the Lieutenant Governor's office. I'd first taken the precaution of asking the Lieutenant Governor's receptionist to accept a package for Mr. Keniry.

"Can you fill this right away," I said, showing the suspect the bogus script. "I'm in a real hurry."

"I'm jammed right this minute," he said, reading the script.

"Can you deliver?"

It worked like a charm. He agreed; I paid and left. While I was inside, Chet Bishop had the store under direct surveillance from a car parked across the narrow old Boston street. An agent's dream, the prescription counter in the Woodard is wholly visible through the large plate-glass window. After I had left, Trooper Bishop watched Christopher Munk fill the script himself and leave, apparently to deliver it to the Lieutenant Governor's office in the State House.

Munk did just that. So we had him for illegal pharmacy practice, plus a narcotics charge. All our case needed was some tightening for court. So I wrote another script for Percocet, using another fictitious MD's name. Despite the obvious success of the operation, Curtin still wasn't too happy, but he took the next one in. I told him the script address, Room 107, but neglected to inform him it was the lieutenant governor's office. Oversight, slap me on the wrist. In hindsight, the third script we passed may have been pushing it with Munk a bit, but the greedy and the criminal don't attend to the niceties.

Finally, when Curtin came out after passing his script, I wrote some more for Valium and Percocet for Chet Bishop and suggested he get them filled hand to hand, which he did. The hand-to-hand idea was an evidentiary maneuver, but it turned out to be a good thing because by this time Curtin was getting some heat from the Lieutenant Governor's office wanting to know what the hell was going on. Being a state employee, Curtin was more sensitive to pressure from them than I, a fed.

Curtin now had more than enough cause and fact to make the arrest. Christopher Munk was surprised. But so was I when Curtin decided to process him through Boston Municipal Court instead of the quicker and more convenient Suffolk County Superior Court, as I had hoped. That may have been to put me in my place.

Next step was a warrant. We wanted to search the place for more evidence and to confiscate the records. I offered to get an administrative inspection warrant, which I can obtain relatively painlessly and quickly compared to the grief I knew Curtin would face in the Boston system. But Curtin still wasn't too happy with me for what he considered indirect pressure and direct interference. He said he would get his own search warrant, thank you. I backed off on the warrant. We called it a day on Beacon Hill.

Despite Curtin's pique, I considered it a successful operation. We had shut down a diverter. Back at my office, I made the mistake of telling my boss, Dennis Johnson, everything. Exactly the way it happened, including my quasiundercover role. He positively hit the roof.

"Overstepped your authority!" he shouted. "Guilty of inappropriate investigatorial behavior."

I kept quiet for a while. Johnson wasn't leaving much room for rebuttal. Technically he was right on every point.

"This verbal reprimand will be followed by a written one," he threatened. "You can bet your sweet ass on that!"

While Johnson was ranting and raving, I was thinking what a great day's work I'd contributed to: the arrest of a diverter alleged to be a big smuggler, and the shut-down of a store that constituted imminent danger to the public. In other words, I saw my job description fulfilled.

I told Eddie B. what I finally told the boss to do, reacting to his "verbal reprimand" bullshit.

"You said *that?*" Eddie asked, unbelieving. "Not only anatomically impossible, also inadvisable to tell your boss— not if you want to keep your job."

"The whole thing was out of character for both of us. Maybe it was the heat wave. We're both hotheaded Irishmen. Fortunately we understand that about each other now. We're still friends. But I wasn't through with the case yet."

At seven-thirty the next morning the white hats met in front of the closed pharmacy. We couldn't enter and search for evidence until we had a search warrant. John Curtin went off after his warrant; Pacifico, Bishop and I waited in front of the store. Beacon Hill neighbors and customers walking by about their morning business saw us there and the store closed. The more curious and neighborly types stopped to ask questions. Being the most diplomatic and polished, Pacifico fielded those with his own innocuous, imaginative answers while we stood around trying not to look like cops.

During our wait in the warming morning sun it was obvious how few customers the Woodard was missing by not being open. Parking was next to impossible, and there

wasn't enough foot traffic to make a modern pharmacy profitable. The decided lack of business was added confirmation
that Christopher Munk was not making a mint here. It required no great stretch of the imagination to see that for him
to maintain his lifestyle and keep up with the Joneses, he
had to have something more than this going for him.

The day grew warmer. By noon it was hot. By two the
humidity was right up there with our patience levels. Where
the hell was Curtin? By four we were boiling in the heat and
I had a case of the I-told-you-so's. I figured Curtin might
have been having trouble getting a warrant for the whole
pharmacy because he only had the probable cause of the
four scripts. I had wanted to use Suffolk court or just get an
administrative warrant in the first place. The bitch list grew
longer as the day wore on.

Just after four, Marylin Green came by, curious to see
what was happening. In the shimmer of pavement heat she
looked to me like an angel of mercy. Since she was the
manager of record, I saw nothing to prevent her from opening up. Not for the public—but for getting us out of the hot
sun to wait inside. This would at least alleviate some of the
curiosity of the staid Beacon Hillers. I knew John Curtin
wouldn't like it because it smacked of irregularity to enter
the premises without a search warrant, but I told everyone,
"No search—just to get out of the heat."

At about four-thirty I sent around the corner for some
sandwiches. It had been nine hours since our arrival. We
hadn't eaten all day and Curtin was still nowhere in sight.

Some Massachusetts pharmacies have special limited licenses, permits to distribute *spiritus fermenti,* for medicinal
purposes. In the past especially, this privilege was often
abused as the pharmacy sold liquor on Sundays or after
hours, when the drugstore might be the only place a partier
or someone needy and desperate enough to pay the price
could go.

The Woodard must also have had a beer and wine license
because they had a well-stocked cooler—from which

Marylin Green offered us a cold beer to go with our sandwich on that ninety-degree broiler of a day.

No sooner had we popped the tops on the frosties than in walked Curtin. Sweat pouring off him, he walked directly to the Rx file, seizing only the four scripts we'd passed the day before. I'd been right, unfortunately. Those prescriptions were all he could obtain a warrant for.

I felt some anger at the daylong wait, mixed with some embarrassment for John, because it could've happened to *any* of us. About then Curtin looked around at us. He noticed the beer and—va-va-voom! Remember, Curtin makes Refrigerator Perry look like Pee Wee Herman. So when he bellows or threatens, people listen.

Marylin Green managed not to wet herself in fright. I'm the one he targeted of course, from the residual feelings from yesterday's action.

"How the . . . who do you think . . . ? You'll ruin my career. We go back a long way. You're deliberately screwing me!"

I don't take this type of criticism well. Especially when it's expressed publicly. I tried.

"John, I'm on your side. We've been waiting out in the hot sun for nine hours. A quick beer with a sandwich. For all we knew we had another eight hours to go here, so what's the big deal?"

By way of response, Curtin stomped out, ordering a head-shaking Chet Bishop to follow his lead.

"Come on—we're outta here."

I'm six-foot-four, and 240 pounds but I wouldn't want to tangle with Curtin. Bishop complied even though he didn't understand. More verbal pleasantries were exchanged between us as they headed out the door. Trailing Curtin in bewilderment, and no doubt fed up with our antics, Chet Bishop suddenly announced, "I want out of this f'in unit right now." He slammed the door of the state police cruiser.

Pacifico and I were left in the store, still angry and speechless, but most of all embarrassed. We thanked her for the beer and bade Marylin Green adieu, calling it a day.

Back at the office I purposely neglected to write up the affair. I took the mature stance: if those who were angry at me for trying to do my job wanted a report, they could come and ask for it.

"But that obviously wasn't the end of the incident," Eddie said. We were inside the Garden now, wending our way up the concrete ramp in the bowels of the building toward our section.

"Pretty much the end of *my* involvement," I said. "The rest I learned from Curtin after we'd both cooled off enough for us to be friends again."

Christopher Munk was released, free on bail the next day, and the store was back in operation. Obviously, we were going to need evidence more substantial and compelling than four scripts to nail Munk. The DIU still had the active cooperation of Marylin Green. Wanting filmed evidence in order to stand up against any clever defense in court, the troopers started this new phase of their investigation by setting up a hidden camera in the prescription area of the store, then monitored it from the basement.

The first thing that happened was that some guy in a Capitol Police uniform turned up, and the camera recorded him going behind the counter, where he pocketed a bunch of Percodan.

"But you don't want him; you want the owner, so you let him slide," Eddie speculated.

"Close . . . Here the plot thickens. At first, they figure the guy is impersonating a cop. It's done often enough to gain entrance to otherwise restricted areas. The troopers do a side investigation of him, find out the Percodan pocketer is our informant Marylin Green's boyfriend—who happens to be a narcotics addict! All of which she'd neglected to tell us."

"Convenient. Addict having a pharmacist for a girlfriend."

"Told you it thickens. We find that the addict boyfriend, Link, is indeed a Capitol Police officer. Not only that, but further investigation discloses that Carol Bower, the night relief pharmacist, is also a junkie we've already tracked through several overdoses and mix-ups in drug-related criminal offenses."

"Wow—finding the Woodard was like stumbling across a treasure trove of whacked-out druggies! You narcs should set up a few places like that, save a lot of running around."

I ignored Eddie.

"They decided to take a closer look at Marylin and her boyfriend, and they discover she is a narcotics addict too. Together with her rogue cop boyfriend, they were stealing dope from the store. I don't know what got her onto the boss's case, but she brought the house down on herself and her boyfriend in the process."

I ended my recital then as we took our seats in the Garden and the Celtics took the floor. Eddie was shaking his head and laughing.

The overall results of the Beacon Hill Caper were many: Owner Christopher Munk was arrested and eventually found guilty on all four counts. Three years probation and a thousand-dollar fine. Store closed, corporation out of business. Munk is now suing the Board of Pharmacy for unspecified damages. Claims a violation of his rights.

In time, the consequences of flirting too long with addictive substances were visited upon the scions of the famous Beacon Hill families whom Munk was allegedly supplying. Their story hit the newspapers. One died of an overdose, another entered a drug treatment program.

Officer Link, Capitol Police, was arrested.

Chief Beaulieu, Capitol Police, retired on a disability pension.

Trooper Chester Bishop was transferred by request to Essex County Drug Task Force.

With everybody ticked at me I never bothered to write the report. Couldn't find a way to make it look even slightly complimentary, no matter how I cut it. The only defense I have is being human. It's the same defense I apply to John Curtin and my boss, Dennis Johnson, in order to see their side of the action. The story never even got told until today.

I'm the only one left on the same job, and like a lot of life's crazy bounces, I got a promotion soon after the incident.

The informant, Marylin Green, was given great leniency in light of her cooperation. It's a shame, especially for someone with her potential and her past record of achievement, before addiction. But as she was a user who refused help, her end was predictable. Marylin Green was found dead of an overdose of drugs.

10 Operation Atlantis

OPERATION ATLANTIS WAS THE CODE NAME given the overall program, spearheaded by the federal government, which attacked burgeoning smuggling activity along the Maine coast. Among its many achievements, Operation Atlantis snagged the largest haul of contraband drugs ever seized on the entire East Coast until that time. The ins and outs of the operation were so complex it'd be impossible to describe it all. My involvement in Atlantis really started as the operation was spectacularly winding down.

The operation ended with the seizure of the *Onolay,* a large luxury yacht that had transported forty thousand pounds of Colombian marijuana to the American market. The benefits: shutdown of a very major smuggling operation with ties to the Mafia and international organized crime, and the arrest of thirty-two persons. The case stretched from the rockbound coast of Maine, down to the Colombian marijuana fields, over to Marseille, France, and points south.

One amazing feature of the operation was that it lasted only a few short months from inception to conclusion. Whoever first said timing is everything probably didn't know they'd made the most profound utterance of all time as far as law enforcement work is concerned. I did not become involved until the end of Atlantis. I was feeling some heat against the system because I'd made a beautiful case against a real slimeball in another part of the Pine Tree State and couldn't get him convicted for anywhere near what he deserved.

"Doesn't anybody want this bum behind bars?" I'd yelled out in frustration. I'd watched a local pharmacist infect his own community with illegal pushing and the community at large with importing large quantities of drugs for a nearby prep school. Having built a solid evidential case with more than enough to convict the guy, I wanted him put away for a long time. I was burning because I couldn't get anybody in the judicial system to work on the case to put him away. My initial perception was they all wanted the quick fix—plea bargain him down to what I felt was only a slap on the wrist for his crimes.

"The real reason no one's interested in your small fry, Jack, is they got so many big fish cooking right now." I was so apprised by an older, wiser veteran of the courts. It was all timing.

So here I was in federal court, still trying to get my druggist hooked into the judicial system and wondering why I couldn't get anywhere, when I finally began to get the drift.

For starters, there were only two US attorneys in the Bangor court. And they were already buried under an avalanche of paperwork trying to handle the arraignment and disposition of thirty-two defendants from a recently executed phase of Operation Atlantis.

A common legal ploy by defense attorneys is to create a barrage of time-consuming to-process paperwork in an attempt to dismay or discourage the opposition. Particularly if the prosecutor's office is, as normal, already too busy for the personnel in the office to handle. The supposition is that the prosecution team, faced with an ever-growing mountain of work, will throw up their hands and accept a compromise that lets the criminal off more easily than if they'd pursued to the full extent of the law by processing all the paper. For prosecutors interested only in their conviction rate as a springboard to private or political success, it is also a means of a sure, even though lesser, conviction. And if an inexperienced attorney isn't prepared or confident of his legal footing, a plea bargain with less work and elimination of the intimidating mountain of paperwork can look pretty inviting. The legal defense team for the suspects in Operation Atlantis created a veritable snowstorm of paper. Standing against the flurry, Assistant US Attorney James Brannigan had all he could do to field the hundreds of briefs, depositions and other legal papers flowing from the Boston offices of Oteri, Weinberg and Markham.

I have a pet opinion I call the slime-filled balloon theory: when you squeeze one end of a criminal operation the stuff squirts out somewhere else. After the criminals had their own way in the south for a long time, the feds put some concentrated pressure on the smugglers and dealers, putting many behind bars. Needless to say, a percentage oozes through the cracks in the best operations. As pressure has mounted against La Cosa Nostra, much of their heroin operation has been commandeered by less structured and less disciplined (though no less eager) groups of Chinese, Nigerians, Mexicans and Pakistanis. The mob has adapted, bringing larger amounts of marijuana and cocaine overland through Mexico into California. And by sea and air into New England. As the squeeze got tighter in Texas and Florida, the slime had to squirt somewhere. And so—Operation Atlantis.

Bryer's Neck, Boothbay, Maine. Except for about six weeks in midsummer, it's one of those places about which they say, "you can't get there from here." The remote and beautiful rugged coast of Maine is the perfect place to land megamillions of dollars' worth of imported marijuana and cocaine. Despite the vast size of the state and its laid-back reputation, Maine has one of the very finest antismuggling units in the country. It needs it. The state police division of special investigations has a most creditable reputation for honesty and accomplishment, but the numerical odds favor the criminal.

Agent Robert Watkins knew that the Maine coast with its

thousands of secluded inlets and sheltered bay areas—formerly home only for lobster fishermen and tourists—were now regarded as perfection for modern smugglers. Watkins spent a great deal of his time keeping in touch with the locals along the coast and observing the day-to-day life of the Atlantic villages.

A member of the crack antismuggling unit of the Maine State Police special investigations arm, Watkins knew the Damariscotta River area belied its serene geography by being a hotbed of smuggling activity. The previous year a major bust had taken place on the Damariscotta near Bryer's Neck when a drug-laden yacht was seized. Watkins was familiar by now with most of the potential smuggling spots in the area. He paid special attention to the unguarded coves and secluded spots along both banks of the tidal river that offered deep-water docking for boats large enough to haul big loads of drugs. His antenna went up when he learned that an outsider, John Russo of Brooklyn, New York, had rented a secluded property near the mouth of the river as it meets the sea. The location was only a few hundred yards from where the antismuggling unit had successfully seized a major cargo of contraband the previous year from property owned by Michael Larsen.

Knowing the octagonal old house with the grounds and dock on the river were rented by someone he didn't know was enough to alert Watkins. He maintained a loose surveillance on the property over the long Maine winter. Nothing untoward. He thought perhaps he'd been unnecessarily suspicious. He did put out some informational feelers with several enforcement agencies though, just as a matter of course.

Watkins's curiosity was further piqued by the commercial plates on Russo's pickup truck. Tracing that, he eventually found connections to a fleet of six trucks that Russo had registered under a series of fictitious names to a hotel address in Portland. Interesting. Imagine then, what he thought when he discovered Russo's name was really John M. Palmetto, Jr., of Brooklyn. Why did he need an alias and why all the subterfuge?

Watkins watched more closely. Nothing. Until spring.

Watkins was passing the time of day with the local real estate dealer. "Anything new, Eph?"

"Ayuh," the realtor responded.

"You gonna tell me 'bout it or do I have to subpoena you?"

"Well sir," the realtor said, smiling with his eyes. "That fella you was askin' about, Russo?"

"Rented the octagonal house," Watkins said, impatiently.

"That's the one, the renter of the river property. He's complainin' that his gangway and dock hadn't been properly set for use."

This seemingly innocent information intrigued Watkins immediately. He knew that the house was on a deep-water location that could accommodate docking large boats suitable for international smuggling.

The bee was really loose in his bonnet when about the second week of April it developed that the renter was now doubly angry because the dock work was so slow and he was in a big hurry.

This suggested some type of deadline; something most Downeasters don't bother with or cotton to. The urgency suggested to Watkins that Russo, or John M. Palmetto, Jr., wanted the dock ready for something other than some sport fishing, as he claimed.

The DEA in New England has a reputation for sharing the wealth. We have access to the best and latest national and international intelligence and don't mind sharing it with the locals. At least I stress that cooperation with the people I've trained, and it has paid off. Others, like agent Mike Cunniff in Maine, agree. Watkins had contacted DEA agent Cunniff as soon his suspicions had become more than fantasy. Mike has a reputation for being one of the hardest working in the entire agency. Cunniff heard Watkins out and drew the same conclusions as the Maine trooper: something smelled fishy at Bryer's Neck, and it wasn't the halibut.

Cunniff, working with Watkins and two others from the Maine antismuggling unit now put the rental property under more active surveillance. The cooperation between Cunniff and Watkins marked the beginning of a pattern of exceptional interagency cooperation, the hallmark of Operation Atlantis. I've mentioned time and again how effective an anticrime weapon simple communication among the good guys is. Before the brief operation was concluded it would involve active participation and cooperation from police and sheriff's departments up and down the East Coast, including Bath, Wiscasset, Portland and Boothbay Harbor, Maine, and Gloucester, Massachusetts. There was also help from the Department of Marine Resources, US Customs and Coast Guard, and the DEA in several continents as well as the French Federal Police. By case end there were nearly a hundred different departments and agencies involved.

As work on the suspect dock and float neared completion the third week of April, reinforcements were called for by Watkins and Cunniff. They sensed that whatever was going to happen would happen soon. The riverside surveillance was now increased to twenty-four hours a day.

It soon paid off. On the evening of April 26, Robert Ruel, an agent of the state antismuggling unit concealed in an observation post across the river, opposite the suspect Russo property, spotted a large motor yacht coming upriver from the ocean—without running lights! The suspect oceangoing vessel approached the dock rented by Palmetto. After a hurried radio dispatch Ruel was quickly joined by Cunniff and two coastal wardens. Cunniff burned the air with messages, requesting information almost as quickly as he could talk. He advised Sergeant Paul Hooper, the Maine state cop supervising the antismuggling unit in the Boothbay area.

Practically the first response Cunniff received to his information requests was about the yacht *Onolay*. Of British registry, the eighty-one-foot motor yacht had been purchased in southern France by Parus Ltd. of Gibraltar. The owner was listed as John Peterson, New York, New York, a nonentity. Not a person who didn't count, but literally a person who didn't exist. The crooks had taken some hints from the ward politicians who registered voters from the cemetery in close elections.

The vessel had sailed from Antibes to Gibraltar in March then to Martinique, from where it departed for Aruba in mid-April. That was its official itinerary, anyway. Captain of the *Onolay,* Robert Rangus, had filed papers in Aruba that he was bound for Le Granadine. Bryer's Neck, Maine, is a bit north of that. Captain Rangus was a long way off course.

Setting their plan in action, Cunniff and Watkins moved to the other side of the river as their prewarned troops took up their positions. They formed a tight ring around the property that covered all roads and paths. The Coast Guard moved to block escape by water. By one in the morning the two agents were creeping down a woods path near the dock and the rented house. They were close enough to make out the sounds of several different men speaking, coughing, sneezing and swearing. In the dark they couldn't see much, but they could hear the metallic slam of tailgates closing and figured they hadn't set up their encircling ring any too soon. The most intriguing sound of all were the noises of soft, heavy objects striking wood. To the trained ear they could only be bales. As there wasn't much cotton grown in Lincoln County, Maine, Cunniff figured it was a good bet the bales were marijuana.

Judging from the number of bales dropping and truck tailgates slamming, it had to be a great deal of marijuana. When after an hour they were convinced they could wait no longer, the agents signaled the antismuggling unit by radio. They in turn called Hooper, who ordered the men to close the net ringing the property.

Cunniff and Watkins drew their weapons. They positioned themselves on the main dirt road that led to the house and dock from the paved road so that they could intercept any trucks leaving as well as be in place to direct police vehicles into the area for the mass arrests. Simultaneous with the roadblock and the flight deterrent teams going into position in the ring around the property, Robert Ervin of the Maine

State Police and Chief Petty Officer Sullivan of the US Coast Guard sealed off the mouth of the Damariscotta River and any potential escape by boat.

The motorized troops arrived like the cavalry in the old westerns, except that it was dark and cold. When the spotlights went on, Watkins and Cunniff saw so many crooks milling around in their beams it looked as if they were downtown at noon. The black hats knew when they were beaten. Hands went up as if someone had called for a vote at the town meeting. Captain Mel Graves of the DSI read the boat crew their rights. Some trucks had already taken off. Cunniff hoped they'd be picked up at the roadblocks.

At three in the morning one of the roadblock teams scored what turned out to be a big hit when they stopped a truck with its radio tuned to the police scanner. Inside were Sal Donziello, kingpin of the operation, his bodyguard and hatchetman Petie Oldo, and "Big Joe" Tasso, a reputed Mafia soldier. Russo fled, somehow escaping the dragnet. He eluded police until his arrest in Lido Beach, New York, eight months later.

In all, thirty-two arrests were made in this segment of Operation Atlantis. After search warrants were issued by US magistrate Melvyn Zarr, tons of property were seized, including the million-dollar yacht and forty thousand pounds of Colombian gold—536 seventy-five-pound bales! And one suspect who turned informant.

11 The Burning

I WAS SPENDING A LOT OF TIME IN MAINE THAT
spring. On May 15, pursuant to a court order by US district
court judge Edward T. Gignoux, the 536 bales of Colombian
gold seized from the *Onolay* at Bryer's Neck were transported inland to North Windham, a crossroads town near
Sebago Lake. The Idsom Corporation in Windham had been
contracted for incineration of the South American dope. I
was one of twenty agents assigned to witness and monitor
the burning of the contraband seized in Operation Atlantis,
which took from seven-thirty one afternoon to five the following afternoon. I watched an awful lot of expensive leaf
go up in smoke. I couldn't help but see the irony of man's
destruction brought to this idyllic rural setting. On the flip
side, my comic sense was wondering what the result would
be if the mooses upwind were sniffing the clouds of stuff we
were sending up.

I guess I was in a philosophical mood that day: Here I
was, out in the middle of nowhere compared to Boston or
any urban crime setting, yet realizing how the tentacles of
crime could reach even here. We were incinerating this garbage only a few hundred yards from the CVS pharmacy
where I'd recently nailed a gonzo pharmacist who was using
and selling drugs from behind the counter. He was a different and singular outpost on the criminal supply line from an
MJ field in Colombia, but it all ended up in the same place,

in the vein and brain of some American kid. And it doesn't matter whether the kid is from Times Square or Boody's Corner, they end up just as zombified.

Or dead.

Mike Cunniff, the hotshot agent largely responsible for coordinating Operation Atlantis and grabbing the contraband we were burning, must have noticed my pensive mood.

"Whatcha musin' on, Jack?" he asked at a break, offering me a cup of coffee.

"Congratulations, Mike, great job," I said, accepting his offer of sustenance. "Just kind of thinking about where all this dope came from and connections, circles, how things seem to go around."

"I *think* I know what you mean. Yeah, it's nice to think that something like this," he said, nodding to the rising cloud of smoke, "disrupts that circularity somewhat."

"Nice to know we can break some connections. Whether a person makes it, grows it, sells it or uses it, in a way they're all connected. Some guy smoking a bone in his own living room has a hard time maybe seeing he's helping organized crime, but the profit from the sale of his joint has to go somewhere—and it sure ain't the chamber of commerce."

"Amen. Even if he grew it himself, that's illegal, and he's 'rending the fabric of our society' as the professors would say."

"Christ, *we're* starting to sound like professors," I said. "But a lotta people believe there are no such connections, that organized crime doesn't exist, that the Mafia is a myth."

"Too many connections to be coincidence. Take this case. Look at the connections and tie-ins and see what you call it," Cunniff said, settling back in his chair. "I'll walk you through the case, you draw your own conclusions."

I grabbed a chair for myself, eager to hear his inside view of Operation Atlantis.

"Of the thirty-one defendants who were arrested, Sal Donziello, aka 'Bo,' and Danny April play the most significant roles in setting up the *Onolay* deal, or what we called

Operation Atlantis. Bo Donziello's been known to be involved with big-time marijuana trafficking back to at least
1975. He was smuggling multi-ton loads from Colombia
into Florida. Then he supervised transportation of the stuff
from the Fort Lauderdale area up to Brooklyn."

"Big loads? What'd he use, planes, trucks?"

"A fleet of specially equipped cars. And a specialized
method of operation. You can see some of the same organizational imprints in this Atlantis setup—the fleet of trucks,
the compartmentalized 'crews' . . . Nobody can rat out
anybody except others on the same level of the pyramid as
themselves. The group established a base up here in Maine
when federal pressure began to increase down in Florida,
about 1976. In the fall of '77 we grabbed the steam vessel
Lusiada in a major smuggling bust just up river from the
rental property where this all came down. The antismuggling unit hasn't made any prosecutable connections yet, but
notes we found on Bo Donziello suggest some of these same
people have been used in other big operations here in Maine.
Doesn't matter, we got them this time anyway. But it gives
you a hint of some of the volume of drug traffic now, just in
Maine. It takes organization."

"The pyramid structure sounds like Mafia," I said.

"Donziello and Danny April designed or at least imple-
mented an elaborate *modus operandi* intended to minimize
any possibility of detection of themselves the higher-ups and
to frustrate investigative efforts of any law enforcement
agency in the event of an arrest by any subordinate.
Donziello and April each had their own separate crews of
underlings and soldiers all arranged in an organizational
chart with the traditional crime family configuration of
soldiers and capos."

"It's a wonder you got them."

"Luck, mostly. Ideally, each underling only knew his immediate superior in the organization, further insulating
those at the top. Most of Donziello's crew only knew him by
his nickname, Bo. Almost all his workers were recruited
from friends, or friends of friends. Every worker, when

hired, was vouched for in some fashion. Nearly all of them came from the old neighborhood in Brooklyn."

"To guard against infiltration by undercover cops."

"Exactly. Theoretically, each employee had one contact, who in turn knew only one contact. Donziello gave his most explicit, his most incriminating instructions only to his most trustworthy associate, who passed on the orders. As you know, this guy's known as a 'buffer' in the underworld. After the buffer had given clear orders and expectations, the kingpin need only speak in a roundabout, unincriminating way to be understood.

"Although Bo sometimes personally worked or supervised a shipment or pickup, his instructions to those less trusted were always in this underworld doubletalk. And, of course, no one ever dared to ask for a clarification. A good writer could probably make an excellent comedy out of some of the potential for error there."

"May already have," I said.

"The major cohesive element among Donziello's smuggling crew and teams of drivers and other workers was his constant and repeated allusion to the fact that he was 'backed'—meaning sponsored and supported by 'unidentified Italian-American organized crime figures.' True or not, it's obvious Bo enjoys playing the role of godson. He drives a new Mercedes and employs our defendants Petie Oldo and Joey Tasso as bodyguards."

"How did Bo avoid detection down south if he was running such a big show?"

"As I see it, there are three great potential weaknesses in a traditionally run organization of this type, Jack. Bo had them covered. He must have studied and learned well. The first is that great care must be taken to insure that the day-to-day illicit activities of the group don't expose them to detection. Make sure nothing they're doing on a regular basis calls attention to their operation. From the beginning, Donziello had insisted that none of his employees look or act anything like what might be considered a profile of a smuggler. For example, he insisted all of them dress in a certain Sears polyester style that didn't vary too far from middle-class America. And made them all maintain a clean-cut appearance as far as beards and hair and that stuff went, nothing too far out."

"The IBM of the criminal world."

"The FBI dress code, you got it," Cunniff smiled. "He even picked what he figured were middle-of-the-road cars, pun intended. In Florida, his fleet of sedans were Plymouth Fury III's. All properly registered, except that the company they were registered to was bogus. Outwardly they were standard to the point of blah—which is the way Bo wanted them to look to any observant law enforcement people on the roads between Florida and Brooklyn. The cars were equipped with adjustable air shock absorbers to balance the heavy loads of marijuana carried in the trunks. Between trips, the conservatively dressed, businessman-appearing drivers parked their conservative-looking automobiles behind closed doors in Florida warehouses rented for just that purpose. Cars were supposed to be used for business only. No joy rides.

"On trips, drivers were instructed to stay within the speed limit and do nothing to draw attention to themselves. They were specifically warned to stay off the Jersey pike to avoid the effective measures of the New Jersey State Police. Drivers were always paid *after,* never before a job, so that indiscriminate spending wouldn't louse up the operation. All these guys we caught in the Atlantis coup, except for the ship's crew, were brought up here to Maine from Brooklyn and Florida. This thing was well planned. They had expected to be in the area for about ten days to be on the safe side, be prepared before the *Onolay*'s arrival. They'd been instructed to blend into the area, to pose as out-of-state sport fishermen. They had done this type of subterfuge successfully before and are reportedly extremely ticked at Palmetto for blowing their cover by demanding work on the gangway and float. Of course, the fact that the *Onolay* arrived so early caught them a little off guard.

Helped us bag them, too," Cunniff said, smiling.

"My philosophy too," I said. "Better to be lucky than efficient. Or something like that."

"Secondly, using approved Harvard Business School techniques, the organizers must insure against the whole kitty being lost in any one catastrophe. Also called 'spreading the risk.' Planning to cut losses in case of a seizure, Bo broke the money and drugs into smaller units as soon as practically possible. If we grab a shipload like this it murders an organization; grab a bale, they hardly notice—or they notice, but they can recover. So Bo always staggered the schedules and routes of his load carriers and money couriers skillfully, leaving as little to chance as possible. Each of Bo's drivers knew little concretely except that he picked up an innocuous-looking car at some hotel or other anonymous location and that he'd usually deliver and walk away from it at an equally unremarkable location at the destination. In this Atlantis case, once the ship was unloaded the trucks were supposed to disperse the bales to five separate 'stash' houses, like the one rented by Roy Como on Knickerbocker Lake. Then they could be transported to New York or wherever from there—again, minimizing potential losses. If one house got knocked over in a raid, it still left four. You can see how huge the profits must be to allow them to abandon ships, trucks, houses and planes with such impunity."

"I can."

"Finally, organizers like Bo have to inspire the loyalty of each of their workers and take precautions against defection such as has happened here. We are developing an informant. Bo relied heavily on his reputed association with the mob to keep his employees faithful to him. Aside from the threat that connection implied, they also were repeatedly reminded that Bo had established a legal fund of fifty thousand per man, in the event they were ever caught. They were also assured that if something unforeseen happened in their legal defense, or they had to take a fall, they'd receive a large lump sum if they went to jail, plus expense money inside. They were warned that if arrested due to some screwup of their own, they'd be bailed out financially, but that they'd be expected to work off whatever the organization expended on their behalf. That went for speeding tickets too, which of course could endanger the whole organization by focusing attention on it.

"We have it from our informant that Bo has already sent word around to the various home locales of the other defendants that 'everything will be taken care of.' The defendants all claim in front of Judge Gignoux to be paying their own legal defense, but Bo and Danny April are springing for everyone's bail, as well as lawyers fees, travel, lodging and spending money during all the pretrial conferences and hearings. He's also paying 'prison salaries'; all in exchange for not talking to the authorities."

"Sounds like a great guy to work for. Better than Uncle Sugar," I said.

"Except that when one of the defendants residing in Florida suggested perhaps the compensation could be a little greater, one of Bo's lieutenants, Big Joe Tasso, allegedly suggested in rebuttal that said defendant come to New York 'alone.' "

"For negotiations, no doubt. Possible termination of contract."

"Right."

I finished my coffee and mused upon connections, my thoughts trailing away like so much smoke in the breeze. Our break was over, but I wanted to hear more, so the night after the burning of the bales Mike and I continued our conversation. Being one of the few Irishmen I know who doesn't drink, Cunniff had coffee while I went for a few beers. I wasn't due back in Beantown until the following day, the taxpayer was footing the bill for my room, and I needed something to wash down the sickly sweet smell of the smoke from twenty tons of Colombian Maryjane.

Some of my most productive liaison work has been done in these relaxed beer and gripe sessions on my own time. I've made some great friends over the years and the suds sessions have also helped me determine who'd be the most reliable men in a pinch. Off the job, Cunniff was in an even more expansive mood than he'd been on break during the burning.

I was fascinated with the complete background information we now had on this phase of Operation Atlantis, thanks to one of the defendants turning government informant and some exceedingly thick investigative files going way back on a few of the smuggling syndicate's soldiers.

"I've had and used CIs before," I told Mike. "But usually they were just passing along hearsay information or only slightly involved. I can't really recall having an informant so willingly fill me in after the fact like your guy."

"He was with the organization a long time. He knew a lot of the principals—since he was a kid, really. As for willingness, he was pretty sure they were about to finger him anyway, so he decided to come with the good guys for some protection."

"How about the other guy, the soldier?"

"Pat Gerando. He was a long-timer too, and off and on he was in enough trouble so that between his record, what we know, and what the informant told us, we have a pretty clear picture of this from the start to finish."

When I asked if Pat Gerando was from Brooklyn, like so many of the participants, Mike Cunniff hunched his shoulders and launched into a long story of the gang connections that eventually landed some boys from Brooklyn in Bryer's Neck.

"According to the old New York police blotters, these guys almost all started out in the same neighborhood in Brooklyn, or were recruited by someone who did," Cunniff began. "Pat Gerando said Bo Donziello had employed a large number of men in his present organization as couriers and soldiers in his other smuggling ventures before this operation, and that they were almost all from the old neighborhood. Recruiting and holding people, and keeping them in line, was easy for Donziello: first, because he paid well; second, because he promised protection; and last because he constantly portrayed himself as 'connected.'

"A lot of these men picked up on the Damariscotta were

tied to each other through juvenile crimes starting back in the fifties. When Pat Gerando was fourteen or fifteen years old he hung around with a group known as the 'Avenue L Boys.' One of the associates from this operation that he met during his Brooklyn youth was Donziello's brother, Scampi. Pat Gerando first got to know the brother when Scampi began dating a girl who lived next door to Pat. Scampi Donziello would later introduce Bo to Gerando, and their association flourished.

"Another friend was Donny Dutch, who was in the Avenue L gang and used to steal cars for joy rides when he and Gerando were fourteen."

"Typical All-American kids," I said.

Cunniff laughed. "These kids didn't have yo-yos or frisbees. They played with General Motors master keys or carried screwdrivers to pop ignitions with. They stole a lot of cars until the night they went out with Danny Syventro and stole a red Chevy. Syventro's supposed to be a karate instructor in Naples, Italy, now, but that night he was in the back seat during a wild street chase until a bunch of smoking police cars finally corralled the lads. Pat Gerando's father bailed him out but ended his days as an official Avenue L boy.

"Gerando went away to the Navy and lost track of Donny Dutch for several years until one night back in the old neighborhood he bumped into him in Cavanaugh's Bar. Donny Dutch said that in the interim he'd become an electrician's apprentice, gotten married and addicted to heroin —not necessarily in that order.

"Gerando wasn't in the best of shape financially. Donny offered to put him up in the Canarsie market for the night and sell him a false birth certificate so he could get a driver's license to make up for the one Gerando had been forced to surrender for violations. Gerando said no—he had his own sources for such documents.

"In the early seventies Gerando moved to Florida, where he started an upholstery business. There he met, and occasionally hired, an old pal, Vance Nicola. Nicola had been a hippie living in a commune and sometimes worked as a tree surgeon. He cleaned up his act, shaved, and during the next year started driving around in a silver Chevy belonging to Bo Donziello and disappearing fairly frequently on extended trips to Colombia and New York.

"After meeting another old friend, John Shick, at the Flying Machine Bar in Fort Lauderdale, Gerando started buying and selling pounds of marijuana and cocaine in order to pay for his own marijuana use. Several of the men started seeing each other in Florida now, including Robert Ogden and Scampi Donziello.

They met often at Shick's house, which seemed to be used as a staging area for loads of drugs going north. In time Gerando also renewed acquaintances with Jimmy Viggi and Joey Omeni, two other pals from the old gang. Viggi made a living selling marijuana to some hippies in Pompano Beach, off the Dixie highway.

"Gerando expanded his horizons a bit now, even going to Mexico via Dallas to oversee a consignment of marijuana for Joey Omeni. In Mexico he went into the mountains and met the farmers who grew the weed. He later bragged that that was where he met Lolita, a woman whose father allegedly had been a hit man for a former president of Mexico. Lolita and her Texan boyfriend guided Gerando around Mexico City and Veracruz and helped him with car rentals and other details involved in setting up the buy. Gerando was doing fine on his first international venture until a discussion arose, after Joey Omeni arrived, as to which landing strip would be used to bring out the load. Things went a little strange when Omeni took the buy cash with him and went to check things out, saying he'd be back in ten minutes. When he hadn't shown after eight hours, Gerando had to charter a Cessna six-seater to get himself to Mexico City, where he could get a flight back to the States.

"Once home, he received a call from Omeni's wife, who told him that Joey and his pilot had been arrested in Boca Raton. The marijuana had been safely offloaded prior to the bust. She asked Pat to rent a miniwarehouse and pick up the five-hundred-pound load from Timmy Teschi.

"Loyal soldier Gerando took charge. He rented a van and went to the sign shop owned by Teschi, the associate temporarily charged with holding the dangerous cargo. Stacking the van with a load of marijuana-laden cardboard boxes, he first took it to a warehouse rented by Omeni. Then it dawned on him he couldn't keep the stuff there. Not only was the space rented under Omeni's name, but it contained a disassembled home Quaalude laboratory and several fifty-gallon drums of chemicals. He picked the stuff up and moved to a new location.

"This loyalty earned Gerando big-time respect and some heavy commission profit on the load when Omeni got out of jail, as well as the use of Joey's 450SL Mercedes while he was in the clink. Things went well for Gerando until big heat came down in the form of a police raid on Omeni's warehouse/laboratory. Gerando took the hint. He decided that was a good time to visit his parents in Arizona.

"When he returned from the desert sabbatical he began working regularly for Bo Donziello. After some security and employment tests, which included several false starts to check his reactions and shaving off his mustache to attain the clean-cut image Bo preferred, Gerando was finally trusted with a trip. At first he wasn't trusted very far. He would be sent to a parking lot where he'd park. Leaving the ignition keys in the ashtray, he'd walk away for an hour or so and come back to find his car riding slightly lower on the springs. The car had been taken away and loaded with marijuana or coke, but never having seen who took it, Gerando couldn't testify—nor, unless he looked in the trunk, did he know for sure what was in there.

"Once loaded, he was warned to stay away from any other fleet drivers encountered on the road north, and especially to avoid the Jersey pike on his way to the drop-off point, the Golden Gate Motel in Sheepshead Bay. All drivers were issued special keys that broke off in the lock if they attempted to open the trunk. They hoped in that way to discourage a less-than-hardnosed cop if they ran into a police search on the northward route.

"Gerando did well, earning $3,500 per loaded trip and $500 per empty: four grand roundtrip, plus all expenses. Truck drivers earned about $10,000 per trip, or ten bucks a pound, carrying thousand-pound loads.

"The outfit based trust on performance. If you performed according to their expectations you were trusted. If you varied from the norm or exhibited too much individualism, you were suspect. Gerando was eventually given the extra responsibility of overseeing all maintenance for the syndicate's fleet of vehicles, which he contracted for at OK Tires in Pompano Beach, under the name of Dinny Forest. He continued to drive, occasionally vacuuming enough marijuana debris from the trunk of an empty returning to Florida to roll himself a joint.

"His only problem with courier duty came when, after picking up a $300,000 package of money at Bergen Beach for a Florida delivery, he was accused of being short a hundred thou upon delivery. It was quickly straightened out. Obviously, he lived.

"Gerando was one of those requested to be on more or less permanent stand-by duty for offloading incoming marijuana boats. He was kept busy with other chores also, like flying to New York for a meet in Greenwich Village, then a quick trip down to Harrisburg, Pennsylvania, to change the registrations on all the Plymouth Fury fleet. Great pains were taken in some areas of cover, and these details show, but then they'd do something really stupid, like lose the phone number of a hit man, or leave a dope-laden truck in Fall River, Massachusetts, instead of Falls Church, Virginia."

"Like the gang that couldn't shoot straight," I said.

"Thank God they do blow it once in a while," he said. "If they were all geniuses, we'd never catch any of them."

"Did this outfit ever come close to getting caught before the *Onolay* job?"

"Some of them almost didn't make it *to* the job. Just a few months prior to the Maine deal, several of them came *this* close to getting bagged in a roomful of guns and money in New York."

"Choir practice at St. Mary's."

"The Donziello soldiers were sometimes called on to babysit piles of money—say after a drug deal, and before the loot had been spread around. Drug deals are always cash of course, and a couple million in fives, tens and twenties makes a pretty good-sized pile. Could be conspicuous."

"I have the same problem."

"To you and me it sounds pretty bizarre, but I suppose they get used to it. Babysitting a million or more was a fairly routine job for the men in this outfit. This near-fiasco that almost got them bagged happened in an apartment in the East 90's, near Flatlands Avenue. Big Joe Tasso and his wife Sharon were already there when Gerando showed up, as ordered. Also present were Al Dutch and Mo Bottle. Not long after, Bo and his shield, Petie Oldo, showed up. Bo was carrying a plain cardboard box about a foot square. 'There's supposed to be $750,000 in here,' he announced, pointing to himself and Petie. 'We counted it twice and got it different both times. I want youse to help us count it again. Then we got another pile in the bedroom's gotta be counted.' Donziello put the money box down in the middle of the floor. There were now seven people present in the Brooklyn apartment. Drinks were refreshed and everybody took a pile of greenbacks and started counting. It was something of a party atmosphere with the sweet smell of money mixed with the scent of small amounts of cocaine, some Thai sticks for spice and the aroma of several pounds of marijuana wafting from the back room."

"Sounds kinda homey to me, like Ozzie and Harriet and the kids wrapping presents at Christmastime."

"Yeah, well, the party must've gotten a little loud, what with all the comings and goings in the apartment. Hearing the ruckus, a neighbor figures a burglary is in progress and calls the police. So in the midst of the counting and the talking, and stacks of money spread all over the apartment, the cops respond to the neighbor's burglary summons and come knocking on the door. Not knowing it's the law, Mo Bottle pulls his .38 and goes and opens the door a crack. Seeing the fuzz, Mo slams the door in their faces and yells, 'It's the cops!'

"Can you imagine what a scramble? Thai sticks, guns and piles of money flying around the room, everybody trying to hide. The marijuana, coke and all the extra guns were stuffed into a closet. Mo Bottle and the extra bodies all went into the back bedroom. Donziello ordered them to leave one pile of dough, about a hundred thou, on the table and for Petie Oldo to let the law in.

"Gerando and Donziello greeted the cops, giving them false names and explaining to them that they had a retail store nearby and the money on the table was receipts they were counting before going to the bank. For whatever reason, the cops bought the story. It may be just as well they did. They could've been gunned down from the back room. Donziello was bullshit because the cops had gotten in, but mostly he was bullshit because they had to start counting all over again.

"Gerando was given the job of bringing about a quarter of a million of that pile to Florida. He had the load in the trunk, wrapped in brown paper, when he was stopped for speeding in South Carolina. He was asked to open his trunk. He stopped breathing for a while but the cop didn't ask what was in the brown paper. The search was only an extension of the speeding violation. He gladly paid the twenty-five-dollar fine. In cash.

"Gerando was soon summoned up north to New York again to help with a twenty-bale shipment. When that was finished Bo Donziello and Petie Oldo took Gerando out for a spaghetti feed in Brooklyn. Gerando could tell something special was up. Over the Italian food, Bo handed him two thousand dollars, instructing him to use it to buy provisions the following day for a 'deal in Maine.'

"Donziello was planning for the arrival of the *Onolay* in about ten days. Little did he realize he had a date with the antismuggling team in little over twenty-four hours. Gerando was told to get fruit juices, soda, food and beer. He took notes. Donziello instructed him to get fresh fruit for the boat crew and to be sure to bring vacuum cleaners. During the spaghetti, Oldo was a nervous wreck. His wife was due to have a baby any moment. Donziello also reminded Petie to pick up pumps and more vacuums from an unnamed source. Planning was inclusive.

"About the time the spumoni was served, Oldo got a call from his babysitter that his wife had gone into labor. Petie left for the hospital, but there was never any question that he would be there on time to leave for the smuggling operation. First things first.

"At seven the next morning Petie woke Gerando up with the news that his wife had delivered. They went off to the Canarsie Market and the A and P to fill their food order for the north woods. To Brooklyn guys, going to Maine seemed like a polar expedition.

"Along the way they stopped near the Italian-American Social Club to check on the pump man, who turned out to be Charlie Vox, another old acquaintance. Vox loaded tools, fittings and extra parts onto the truck. They rendezvoused with Big Joe Tasso, Vance Nicola, Edsel Webb and several other of the defendants. When someone mentioned it might be cold in Maine and that several of the boys came down sick during an offloading the previous year, there was a mad dash back to pick up warm clothes.

"That's what I mean about meticulous planning mixed with dumb oversights. They'd thought of beer and vacuum cleaners, but no one had given any thought to what weather conditions might be in Maine. Lucky it wasn't an African safari.

"Vance Nicola's mother and Big Joe Tasso's came up with an extra supply for the single guys in the operation. Mrs. Nicola also cooked them up a big spaghetti feed before sending them off.

"Full of pasta, Bo Donziello marshalled his troops, sending them out in convoy. Seven trucks, a Mercedes and a

Plymouth Fury. The CB traffic amongst them sounded like Italian army war maneuvers. After stopping several times in Connecticut and New Hampshire for food and gas, the convoy made it to the Sheraton in Portland, Maine. They planned to spend the night. Danny April, second in command of the operation, returned from a phone call to the house in Bryer's Neck, agitated in the extreme. 'The freakin' boat's dockin' *now!*' he screamed, rounding up the gang. The boat was about a week early. They were at that point an hour and a half drive from their destination. Finally reassembled, the convoy left the Sheraton at top speed.

"Down the road a piece, in Bath, Patrolman Ira Cohen spotted Gerando speeding, took chase and signaled him to pull over. Gerando had time to radio and warn Donziello he was being stopped. He then shut off the CB as the trooper approached the car, before Bo had time to radio back. Cohen informed them they were stopped for speeding.

" 'Were you following another truck?' Cohen asked, wondering if they were in convoy.

" 'No way,' Gerando lied, digging out the registration. Hoping to distract the officer, Charlie Vox pulled out a map. He told Cohen they were heading to Canada. He then asked directions to a motel, a gas station and an Indian reservation.

"We learned later that the others would have gladly strangled Vox for asking that stupid question about Indian reservations. Cohen was suspicious of this mixed bag of nuts, but it wasn't that question that got him. They were just plain suspicious. He decided to trail them for a while.

"The motel was in the opposite direction from where they were headed, so they had to make a U-turn to make it look good after getting their ticket for speeding. Now they were really in a bind. They couldn't miss the shipment, but they didn't dare draw attention to themselves or the operation. After missing a couple of exits they finally hit the right one for the gas station the trooper had directed them to. It was closed. They debated checking in to a motel for an hour just in case the trooper was still around but decided to chance it.

"Back on the highway they realized they were still being followed. They didn't dare chance leading a police officer to the smuggling site. They couldn't stop the cop and ask him why he was following them without drawing more attention to themselves. They passed up the Boothbay exit and thought they'd missed their secondary exit when it finally materialized—after what seemed like hours of driving while being followed.

"All this time the operation was going down, down on the Damariscotta. The boys decided to keep the cop on their tail and lead him away from Bryer's Neck, not knowing of course what was happening there. Fuming, Danny April mapped out an alternate route they could double back to the coast on once they were free of the cops. It never happened. The roundup order was given from Operation Atlantis. Before they reached the exit for the alternate route they were stopped again and arrested for conspiracy to smuggle.

"So ended that part of the gang's active participation in Operation Atlantis," Cunniff said. "It was all over for all of them except for the courts. And the way that's being handled is just more proof that Bo Donziello was running more than a one man operation."

"Connections," I concluded.

The DEA, Interpol, various national and international police forces, and the Maine antismuggling unit had combined to make the *Onolay*'s haul of twenty tons the largest seizure in history until that time, as the *Lusiada,* another state of Maine haul, had been before it. There was no question that Maine had been discovered as a desirable spot to drop illicit drugs. The stakes were escalating constantly.

As the criminals dispatched more and more loads of drugs northeastward, the authorities were trying to stem the tide, or at least make it so expensive it hurt. In the two short months following the *Onolay,* the Atlantis team seized another monster haul on Mt. Desert Island, and on June 20 they sank yet another drug boat in picturesque Bar Harbor. Both these shipments were bigger than even the *Onolay.*

I was keeping in close touch with Mike Cunniff, always

being on the alert for any fallout intelligence that might help cases I was working on, or just for future information.

"Been pretty busy up in these parts, Mike."

"We're still getting stuff from Atlantis. One smuggler committed suicide and Schaefer was found dead."

"Schaefer, one of the guys you grabbed at Bryer's Neck?"

"Thomas G. Found dead in Brooklyn. Kings County medical examiner characterizes his death as an accidental drug overdose. Other indications and information we have suggest he may not have ingested the drugs voluntarily; or at least the drugs he took weren't the ones he *thought* he was taking."

"Strictly opinion of course, but it sounds to me that, like the bales of sweet leaves we took to Windham, he got burned."

"Officially, it was an overdose," Cunniff reminded me.

"Right, overdose."

"You can expect more overdoses in the near future if things don't tighten up."

"Meaning?"

"They're starting to fall out. The old gang isn't hanging together in the aftermath of the bust. Stems from the time they were all in the holding pen in Portland and Bo Donziello was bragging everything would be taken care of. Seems he isn't taking the care everyone would prefer. But those who ask for more are having accidents."

"Strange."

"Yeah. The way it started, they're all in there and Bo Donziello is screaming at everybody to calm down. After all, he and Danny April had just dropped two million dollars apiece on the aborted operation. That had some effect. When he said everything'd be taken care of, they remembered the fifty grand legal fund he supposedly had in reserve for each man and the fact that he was 'connected.'"

"That helps."

"He needed time to round up some cash and corral his lawyers. There wasn't any real panic then because even those crew members and hirelings on the lower rungs who didn't know Bo had seen him set this operation up and knew his reputation. They also knew of the incredible profits made in smuggling. They'd all heard the stories of the Loveboats, the Caribbean cruise ships whose drug loads were a lot more valuable than the ships themselves. Bo said he dropped millions, but millions shouldn't be a stumbling block for someone in the astronomically profitable drug scam. Especially someone connected. Pat Gerando remained a standup guy. He suggested to Bo that they bail out first those soldati most likely to crack first. He even volunteered to stay with Tony Bottle, because Tony was so young and might need some bucking up."

"Loyal," I commented.

"Gerando's loyalty didn't pay off in the long run. He was bailed out finally with Rangus, the ship's captain. They were given a grand each and spent the next week, expenses paid, at the Parker House Hotel in Boston, waiting for their hearings. At this time they were going through a lot of subterfuge trying to convince Judge Gignoux that all the legal work wasn't being paid for by one source. They wanted him to believe that each defendant was paying separately for his own defense. A little perjury never slowed the mob down. Truth can cause complications."

"Separate defense makes it more expensive and difficult for the prosecution to pursue," I remarked. "Also, a common defense practically admits conspiracy."

"Bo would dole out money to the defendants either through a lieutenant, or one of the lawyers might deliver a few hundred for walking around money. Most of these transactions took place in the courthouse men's room."

"I'll refrain from the obvious comment regarding the appropriateness of that location," I said.

"Things started to break down when one of the newer men began complaining about the supposed 'connected' outfit paying off peanuts in men's rooms. Another, free on bail on the Atlantis charge, got busted on a coke charge in Florida and asked the outfit for fifteen grand, to retain a lawyer. Donziello said, 'Go ahead, get one supervised by Oteri,' and that he'd get the money. In the meantime, Pat Gerando was offered ten thousand dollars to plead guilty, accept a plea bargain and do seven months. This escalated to ten months and finally to a year, plus two years probation. This somewhat weakened Gerando's confidence in Donziello and his promises. He finally complained."

"Not always the wisest course, I've heard."

"Big Joe Tasso contacted him down there in Florida. After realizing Gerando wasn't to be easily quieted in his claims, he suggested Pat come to New York to straighten things out. The clincher for Pat was when Big Joe stressed Gerando should come north alone."

"Come alone, the better to snuff you my dear."

"I think that's what Gerando figured. Anyway, the mob's behavior helped him decide it was healthier to come over with the good guys."

"Didn't want to contribute to the stats? Be victim of 'apparent gangland homicide,' as the papers would say. Mafia?"

"You tell me, Jack, you tell me."

12 Rolling with the Punches

ONE THING I'VE HAD TO ACQUIRE SINCE JOINing government service is an ability to roll with the punches. This is a necessity as a sanity preserver anytime, but especially in situations over which you have no control. Lack of control is frequent when a large bureaucracy is your employer and supposed ally, and the criminal element is your adversary. Standing between those two, if you can't accept the things you cannot change, you'll soon be pasting on labels at the cracker factory.

I've also learned that what sometimes looks like a pain in the ass can turn out to be a blessing. As much as I detested Herald Clarkey, the speed-dealing outlaw pharmacist from Maine I had nailed, for example, he indirectly saved my wife's life. At least it certainly helps to look at him that way, because he has no other redeeming features that I know of.

I started after Clarkey in the first place when I received an "excessive/suspicious order" from our Phoenix DEA office. Under the Controlled Substances Act, manufacturers, distributors and wholesalers are required to maintain an internal control system that picks up any unusually large orders or deliveries of any one substance to any one source. Once an order has been "redlined" as being suspicious or excessive, the manufacturer or distributor is required to notify the nearest DEA office.

Phoenix DEA had received notice from the R. J. Legere

Co. of Phoenix that Clarkey's, a retail pharmacy in Bethel, Maine, was ordering three types of speed dosage units of a hundred thousand to a quarter million *per order*. Related chemically to amphetamines, the drugs were phendimetrazine, phentermine and diethylpropion, all of which are used legally in short-term treatment for obesity control.

In the foothills of the White Mountains, Bethel is the largest town for many miles around. The population is about 2,500, and even if the cows were on diets all those pills couldn't have been consumed in Bethel. I thanked Phoenix and started checking.

I had the solid beginnings of cause for a case against the owner and pharmacist, Herald Clarkey, when my initial investigation showed him ordering well over a million units of the same stimulants from several different pharmaceutical houses in Connecticut, New York and Colorado as well as the Phoenix firm.

Through routine legal inquiries I gleaned other information about Clarkey. He owned two airplanes, a single-engine job that he docked on the lake behind his house in Bryant Pond and a twin engine he kept at his private airstrip, the Colonel Dyke Airfield in Bethel. It appeared that Herald was doing very well financially in the small-town pharmacy, or else he had inherited. Local law enforcement people told me Clarkey had been a prime suspect in several criminal investigations, but that they'd never been able to pin anything on him that stuck.

Adding other peripheral information gathered on Clarkey to this, I soon was ready to go to Maine for some on-site work with Red Eyes Houghton. Up there, we planned to hook up with our liaison, Debbie Conroy, an agent with the Maine Department of Special Investigations, the same outfit that had been so successful with the smugglers. I was ready toward the end of January, but a few things got in the way.

I was leaving for northern New England on a Wednesday morning. I wasn't leaving from the office but from our shoreside home in Scituate, so I was home later than usual.

Red Eyes wasn't expecting me to pick him up until after nine, when we'd go after the administrative warrant.

It was not only a welcome break in the routine to be leaving a little later, but it gave me a chance to spend a few extra minutes with my expecting wife, Jane. She'd had an ectopic pregnancy some years before, so we were kind of walking on eggshells through this one. I had just gotten our daughter, Janerie, out for the schoolbus and was getting set to leave myself, when Jane suddenly collapsed to the floor, unconscious.

Suffering what the doctors called a "severe abdominal catastrophe," Jane lost six pints of blood and the baby. She had to have surgery. Clarkey and his speed-dealing in Maine went on the back burner then as I took a few weeks off work to help out with Janerie and things around the house and to be with Jane as she began her recuperation.

Then, going back to the job, I had some pending court appearances to handle, so I delayed going to Maine again. I didn't mind as Jane was still bedbound and rocky only three weeks after the surgery. The investigation stalled, but Clarkey wasn't going to go out of the profitable illicit drug business voluntarily; he'd be there for us when we picked up the pieces again.

Mother Nature then intervened in the form of one of the worst blizzards in history. It hit so fast and with such fury that I barely made it home from Boston. When I did, the raging Atlantic looked like the parting of the Red Sea. Our house was one of the few in that part of Scituate not swept out to sea or severely damaged. But without heat and electricity, with gas leaks and flooding everywhere, we had to be evacuated by the National Guard. Clarkey had received another lengthy reprieve.

As I said earlier, I'm grateful to him: working his case meant that I was home that day that Jane collapsed, and I'm sure I helped save her life. But the more I learned about him, the more I wanted to stop him. By this time I knew that he was getting speed from at least four suppliers and had done over a million dosage units that year. I could only speculate what else he was doing in the line of drugs, but I could imagine the effects of that quantity of speed in rural Maine.

The third week in March we went after him. The best procedure seemed to be to start with an accountability audit and investigation at the pharmacy, whereby Clarkey would have to show us where all the drugs he'd ordered had gone. Needless to say, we figured he'd have a tough time showing scripts for a million doses in a town of 2,500.

Oxford County sheriff Alton Howe told Red Eyes, Debbie and me that Clarkey had often been suspected of criminal activity but seemed the untouchable type that was too big or slippery for the locals and too insignificant for the feds. He described Clarkey.

"About five-ten, 180. You won't mistake him, his face is frozen into a sort of grimace."

The sheriff explained the local story went that the slight facial disfigurement happened when Clarkey was forced to bail out of a military aircraft. Still an expert pilot, Clarkey had flown during the Korean War. This "grimace" figured heavily in Clarkey's sentencing later.

"You be careful," Sheriff Howe warned as we left. "Clarkey always carries a pistol on him, and he's got plenty other guns hidden around that pharmacy. I think he's the type to use 'em, he gets in a tight spot."

"Thanks, sheriff." We shook hands around.

"You get the little bastard—he's up to something."

One thing had us baffled so far. None of our meetings and interviews with various Maine authorities had revealed any exceptional use of speed or high incidence of speed-related arrests among the criminal population they were familiar with.

So what was Clarkey doing with a million hits per annum? No one had a clue.

March 17. With Red Eyes and Debbie Conroy, I presented the inspection warrant to Herald Clarkey at his pharmacy on Main Street in the quiet town and famous home of Gould Academy. I flashed my shield. He didn't seem impressed. I laid my credentials on the counter for him to have another look.

"Any weapon you're carrying, produce it now," I said, folding my arms as though I had a shoulder holster underneath my suitcoat.

Clarkey pulled out a .45 automatic that could blow down brick walls.

"Unload it and place it on the counter," I ordered. I figured I didn't have a weapon, why should he?

He did. I breathed a little easier.

A lot easier.

I may have intimidated him somewhat physically, but in response to my questions he acted as though I were right off the boat.

"Where'd all these stimulants go?" I asked. Clarkey of course didn't know what I knew already about his operation.

"Gould Academy," he said. "Some corporations've been having a lot of retreat sessions over there." I guess he figured he could tell me anything and I'd believe it. He wasn't taking me very seriously. I loomed over the counter at him, my nose inches from his. His grimace tightened.

"Mr. Clarkey, I'm a federal investigator. I'm from Boston. My name is Crowley, and I'm in Bethel, Maine, on *Saint Patrick's Day*! Do you think I'd be here unless I meant business?"

He was slightly more civil after that. As expected, Clarkey didn't have any immediate credible answers for where the huge amount of drugs had gone. We worked Bethel and the neighboring area for a few days, interviewing people, handing out subpoenas for his bank records, postal and shipping receipts and telephone toll records. The toll records were easy in the town where Clarkey lived. You just asked the one and only operator. Bryant Pond, Maine, was the last crank-operated telephone system in the country.

At least the mystery of the speed was clearing up. With the help of Bethel police chief Bob Stearns and the leads we were developing, it looked pretty certain that what Clarkey was doing was ordering the massive quantities of stimulants through his pharmacy, then flying them down to Florida in his own plane. In the South he was swapping the speed for marijuana and cocaine, which he brought back for sale in Maine.

All our investigative activity wasn't doing much for Clarkey's reputation or disposition, but it was difficult for us too, as none of this investigation was conducted undercover. The suspect knew most of our moves as we made them. The rest he could figure out by the type of questions we asked his neighbors. Finally, I had enough evidence to take to Assistant US Attorney Jim Brannigan.

Shorthanded, Jim was alternating between the Portland and Bangor offices and was too busy to be polite.

"Bring it to me airtight, Jack, and I'll design a complaint that'll get him convicted. Weak in any area, I'll drop it—I'm too busy."

"Agreed. Just one request."

"Shoot."

"During the grand jury hearings ask him where all the drugs are going."

"Gotcha," Brannigan smiled. He knew the reason I asked.

If we couldn't find out where the drugs went to through our investigation, it was a shot Clarkey would tell us under oath. Secondly, if he refused to divulge that information, then under the grand jury rules he would be held in contempt and could be incarcerated for the length of the term of the grand jury, up to eighteen months. It was leverage, and a strong incentive for coming clean.

In the course of our investigation we coincidentally uncovered an insurance swindle. Clarkey claimed a death benefit on a deceased employee. Naming himself the beneficiary, Clarkey had taken out a policy on a part-timer he knew to be dying of cancer.

Things were looking pretty good for our case. Except that was about the time of the seizure of the *Onolay* as part of Operation Atlantis and an already overworked Jim Brannigan had his hands full. I began to worry. Just as the preponderance of evidence was showing Clarkey as running an even sleazier operation than I'd originally figured, the case was sliding toward the far back burners.

For his part, Clarkey was gumming up the works by producing false theft reports to the grand jury. He claimed that most of the speed had been stolen in an amazing series of thefts at his establishment. I was able to prove his claims false, and he eventually changed his innocent plea to guilty, but it took time. When I left active participation in the case Clarkey was facing up to twenty years in prison. Once the investigator has done his thing and then sold the case to the prosecutor, it's pretty much out of his hands what happens after that. Events don't always go the way we planned. Especially when they are happening three hundred miles from your office.

Adding to the DA's workload was continued success in the form of another grab by the Coast Guard, DEA and Maine DSI of the steam vessel *Southern Belle,* and another six tons of marijuana. It wasn't the six tons that caused the problem but sixteen new defendants arrested.

Next thing I knew Clarkey, instead of the twenty years I expected, got a *year* imprisonment and a paltry three-thousand-dollar fine! I was bullshit!

I consoled myself with the fact that we had shut him down and stopped the diversion flow of drugs. Clarkey's license to dispense had been revoked, and I suspect that in small-town Maine he was anathema.

When I later suggested to Brannigan that we return Clarkey to the grand jury, he refused, insisting that part of the plea bargain deal with Clarkey was that the case was over, period.

"He asked for leniency due to his condition," Brannigan said.

"What condition?"

"Heart. He'd obviously already had a stroke; see that paralysis on one side of his face?"

Brannigan had been had.

But Clarkey didn't get the last laugh. He still got nabbed on the insurance fraud. Then, with investigative information I'd developed working our case, I contacted the Maine Medicaid fraud unit, who nailed Clarkey with another two years prison time and thirty thousand dollars restitution for what he'd bilked in Medicaid payments for prescriptions fictitiously filled and for which he billed Medicaid.

I'll pat myself on the back for that, but I missed the boat elsewhere with him. If I had it to do over again today, my investigation would have concentrated on his assets, and I'd try to seize his house, his two planes, airfield, pharmacy and other commercial real estate. Get 'em where they hurt.

A valuable lesson—it'll have to go under the category of being satisfied with what we did get. I'm not losing any sleep over Clarkey. If I look at it from the right angle, he saved my wife's life. See, I'm rolling with the punches.

13 Undercover Reverse Sting

MY SERVICE WITH THE DRUG ENFORCEMENT
Administration has been unusual to the extent that most
DEA people get moved around a lot. Except for temporary
duty assignments and occasional training in faraway places,
I've been stationed exclusively in New England. There have
been trade-offs for that privilege in terms of career advance-
ment, but I've been satisfied.

Of course, the case work of my assignment rarely remains
limited to the six-state region. My part of an international
investigation may originate or end here, but the nature of
the drug business is such that there are always threads leading to Montana or Montezuma, Mexico, Oregon or Oman,
Jordan.

Given the international character of the drug trade and
the state of modern transportation, it hardly matters where
you are base-stationed anymore. Global cases require agents
to be globetrotters, or at the very least global communica-
tors. A good percentage of the most abused nonprescription
drugs, heroin, coke and marijuana, originate from Asian,
European or Central and South American sources. Whether
it's called *petillo* in Bolivia or *crack* in Boise, the product is
the same. And causes the same destruction of lives.

Nuclear-age communication and transportation help
make the modern criminal extremely mobile. That's due
both to the nature of the business and the criminal's choice

—mobility increases the odds of escaping detection and capture. The bad guys can use laser technology, computers and satellite communications as easily as we law enforcement people. For that matter, they sometimes have the innovative equipment long before we do because they don't have a cumbersome bureaucracy to fight for appropriations.

It has indeed become a very small planet.

As evidence custodian for the Boston DEA office (one of several collateral duties) at the time of the following reverse sting case, I had been put on notice that I might be asked to supply some bales of confiscated marijuana as flash in a Maine sting. The evidence custodian has charge and responsibility of all seized property, including drugs. We periodically destroy the bulk of the inventory but always keep some of the real stuff on hand. We sometimes use the confiscated drugs as front in undercover operations. The marijuana or coke might be used as a lure to snag a buyer or to establish eyeball credibility with criminals to get deeper into their organization or as props in elaborate sting schemes. The good guys have to be inventive too, not just to make arrests but to help insure they stay alive while doing it. There have been too many grisly newspaper stories featuring the corpses of drug cops whose cover wasn't good enough.

In a standard undercover drug operation the good guys pose as buyers and obtain evidence of the bad guys selling them drugs. A sting is simply a reverse of that procedure— the good guys pose as *suppliers* and attempt to net distributors. This reverse undercover operation began a couple of years ago in the fall.

Early October in northern New England is stunning visual proof of a loving God. I was in Portland, Maine, conducting an investigation on a wholesaler conveniently located near Riverside, the truly outstanding golf facility of that city. It wasn't a back-breaking job, either. I'd been told that I might have to supply some bales of marijuana for front in an undercover investigation my old friend Mike Cunniff was running with Harry Bailey of the Maine State Police. Easy enough. Given that my own assignment was only a mashie shot away from one of the finest and most picturesque public golf courses in the United States, and that I was kind of on standby as far as providing the under-cover dope, I was considering the least I could do out of gratitude was sacrifice a couple of Titleists to such a benefi-cent deity.

I was at a window seat in a restaurant in Portland's old port, adjacent to the federal courthouse, when I spied "Big Harry" Bailey, a trooper I'd worked with on previous drug cases, crossing the street from the direction of the court-house. Spotting my wave, Harry stopped and executed a lumbering impromptu Irish jig in the middle of the busy street. Joining me inside, he could barely contain his glee. A guy his size cavorting about the restaurant wasn't everyday stuff in Portland.

His dance raised a few eyebrows until I got him to sit down.

"Hit the lottery, Harry?"

"Better." Bailey informed me I was off standby for pro-viding the bales of marijuana they'd asked for. They'd made their arrests without needing the bales as front. "We just stung some crooks for half a million dollars in cash!"

"The drinks are on me." I congratulated him and asked him to fill me in.

"A beauty, Jack, it's got more twists and turns than what you people in Boston laughingly call streets. Wait—here comes Cunniff," he said, pointing out Mike Cunniff coming across from the courthouse. "He can help with the story."

"Do I have to buy him drinks, too?"

"You're in luck, just coffee for Cunniff."

Like the proverbial bad penny, the story started out here but rolled through Colombia, Colorado and Costa Rica be-fore it came back to Maine. It really began as an offshoot of another investigation then just kind of blossomed by itself, but it clearly demonstrates the value of perceptive field men using their instincts, intelligence and tenacity to hang in there and finally make the collar. And, in this case, to re-lieve the criminals of over $500,000 cash, a BMW sedan, a

Ford truck and, lest we think it's all child's play, a .9mm Luger and a 12-gauge pump-action shotgun.

"The thing didn't start out as a sting at all," Mike Cunniff began the story. "An informant vouched for me being a legitimate buyer and helped put me in touch with Robin Marning, a vintage car dealer in Falmouth. Cars weren't all Marning dealt. Once he decides he can trust me he asks if I'm interested in investing in his cocaine business. He needs float money."

Float cash is the front money required as down payment or earnest money in a deal. It floats from the time a deal is solidified, until the time of delivery. In this case the float would be used for ten days, the time between contracting and delivery. This way the broker or dealer gives away a minute percentage of his profit but never has any of his own capital at risk. Cunniff gave Marning $2,500 of OAF funds for a 2.5-ounce sample to be delivered in nine days.

I was surprised. *"Future* delivery? He must've figured you just fell out of a tree."

"For collateral he was supposed to give me the keys and registration to one of the cars from his dealership—which he claimed was a front to launder the cocaine profits. He alleged his pound supplier was this lawyer, Gerry Vax. Vax reputedly had a huge renewable stash in Florida, from which he not only did local business with pound dealers like Robin Marning, but that he also routinely supplied twenty pounds per month to Denver, Colorado."

"No amateur," I said.

"His offer to me was simple. For every twenty-five hundred I kicked in, or got others to kick in, there'd be a 10 percent cash profit return in ten days—or we could take payment in coke."

"If he was doing so well, why did he need you?"

"Two reasons. Spreading the risk, and expansion. According to Marning, the lawyer wanted to increase his market share up here in New England."

"Sounds like Harvard Business School."

"Harvard should have their expertise," Cunniff said.

"The mob's probably the only ones with higher capitalization," Harry Bailey added.

"So we're all set up to go with this, looks pretty standard; simple little undercover job, get it over with. We set up a meet with the car dealer for him to deliver the two and a half ounces, plus Bailey and me are supposed to be there when he contacts his Florida lawyer source. For whatever reason, the deal falls through. This ticked me off at first but worked to our advantage in the long run. Marning claimed the attorney got ripped off in the parking lot of the Ramada Inn in Portland."

"Us?" I asked, wondering about an undercover snatch.

"No, dammit. He says they got twenty-four thousand dollars cash and twenty ounces of coke—wish it was us. But the ripoff did give me a plausible reason to put pressure on Robin Marning to see if he'd reveal any other sources, or put me onto someone higher up in the pipeline. I kept the pressure up, making him look bad for getting taken. Finally, when I showed up at his home in Falmouth, he reiterated the ripoff story, then said he had to cool his heels on cocaine activity because of legal problems stemming from his other business. I figured that was the end of that but apparently the needling about looking bad had worked.

"To make up for his perceived failure and to repair his self image, he introduced us at his house to Gino Casacco, an interim supplier who was gonna take care of Marning's customers while things were on hold. Now here is where it starts getting good. This Gino gives us two samples, each about 80 percent pure! He brags he's got sources in Florida *and* Boston, so there's never a hitch. Naturally, we express the proper interest. Now he wants to see something denoting good faith on our part, and a demonstrated ability to do something bigger than make single-ounce buys from Robin Marning," Bailey said.

They took Casacco to Maine National and showed him a safe deposit box with a $175,000 OAF flashroll. He seemed satisfied. Moving up from Marning to Casacco made the agents feel they were on a roll. Wrong. They did nothing with Gino. But Gino Casacco did introduce them to Michael "Tuna Mike" Bonita from South Portland. Bonita turned out to be the key. Tuna Mike bragged he had been buying 85 percent pure cocaine at the rate of a pound per week for the last six years.

"He could buy the whole state with that kind of profit," I surmised. "Makes you wonder what he was doing with his dough, if what he said was true."

Throughout the summer the agents maintained intermittent contact with the underworld principals with little of any substance happening. Deals would be proposed, meetings would be made and kept, things agreed to; all "what ifs." Cunniff and Big Harry Bailey were representing themselves as men of opportunity, dealers who would move in whatever direction promised to be the most profitable. For every encounter, Cunniff wore a nagra body wire to record the proceedings. He collected a lot of boring tape.

It wasn't until the end of August that their patience began to pay dividends. Big-bodied Tuna Mike Bonita made noises like something big was coming down. Cunniff and the swarthy Tuna had a meet at Biddeford Airport. As added color and depth to Cunniff's cover, Agent Joe Bock, a pilot, was there posing as a small-time smuggler flying marijuana from Jamaica to the US. While negotiating a price for cocaine, Mike bragged he had associates in Cuba, Philadelphia and Trenton, as well as Boston and Florida. No shrinking violet, Bonita had a tendency to exaggerate, especially about his own importance and connections. The agents learned to test his statements before relying on them. He told the truth about his connections around the country, but they doubted him when he first talked about "Alan."

It was during the airfield meeting that the agents first heard of Alan. Alan was alleged to be a friend of Mike's in New Hampshire who had retired after making a million and a half dollars profit on a single hashish deal in Lebanon. At first the agents figured Mike was just blowing smoke, inventing an associate of Alan's stature to build up his own in their eyes. They expressed an interest in meeting him to discuss his Lebanese connection, just in case there was something to it.

Surprisingly, Tuna Mike agreed to try to set up a meet. Our people were intrigued, but during the next few weeks Cunniff was unable to contact even Tuna Mike.

At a subsequent meeting at the Howard Johnson's Motor Inn at exit 8 in Westbrook, Cunniff, wired as usual, with Sergeant Harry Bailey and Trooper Leslie Bridges, endlessly discussed a variety of potential drug deals with Tuna Mike. No mention was made of the meeting he was to have set up with the mysterious Alan, or of Mike's disappearance. By now their parallel investigations had led them to suspect Alan was Alan Hull, resident of Hampton Falls, New Hampshire, and a leading suspect in many previous major drug investigations. About the time the agents despaired of getting anywhere, Tuna Mike announced he had a group of investors interested in purchasing a large marijuana load.

"I know some guys can handle thousand-pound loads," Tuna said. "Even one guy who wants ten thousand."

"Who?" Cunniff asked, not expecting an answer.

"Guy here in Portland," Tuna said, as expected, before his surprise. "Then there's always Alan. He deals."

Cunniff and Bailey could see the drift. Seeing Tuna was now interested in *getting* drugs, and hoping to learn more about Alan, they started playing it as though they had access to large quantities of marijuana. They intimated that the weed could be quickly accessed if they had a guaranteed buyer of quantity. This is where I would have come in, if needed to supply dope as proof that Bailey and Cunniff were who they said they were—dealers on the dark side of the fence.

In undercover work much depends on impressions. Success, even the difference between life and death hinges on the unspoken—what you can get the other side to believe is true, perception versus reality. The agents had been building their credibility all summer. Here, they wanted to give the impression that they didn't care to be bothered with small stuff and didn't think Tuna was up to their size, but because they respected him they were trying to let him off the hook without calling Tuna a small-timer. Hinting he couldn't pull something off either because he wasn't as well connected as he'd bragged, or that they thought Tuna was blowing smoke altogether, might push him extra hard to broker a deal. They wanted him feeling he had to prove himself to them. Subtle, psychological and circuitous, to be sure, but good agents do this every day. It helps them stay alive. Tuna took the bait.

"What's the going price for the kinda bulk you guys're talkin'?" he said. Appeal to the ego seemed to be the effective lure.

"Two hundred forty dollars per pound—in ten-thousand-pound lots," Cunniff snapped. "That's the off-the-boat price. Delivered to your vehicles, it's $265."

"I think we got a deal. I'll add ten bucks a pound, my broker fee, and quote the price $275. Then you guys can pay me the commission for setting it up out of the selling price."

The operation had switched its focus from an undercover buy of evidence to the reverse, where our side was purporting to provide the cheese for the rats to come and get. The sting had begun.

"Okay, these are the terms," Cunniff said, sensing an end to all the summer's jockeying and false starts. He did some quick figuring in his head and rattled off the figures. "Five percent of the total purchase price as a cash down payment. Immediately—up front to show intent. The balance flashed and counted just before delivery and turned over immediately after delivery. Purchase cash secured in a commercial safe deposit box. We'll count it in the bank. One of your people stays with our people overnight or until the bank reopens the next day to make sure it hasn't disappeared. Once the money is clear we release your man—$2,500,000 dockside price, $2,750,000 delivered to your man's vehicles, including your brokerage fee."

"Sounds good," Tuna said. "I'll let you know."

Another preliminary meeting was held the first of October.

Tuna said his man was interested in a ten-thousand-pound buy, and that if things went through Alan would be willing to pay the higher, delivered price of $2,750,000 because, "in addition to being semiretired, he didn't want to take the risk of participating in the off-loading operation."

The point when a load is being dropped or delivered is considered a highly vulnerable phase of any drug deal. Alan also wanted a change in the payment schedule. Instead of 5 percent down and 95 percent later, he suggested 50-50. By now Tuna had confirmed that Alan was Alan Hull as per our suspicions. Hull's name had been hooked into a hundred drug-smuggling cases in the past, but no one had ever been able to land him. Bailey and Cunniff hoped to throw out the right net to catch and keep him.

Negotiations went back and forth as the supercautious drug dealer felt the agents out through Tuna Mike. It was Hull's exceeding reticence to take risk that had kept him out of prison long enough to be "semiretired." The drug agents knew their cover, and acting had to be flawless or Hull would bolt like a fox from the henhouse—or string them along while setting them up as targets.

Tuna meanwhile used every opportunity to magnify his own importance in the deal, trying to justify his 10 percent commission. Cunniff and Bailey and the rest of our sting team were pleased to be making some progress and drawing closer to a biggie. One hitch arose when Tuna reported Alan Hull didn't trust banks, not since a lawyer had informed him law enforcement people could legally seize the contents of safe deposit boxes. Tuna ruminated how Hull and he had worked together for years; that Hull had been wise and thrifty while he, Tuna, had been a wastrel and had nothing to show for all his hard work. Most illegal drug fortunes are sent out of the country to be laundered or hidden as investments in legal businesses. Hull was reportedly hiding his money stash by literally burying it in various underground sites around New England. For that reason Hull, the careful, eccentric, prospective buyer, wasn't about to put almost three million in cash in a safe deposit box for Cunniff to grab. Finally, a face-to-face meeting was set with Hull for the Ship's Quarterdeck restaurant in Portsmouth, New Hampshire, on the Maine border.

Saturday, October 4. Cunniff and Bailey arrived early for the two o'clock meeting. Tuna showed up late, alone. He said Hull was waiting at the Kittery Trading Post on Route 1, back over the river in Maine. Cunniff pretended extreme exasperation. Last-second switches of time and location are common security tests in drug transactions. Through Tuna, Hull asked that the sellers meet him at the new location and go for a ride.

"He's afraid of being overheard in the restaurant," Tuna explained.

Testing his psychological leverage early, Cunniff rebutted that they'd already ordered some food. "Besides, I ain't riding around with anyone I don't know. Tell Alan to get his ass here or I sell the load to someone else." This was a chancy tack, but in keeping with a selective seller's attitude.

Tuna came back to the restaurant about three o'clock, explaining he and Hull had driven to the yacht club. "I hope you got some extra, 'cause Alan says he has talked to some people and now he can do about thirty-thousand pounds."

"Finish *this* deal, we'll talk bigger ones—where is he?"

Tuna checked his watch. "Out in the parking lot."

Hull was waiting in a Massachusetts-registered BMW. Tuna introduced the dapper, diminutive man to "the smugglers." There was more initial power maneuvering for leverage. Hull wanted them to drive to the yacht club. Cunniff insisted he went for no rides. Hull complained he was used to being trusted in the business. He bragged that the people he usually worked with delivered the drugs then let him pay for them after he had collected from his buyers. They finally sat down together at a picnic table in the restaurant parking area.

"Tuna here says you want five tons. We're ready," Cuniff said. "We're here so both parties can meet; you got any questions?"

"Don't wanna get burned," Hull began. "I'm in semiretirement the last five, six months. Practically hibernation, but I deserved it, I worked hard for a long time. Usually the people I work with front the whole load. I don't like banks, safe deposit boxes."

"Hey—we're flexible, but we gotta get paid," Cunniff shrugged. "We give you the dope. If you don't pay, who we going to complain to, the cops?"

After extended negotiations, Bailey and Cunniff finally agreed to 50 percent of the money at delivery so that they could pay the overhead. The drug agents needed a hefty commitment as a sign Hull intended to go on with the deal, and why not make it worth the government's while when they grabbed him?

"Terms will improve on future deals—if things go smoothly here. We can only let you have ten thousand pounds this trip. Other commitments, you understand?"

"It's a seller's market," Hull agreed.

"The only reason we're considering you *this* time is we got a client hasn't been too cool on the last couple a deals and we're cutting him out. Plus, Tuna mentioned he knew you." Bailey interjected: "No violence, you guarantee?"

"No violence. Some of your people can oversee my operation after delivery. That way you have some control, won't be so worried about me not paying," Hull said, changing the subject. "How's the stuff traveling—bales compressed?"

"Bales compressed, no piggyback. One solid block, double-wrapped with plastic inside, burlap on the outside. Total gross weight will be slightly over the ten thousand pounds. About two hundred bales. We normally discount about two and a half pounds per bale for packing."

"Mmm, superhard press. Things seem pretty solid, then. You actually seen the load?"

"We've been in touch with the boat people."

More preliminary bartering followed, including discussions of what vehicle type Hull should use to match the topography of the delivery location. Winnebagoes versus pickups. Cunniff said he expected "to make delivery next Tuesday, Wednesday or Thursday."

"Must be coming by powerboat then," Hull deduced. "Sail, you'd never be able to predict landfall so closely."

"We can predict it pretty close. We'll let you know Monday which day." At a later point Cunniff would assure Hull that he had a vehicle driving roughly parallel up the coast keeping in constant communication with the marijuana boat. "We'll tell you then what vehicles would be best and where to leave them the afternoon before for our men to pick up."

"That's awful short notice for me to get these vehicles ready. I like to set them up with lease papers in the driver's names so that no one gets bagged just for having no papers."

The agents could see Alan Hull wanted to put no money up, if he could help it. His bargaining method seemed to be to nit-pick on any item that would divert attention from the fact he was negotiating for an ever-decreasing cash outlay.

Bailey cut Hull short. "We only need your vehicles for the one night, delivery in the morning. We've done it this way before, no problems."

"What if there's a dispute over weights?"

"I'll be with the load," Bailey assured him.

"He never had a problem with weights yet," Cunniff said. "It's awkward starting with someone new. We're the ones taking all the risk here."

"Do it any way you're comfortable," Hull said. "I can always cancel if I don't like the setup."

"Us too." Cunniff didn't like the sound of that but he forged ahead. "I just have to see the half-mill flashed right before delivery so I know it's coming. The flash should happen in some public place . . . Maybe a police station parking lot. That way I feel safe. Comfortable."

"I don't think the police parking lot's such a good idea," Hull said, squirming. "Look, I got a lot of liquidation to do with such short notice."

"The money a problem?"

"Look, an emergency, I can put together $400,000 in a couple hours," Hull said, bragging but not wanting to give up his bargaining edge. "It's the vehicles are the problem. I want to do it right. What if you broke the shipment up, delivered it to me in two parts? Then I wouldn't have to front so much money. I'm not used to doing business this way. Semiretirement I told you. Look, I'm out of shape, I even let my hair grow. I always keep a low profile; you guys'd be smart not to come on too flashy with the locals, too." Christ, what a whiner, Cunniff thought.

"We're conservative too, okay?" Cunniff said, anxious to stick to the point, but conceding on money to keep things moving. "But I told you—we want at least half a mill. If you stiff us—what am I gonna do, go to court and sue, say, Hey, Alan didn't pay my money, please Judge, get it for me?"

Hull didn't smile. "I don't like moving a load as big as this all at once. Why not break it into smaller lots and deliver it over a forty-eight-hour period? I just did a hashish deal, used eight rigs. Didn't put over a thousand pounds in any vehicle, spread the risk, you know; keep it separated out? How about doing this shuffle over a couple days with a Winnie all geared with papers?"

"Get babysitters for the load. My rules are we deliver and vacate any stash location all within twenty-four hours. You do it your way, I'll loan you rigs and even let you use a stash for a while, but we're clear," the agent said, motioning to himself and Bailey.

"I gotta think of a way you can be happy and keep your eyes on the reefer, so I don't have to put up so much front money."

"When can you pay the balance?"

"I don't want to put a time on it now. I got a partner just wrapping up another one I gotta see after seeing you. There's a piggyback load just dropped south of Boston we might take a piece of it if the stuff is mature."

"South of Boston?" Bailey asked, carefully.

"Scituate. Thirty-thousand pounds."

"Doesn't belong to us."

"I plan to look at it," Hull said. "That's why I'm semileery of pressed bales. Some guys mix sand in there with the marijuana. I got a warehouse full of that shit."

Cunniff said, "Different clients for different products."

"I heard of people cutting pot," Tuna said, as if it had never occurred to him before.

Hull said, "The market's so good now you can sell anything. I got a customer even wants to buy marijuana seeds from me."

"Give us a vacuum cleaner," Cunniff said. Noting Hull's mood lighten, he sensed a time to withdraw the pressure. "So look, whatever makes you feel good. In the meantime, let's exchange phone numbers so we don't have to keep talking through Tuna Mike."

"When we see it's a go, that will be soon enough for phone numbers," Hull said, caution rising again. "I don't like phones. I'd rather talk face to face. I paid a thousand dollars to fly a thousand miles just to say a few sentences to a guy. I got a few charter pilots work for me. I just came back from the sailboat races at Newport. Should have a license, I fly so much."

"We got airplanes too," Bailey put in. "Tuna there met one of our pilots."

"Lotta nice little airfields around here," Hull smiled.

"Maine is good for smugglin'. We been doing pretty good here since the spring," Cunniff said.

"Yeah, well it cooled down some; for a while there it was swarming! They grabbed a boatload of weed off the Cape, Provincetown; the smugglers were a bunch of idiots. Told the cops exactly in Maine where they were headed. Plus, don't use the Maine Turnpike: the authorities see a zodiac boat even being hauled, they'll stop you and ask questions. We had two rigs were stopped by the state troopers up near the Canadian border, then again down here by New Hampshire by the DEA. That's why I take a nice safe shot down the back roads to my stashes."

Zodiac boats are the durable high-speed inflatable type familiar to proponents of Greenpeace or fans of Jacques Cousteau. Less wholesomely, zodiac boats are favored by smugglers, especially in off-loading operations from a mother ship or for bringing drugs to shore through shallow water. Or in rocky places like the coast of Maine. With wood lath floors to support the drugs and monster engines attached to the rubber craft for speed, they are formidable tools. Though not as fast, smugglers sometimes prefer battery-charged electric motors for silent runs.

Hull explained that he had five hideaways or stashes in Maine, New Hampshire and Massachusetts, none of which was more than forty-five minutes from where they were seated. He claimed they were all safe, and so secluded that one of them had a half-mile driveway and sat on a fifty-acre plot.

Cunniff said, "I'd like Bailey to approve the stash location seeing as he's going to be staying with the load."

"We'll see."

Bailey said, "It's getting down to the wire."

Hull said, "I haven't been in Maine in months. The inspection sticker on the Winnebago is expired. It's easy to register vehicles in Maine under a fictitious name."

"Can we get on with this? Leave a phone number with Tuna if you want to talk with us."

"Tuna has my number, but let's talk pay phone to pay phone, or personally."

They agreed to use pay phones, with Hull insisting everyone use his code, adding the numbers 0, 0, 1, 2, 3, 4 and 5 to the seven digits without carrying over the surplus. "For example, if your number was 617-8340, in code it'd be 618-1685."

Cunniff practiced one to keep him happy. "So it's pretty much settled except for the mechanics of the deal?"

"I won't make a full, complete commitment yet because when I do, I go through with it," Hull bragged, still hedging.

"If you pull out—just tell me ahead of time. I'll deliver to a different client that's waiting," Cunniff said, calling his bluff. Hull backed down.

"Things will open up a little when we're doing something. I just gotta contact some people in California and Colorado, make sure they're not already bringing in loads."

"Do that."

"It's been a good meeting. I'm ready to get back to work," Hull said, rubbing his hands together as he stood. "We'll meet again tomorrow."

After Hull left, Cunniff and Tuna repaired to the men's room of the Quarterdeck. Cunniff tried to get a feel from Tuna of how he felt the meeting had gone.

"I hope everything goes all right, no violence," he said. "And that we get paid. We gotta take care of our overhead first, you know."

"No violence," Tuna agreed, seeming satisfied. "Yeah, the overhead—that's the way Frank from Miami works, too. Hull's a goldmine of information on these things, ain't he?" Apparently Hull had bought the agent's cover. Tuna turned philosopher.

"I done a lot of deals, made big bucks. But just like here, what I done with the dough," he said, indicating the urine flushing down the toilet.

Mike Cunniff shuddered inside, hoping Tuna's statement wasn't prophetic. The recent night's newscast had shown the blood-spattered remains of a DEA agent whose act hadn't been quite good enough.

By arrangement, Bailey and Cunniff met Alan Hull again the next day, Sunday, October 5, in the parking lot of the huge New Hampshire state liquor store at the traffic circle in the historic seacoast city of Portsmouth. Hull was upset. Anything resembling work seemed to tax this guy. He complained to the agents that he'd been driving around all morning making arrangements for this drug deal, as if he was doing humanity a big service. And now, to add to the executive pressures, he'd left his change purse in a phone booth after a call to Tuna.

"You mind waiting? I got to go get that purse." This comment from a mobster, a guy who reputedly had millions buried. "I been punching out figures all night. I'm in touch with some of my group, but not all. Just hate to put up all that cash. Being away from the hustle for a while, I don't want to gamble. Plus, I just met you guys yesterday. And

Tuna's only an occasional associate. On and off. He never yet put together anything substantial, so I figure you guys might be another nothing. Anyway, can you forego the down payment? I mean, I know of some guys in Vegas and Chicago have done it this way, but this is here."

"We want substantial cash—up front," Cunniff said. "Would *you* go on faith, working with somebody for the first time?"

"I understand. I'm just not gung-ho. It's my money. My friends are tied up getting some whiff and some pillows. I did some pillows last week but they'd only been harvested lately." "Whiff" is slang for cocaine; a "pillow" is the trade term for very loosely packed bales of marijuana. Hull gave the officers two numbers, one for a pay phone. Stressing security, he advised them to keep the area codes on separate pieces of paper from the numbers and to first call the home phone, collect. It was a small step toward the trust the agents were trying to build.

"Call me at home tonight. I'll refuse to accept the charges. Hang up, then call me back in twenty minutes at the pay phone."

When Big Harry Bailey and Mike Cunniff later critiqued their meeting with Hull, trying to assess general progress of the case, Cunniff was concerned that they had either been smoothly brushed off by Hull, or else they hadn't set the hook deep enough.

During the rest of the day they were unable to contact Hull by phone. The communication vacuum increased the agents' anxiety. They smelled the real thing here and wanted to keep the deal going. Finally able to contact the middle-man, Tuna, they met him at 6:30 p.m. in the parking lot of the Hu Ke Lau restaurant near the Sears pickup door in the Maine Mall.

"How come you're so hard to get on the phone?" Cunniff found that by pushing Tuna he kept him off balance and got answers closer to the truth.

"I was talking to my bookie. Plus, back and forth with

Alan. He's not happy about coming up with so much cash. But it still looks okay."

"Is this going down or what? I got to recover my overhead or pay it out of my own pocket. I already agreed to cut the down payment in half. We're down to half a million for that guy," Cunniff said, sounding ticked though inwardly relieved the deal was still going ahead.

"Hey, I want to see it go down, too," Tuna said. "But if this doesn't go with Alan, I guarantee satisfaction if *I* do the load. I got a customer right now for five thousand pounds, and I got another prospect in Bangor with $200,000 cash if I got the product. The only thing is . . . No money. You'd have to front all of it for me. I want to get back into a position I can handle these things on my own again."

"Sorry, Tuna. I got a deadline on the overhead. Maybe another time. Get hold of Hull so we can meet again. Tell him it looks like a go for the day after tomorrow, or Wednesday—the latest."

To their relief, Hull hadn't pulled out. A meet was set for the next day, Monday, October 6, at the Burger King parking lot on the Maine Turnpike northbound at Biddeford. Hull seemed more relaxed and accepting of the two undercover agents. Virtually all the details of the operation they had discussed the previous day were agreed upon, with the further refinement that they would get the balance of the payment within twenty-four to forty-eight hours after the flow of product started. Tuna bragged the load would be sold on sight unless it was "raunch."

Cunniff suggested the Kittery Trading Post to Hull as a place to view the money. "Once the money's been flashed, Bailey and you can go inspect the load. You see the load's kosher—you make some code phone signal to Tuna."

"I don't want the money turned over," Hull said, "until Bailey here and me arrive at the stash house."

Tuna: "Why can't Cunniff and me head for the house once you inspect the load?"

Hull: "Because that puts the money and the dope in the

same location. Too risky. He can take the dough to a motel room. Won't be much bulk; it'll be in hundred-dollar bills."

Tuna: "My car'll hold the money all right."

Hull: "I might rent a car. Cripes, this is expensive. My workers got more loot than me out of the last deal, so far. I'm always the last one paid."

Cunniff: "Put the money in a suitcase, willya?"

Hull: "I just got one back from my brother. A good hardcover Tourister I bought in Miami in '79 for other work. Ain't been used in a year."

Tuna: "Am I still getting any surplus off the load?"

Cunniff: "If there is any."

Tuna: "I'll have a place ready for it. I want it."

Hull: "Any preference whether you work days or nights?"

Cunniff: "Daytime."

Tuna: "I like to work when the weather's real shitty, 'cause cops don't like to get out of their cars in the rain."

Hull: "I got a method of moving loads, it wouldn't matter if there was a thousand cops around, they wouldn't catch you. I got a friend, in Cherryfield, Maine, he keeps bees up there. The perfect thing is he takes the hives to Florida every winter and brings them back to Maine in the spring. What I do is pack the middle of his eighteen-wheel flatbed with stuff, then stack the hives around the load. Who's gonna touch it?"

Cunniff, stroking: "Sounds perfect. You really get around."

Hull: "I used to own a restaurant up here; old colonial building I picked up as payment of a debt. Dumped it in '79. Meet a lot of people that way, interesting opportunities. Too bad about the bees though; only good once a year."

Hull talked about alternate routes to his stash houses in Massachusetts and communication codes. He reminded the undercover men that it was a bad idea to transport drugs on the turnpike because the state troopers and other law enforcement people were "really into profiles," especially men fitting the city slicker profile, wearing three-piece suits and carrying fat briefcases.

"Profiles. That's why I dress casually and pretend I'm a drunk when I travel on airplanes. Profiles," Tuna said.

"I pay others to take those risks," Hull bragged. "I got a reliable inside source tells me what the boys look for. They got briefcases with alkaloid sensors inside that beep into an earphone when they detect drugs."

"They even got *old ladies* undercover at the Miami airport," Tuna complained, shaking his head at the DEA's unfair play. "They walk around with drug-sniffing poodles. Imagine gettin' bagged by an old lady with a poodle?"

Hull left after a final complaint regarding the necessity of a down payment.

Cunniff turned to Tuna. "I feel better about this after meeting him and everything, but what's his big problem with the dough?"

"He's cheap, for one thing. Hates to spend money on work he can do himself or risk something he can get others to risk. Hear him about the suitcase? Bought it in '79. God forbid he wouldn't get another use out of it—it probably only made him a mill or two. Just like the cocaine he stashes for his personal use, he literally buries his cash. He heat-seals it in freezer bags and buries it under the ground in Vermont, New Hampshire, anywhere. He admitted to me that the reason he's been so tough in the negotiations here isn't that he hasn't got it—but that he hasn't got time to dig it up!"

"Christ."

"He's got another hash deal in the works too. By the way, don't tell him I told you about any his previous hash deals."

"You've been all right, Tuna," Bailey assured him.

"Just remember, I get the surplus. Hope there's some gold in the load."

"Should be good stuff," Bailey said, thinking the only gold in this deal might be a detective's shield. The gold Tuna wanted was the best, most potent, most mature marijuana.

"Yeah, the harvest in Colombia just ended. I can make

good bucks if there's gold in it. I know what the market calls for . . . Just so long's it's not green."

"Aged like fine wine."

The meeting broke up when a state police cruiser pulled into the lot, spooking Tuna. Though the agents didn't know it, the incident foreshadowed a later glitch that threatened to blow the entire investigation.

After a doubtful night's rest, on Tuesday Cunniff called Hull from a pay phone in Seabrook Plaza near the nuclear power station. The call was a final test of commitment before giving the go order to mobilize the backup forces for the next day's sting operation and, they hoped, bring-down.

Cunniff: "We had a surprise visit from mother last night."
Hull: "Yeah?"
"She brought Mary Jane along."
"Oh?"
"You'll be surprised to see how mature she looks."
"It should be very good."
"She's resting at our house for tomorrow's trip."
"So you want to plan on tomorrow, then."
"Yeah, why don't we meet for lunch?"
"Tomorrow."
"Eleven sharp. Bring the snapshots with you."

Snapshots was the code word for money. The deal was on.

It was time to call in the troops. Because the sting was going down virtually on the Maine and New Hampshire border, the action could spill over to several states. Protocol demanded some diplomacy. The appropriate local and state police departments were alerted. The marshalling point chosen for the backup forces was the state liquor store, not far from the meeting place, the Ship's Quarterdeck restaurant.

Agents Cunniff and Bailey were there early the next day —wired and nervous but confident that everything was ready behind the scenes. The adrenaline was really flowing. They knew they had built a good case for court. Keyed, they sensed the climax of the case and a good bust.

Hull and Tuna pulled into the restaurant parking lot on time.

"What's the load like?" Hull asked calmly. He worried the agents, seeming to be in no hurry. Shit, he wasn't going to back down at the last minute, was he?

"The load's dry and mature," Cunniff said. "Ready to flash the dough?"

Hull started trotting out last-minute reasons for a stall.

He wanted lunch first. The money was somewhere else.

"Take a ride with me," he suggested. "I wanna move around, switch where we show the money. I don't wanna chance being ripped off."

Cunniff came right back at him. "And I don't want to risk being kidnapped, either. Flash the dough right here as planned." Hull backed off. "No guns, see?"

"Let's go inside the restaurant."

"I been to that location too many times."

Eventually, they reached a compromise, agreeing to move up Route 1 to the Kittery Trading Post. Cunniff was confident the backups would respond to the switch. Arriving at the new location in separate cars, they chose the spot in the parking lot where Hull would show his half million earnest money.

"There's a pay phone across the highway," Hull said. "I gotta tell the courier the new delivery spot."

He and Tuna went to make arrangements for the money to be moved. The phone was directly across the street in another commercial parking lot. Because of a road divider, the drug merchants had to drive down the road to a turnaround and come back on the other side in order to get to the phone.

After a few minutes the drug dealers had made the U-turn and were visible again at the phone across the street. Standing by their own car in the first parking lot, Cunniff and Bailey tried to look casual while waiting for the dealers to return. They'd been engaged in this investigation for months. They mentally crossed themselves against Murphy's Law.

While the parties were watching each other across the divided highway, an elderly tourist stopped by the drug agents' car to ask directions. Like all elderly tourists he lingered, making small talk with the polite young men in the parking lot. That, coupled with what happened next, turned out to be fatal for their plans for a bust that morning.

Cunniff and Bailey watched Hull and Tuna get into their car across the highway and pull out. Minutes passed. Many, increasingly nervous minutes passed. No sight of their quarry. Finally, Tuna screeched his car to a halt beside them in the Trading Post parking lot. He was alone. And visibly agitated.

"We seen a bunch of police cars near the state liquor store. Uniformed and plainclothes cops, might even be DEA —a setup!" Tuna was out of his car, stalking back and forth like a trapped animal. "We done nothing illegal—yet. But if you're really smugglers, you guys better scram, too."

Jesus Christ, Cunniff thought, all our work. The jerks spotted the backup! The agents' only hope was to convince the criminals they had no connection with the police.

"Wait—we'll move this whole deal to another state," Cunniff tried, screaming in his frustration and anger.

"Alan's already intercepted the money courier," Tuna said, getting in his car to leave. "Had to run down the friggin' highway after him."

Maine Corporal Norman Auger and US Customs C.P.O. Paul Flaherty, part of the cover team, had observed Hull chasing after the money vehicle, a brown F150 pickup truck. Cunniff wasn't aware of this going on outside his sphere of the attempted sting. He thought, shit—it's off. Well trained in department economics, he shut off his nagra body wire after Tuna left. He and Bailey went back to their car.

Tuna reappeared beside their car before Mike had time to turn his wire back on. "You don't believe what I said about the cops. You think it's just Hull backing out."

"It would've been easier if you'd just been honest," Cunniff accused, playing the role, hoping he saw a chance to keep it going. He aimed at Tuna's pride. "Shoulda just said you couldn't handle the deal."

Tuna slammed his fist on the side of the car. "Call Alan in twenty minutes."

Needless to say, they did. No answer. Dejected, Cunniff and Bailey returned to the Scarborough, Maine, barracks for regrouping and planning. They figured it was all blown away.

More because they had nothing better to try, the agents put through a five-thirty phone call. Though surprised that Hull answered, Cunniff went on the offensive. "What the fuck you doing to us, man?"

"I panicked. I saw all those cops near the the flash point, then saw you across the road talking to some guy at the car. I figured him for a cop and it's all over. Who the hell was he? I'm not suspicious of you guys, just cautious, I guess." Panicked after spotting the backup force, Hull had assumed the tourist was a law officer, too.

"Those cops could've been there for anything—coulda been inspecting the liquor store!" he said.

"Better safe than sorry."

"So what's the story?" Cunniff said. "This business about the cops sounds like a lot of BS."

"I want to meet and straighten this out. I'll even drive to Maine if that's what you want. The problem is you guys just don't know me. I'm an honest person. I give you a 100 percent guarantee that the money is sitting in my house this minute. That's how ready I was. I'm not going to pull something crazy with Tuna's wife and baby there in Maine."

"Bring the money to Tuna's," Cunniff said.

"Families should be kept separate. Somewhere else."

"Gimme a few minutes to think about it."

"I'll drive up now and we'll meet first—" Hull said.

"No more meetings. It's time to do it!" Cunniff laid down the ground rules. "We'll meet in Gray, ninety minutes traveling time from your location. Ten minutes late, we're out of there. Be on time. Flash the money, then you go with Bailey to inspect the load. I'll stay with the money and someone from your outfit."

"Okay, I'll send my men with the money part way now so

they'll have plenty of time. I'll wait for your call back to set the time."

Hallelujah, the sting was still on. Cunniff called Hull back at eight, after remarshalling his forces.

"Nine-thirty, Hojo's service area, mile fifty-six, Gray, Maine. Be on time," he warned.

"The money's already part way there," Hull said. "But how about downtown Gray, rather than out there on the road?"

"Turnpike's better. We already scouted them both out. Be there."

The agents moved immediately north to Gray. On a drive-by at the scheduled meeting site, Bailey, Cunniff and Trooper Michael Vittum noted a pickup truck matching the description of the money courier's vehicle in the south parking lot of the service center. The truck was unoccupied, but they didn't dare look inside. They weren't supposed to know this was Hull's truck. Curiosity could spook the other side before the law was ready. A phone call to the trooper barracks confirmed the vehicle description. Finally—they were sure the money was there!

The cover team was secreted and in place awaiting the signal to close. All they needed now was to put Hull together in the same place with the money. On another ride-by on the other side of the turnpike coming back, they saw two men, later identified as William Tumesce and Al Dore, getting into the money truck. Entering the parking lot they saw Hull's BMW parked about two hundred feet away from the pickup. All right. Things were cooking.

The agents parked next to Hull. They introduced Vittum as an associate without letting on they knew the money vehicle was already on-site. Hull told Vittum about his scare, seeing the police in Kittery earlier. He felt sheepish for pushing the panic button, not going through with the deal, which was precisely how the agents wanted him to feel. Cunniff pushed his psychological advantage.

"I don't want to hear any more about it, all right? You got the down payment?"

"Not with me," Hull stalled, negotiating to the end.

Cunniff, hardnosed, kept pushing, acting as if he didn't know the pickup was there, his life perhaps depending on not letting the mask slip until all the cards had been played. "How far away, and how long will it take to get it here?"

Hull smiled, finally satisfied. "Over to the left, in that pickup. One of your guys can get in back and count it. I got the keys to the back in my sock."

They moved to the truck where the driver, Tumesce, suggested they drive up the pike and he could turn on his revolving light.

"Make it look like a service call, while you count."

"No need to count it," Cunniff said, impatiently. "I know what a half million looks like."

Cunniff ignored Tumesce and moved to the rear, looking in.

He couldn't signal the backups until he was sure. Inside he saw a duffle bag, a file cabinet . . . and a suitcase that looked like it might be the Tourister their quarry had previously mentioned.

That had to be it.

Cunniff went back to the front of the truck. Hull came with the key held out. "It's in the suitcase," he announced.

Simultaneously, Bailey and Cunniff silently signaled their cover team to respond and close in.

The next few seconds are the most delicate and danger-fraught of any undercover operation. Once the silent signal was given, Cunniff innocently asked Tumesce and his shotgun rider, Dore, to kindly open their jackets to prove they carried no weapons, in line with Hull's assurance of no violence. As they accommodated, uniformed backups came into view.

Spying the law, Tumesce rammed the truck into gear and tried to flee, only to find himself blocked in by a Maine trooper cruiser. Uniformed trooper Ralph Libby relieved a fully loaded .9mm automatic pistol from Tumesce's boot. A semiautomatic pump shotgun was lifted from behind Dore's seat. The backups had moved too fast for the criminals to even thing about shooting. All the suspects, including an apoplectic Hull, were cuffed.

Pursuant to federal search warrants, the agents removed $499,360 from the hardcover suitcase in the truck cap and $1,220 from a canvas knapsack in the BMW: $500,580 total asset seizure, not counting vehicles.

The sting was complete.

We were almost the only patrons left in the restaurant when Cunniff finished his narrative. I toasted him and Bailey.

"No wonder you guys are dancing," I said. "A great feeling to beat them at their own game."

"An understatement, Jack. Great ain't the half of it." When the cases were adjudicated, Alan Hull was sentenced to five years for conspiracy. Al Dore, two years. William Tumesce, four, and beloved commissionaire Tuna Michael Bonita also received two years. Not a bad piece of work.

14 Clandestine Classic: Analogs

CLANDESTINE LABS ARE A SPECIAL CHALLENGE to the drug agent. They produce dangerous, bargain-basement ripoffs of legitimate, controlled drugs. There is no control over what is produced and no guarantee of fitness for human consumption. Underground and criminal, clandestine labs pose an extremely dangerous risk to producers, users and those that try to dismantle them.

As much as we enjoy busting up a clandestine lab, it can sometimes be the most perilous part of our job, more perilous even than having cover blown or getting shot at. Aside from the obvious physical danger from the criminals whose lab we are invading, there is also the danger of a deadly explosion from the many extremely volatile chemicals used in illicit drug manufacture. The toxic nature of these same chemical ingredients also makes it risky just to be in the same room. Breathing the fumes created in the production of certain drugs can kill you, and some of them can even be fatal if absorbed through the pores.

Fentanyl, the key ingredient in the production of most narcotic analogs, is a good example. Fentanyl (commercially marketed as Sublimaze or Innovar) is a short-acting, highly potent narcotic that in humans is about *one hundred times as strong as morphine!* Used in medically approved dosages and legally administered, fentanyl is an effective anesthetic during surgery. That's good. Unfortunately, because of its incredible potency, fentanyl is much sought after for the illicit street trade.

Think of analogs as the chemical offspring of a parent drug—of the same family, with many of the same characteristics. A number of fentanyl analogs have been produced that retain the powerful narcotic action of the parent compound. But potency can be an elusive quality. Actual potency of any drug depends on absorption, excretion, rate of metabolism and the ability of the compound to gain entrance to the central nervous system by passing through the blood/brain barrier. The danger of many analogs is that they short-circuit the whole nervous system due to superfast absorption. It's like sending an arrow to the brain.

The strength of an analog, the potency factor that kills the user, depends greatly on the cooking skill of the chemist. "Cooking" is the term used for the combining of a variety of chemicals into illicit drugs. The term comes from the fact that rooming-house hot plates and Bunsen burners are used in the makeshift labs to heat various chemicals and combinations held in Pyrex dishes and beakers. To the uninitiated, the process looks like making soup. And not all the criminal chemists are university graduates. For some, their only experience with chemicals prior to cooking drug analogs was changing the oil in a getaway car. The only way underground chemists know they have cooked a bad batch is when their customer list decreases due to sudden demise. Then it's time to change the formula.

It goes without saying that the chemist is the key man in any clandestine operation. His expertise can mean a steady flow of customers—or his lack can mean a lot of bodies turning up and bringing heat from the authorities. Since about 1979 clandestine fentanyl analogs have been sold on the street as heroin, "street heroin" or "China White," allusions to its similarity to the real stuff.

Overdose deaths are common among users of fentanyl analogs because of the tricky nature of finding the right balance of chemicals in their manufacture. Many fentanyl deaths go undetected and unreported because of the extremely low tissue levels of the substance. Regular, routine toxicological methods fail to detect them. Nor do the clandestine labs subscribe to the Better Business Bureau or submit their product to Consumer Research for testing.

Fentanyl is a drug agent's nightmare because it is so toxic that you don't have to ingest it to be in trouble. Just being in the same room with a concentrated amount such as in a cooking lab is enough to kill. An agent dismantling a clandestine lab can absorb a small amount of the stuff through his *pores* and die because the chemical gets in the blood stream and shuts down that part of the brain that tells him to breathe. During clandestine lab busts, I keep a very close eye on my people, insist on ventilation, and periodically remind them to take a deep breath.

Beyond the danger from bacterial contamination in an uncontrolled production environment, extreme danger to the public exists from the illicit labs because some of the clandestinely produced analogs are so potent that one gram is sufficient to make about fifty thousand doses (about 250 times stronger than heroin). It doesn't take real mind-stretching to imagine the chaotic effect of a miscooked super-drug hitting the streets for a user population used to shooting, popping or snorting stuff that's been cut ten to twenty times.

Meperidine is another synthetic narcotic that has been frequently mimicked by clandestine laboratory operators, but the popular analog compound MPPP is about ten times yet more potent as an analgesic than Meperidine. Its recommended dosage should be about that for morphine. *Should* be. But remember, the average patron for the products of clandestine labs isn't interested in prescribed dosages. Nor is he always in shape to remember how much he took after the first hit.

There is also a neurotoxic byproduct, MPTP, commonly formed during the cooking of MPPP. Neurotoxic translates to brain-frying—if taken, MPTP frequently leaves the user in a state similar to a severe case of Parkinson's disease. The neurological damage produced by exposure to MPTP is irreversible and appears to worsen with time. Maybe forgetting to breathe is better.

In addition to the danger to agents posed by operators and explosions, there are invariably volatile, burning acids to contend with when busting up clandestine labs. Drug agents are strongly advised to have a chemist on hand whenever possible while making a clandestine bust—for several reasons, including safety and identification of unstable substances. They should also, if it can be arranged discreetly, bring along the local fire department. Lithium aluminum hydride, almost always used in cooking speed, is so volatile it will explode if you look at it cross-eyed.

Most clandestine labs are involved in the manufacture of substances not included in the Controlled Substances Act list. These substances, or "new" drugs, are made by formulating an analog. Simply, an analog is a variation on a theme. Take a standard chemical formula, Librium (chlordiazepoxide) for example. The parent drug is benzodiazepine. Using the original formula and altering or substituting just *one molecule,* a chemist can create a "new" drug, an analog. This new drug, the child, is now slightly different in molecular makeup but retains many of the parent drug's properties and, most importantly, produces many of the same effects as the original.

Why do criminals manufacture analogs? Many safe analogs of common drugs are available on the legal market and have similar psychoactive and therapeutic effects as the parent drug. But the big profit is in the illicit analogs. Legal manufacturers of safe analogs are subject to expensive and profit-eating governmental controls. Librium is on the controlled substances list so *illicit* manufacture of it is punishable by law. But create some slight molecular variation on the theme—invent a drug that's not quite Librium and not on the list of controlled substances—and you can manufacture and distribute it all day long without fear from the law. Simple capitalism: "cook" the analog at a fraction of the cost of legal manufacture and sell it at a multiple of the legal prescription cost. The new entrepreneurs.

The government is in a legal bind. Substances can't be prohibited before they are created. And a newly created analog takes time to identify and prohibit. A new analog is especially attractive to the underworld because until we identify the new substance and get it specifically included under the Controlled Substances Act (which can take up to a year), the manufacture and distribution of that substance is *legal.*

Let's say *(a[b[c)* is the chemical formula for Librium. Librium is on the CSA list so that illicit manufacture or distribution would be prosecutable under the law. But suppose a criminal hires a chemist to cook the formula with a slight twist, *(a[(b—)[c).* The new formula is close enough to the original to have similar effects, meaning the addicts and recreational users will buy it. But the new formula isn't on the CSA list, so he can't get locked up for making and selling the stuff. Yet.

Additionally, an extralegal chemist can create a whole *string* of barely different compounds ready to be produced as soon as the authorities *do* ban the previous analog. Because they differ molecularly from the specific controlled substance, he's safe for a while. Not being under the CSA, the authorities can't go after the criminal and his chemist for manufacturing or distributing the analog. Which would *you* rather deal, illicit substances listed under the CSA, or legal analogs?

I don't mean to paint a rosy picture for the potential clandestine analog producer. Aside from the obvious problem of your customers dying if your formulae aren't right, there is the cost factor. Though a fraction of the cost of legal manufacture, it still takes big bucks to equip and set up a clandestine lab. The criminal must acquire chemicals and other supplies to produce analogs. And personnel. Even incompetent chemists are expensive. Explosions happen often, if you're not careful.

Then there is distribution and sales of the product to either oversee or farm out, perhaps to a motorcycle gang. Or permission might be needed from the syndicate, whose geographical area the lab is in. Analog production isn't for everyone off the streets.

The majority of clandestine labs content themselves with producing the closest thing they can get to popular drugs like Librium, heroin and speed. Other clandestine operations have become highly sophisticated, contained units manufacturing the chemicals and even pressing them into pills or capsules, rather than marketing the raw powder. Some criminal labs are even packaging their product prior to distribution, just like the real labs. In one way, this has *helped* law enforcement people because the specialized machines needed to make tablets and capsules can easily be traced through equipment sales companies and auctions. The mere presence of one of those machines outside of a known pharmacological factory is a pretty good indicator of foul play.

When sniffing out or sifting evidence of a clandestine lab, another tipoff is the presence of large windows and exhaust fans to dissipate the smoke, heat and odor of cooking. The sinus-piercing chemical odor of ether or ammonia is unavoidable in analog cooking. All labs produce a stench both pervasive and noxious. Cooks can't stand an unvented kitchen for long.

Another source of leads to clandestine labs are the mail and express-company deliveries from chemical or equipment manufacturers. Inside informants or undercover agents are the best sources of information. Lacking that luxury, we sometimes have to rely on electronic aids.

The following case developed for the DEA as two distinctly separate threads. It involved two different motorcycle gangs, in separate states and separate investigations. Eventually the threads were interwoven into a classic case of clandestine lab investigation and disruption—except that in this case a prebust explosion threatened to blow away most of our evidence, and one of the chemists was shot trying to escape.

Thread number one involved the shipment of a load of P-2-P from the South, up the East Coast. P-2-P is a precur-

sor for speed, a key ingredient in its manufacture. One gallon of P-2-P combined with other readily available
chemicals makes eight pounds of speed. Important stuff.
Since 1980 it is on the CSA list and its use is strictly monitored. The shipment became a controlled delivery, trailed by
agents monitoring an electronic signal from a beeper concealed inside the load. All that was known initially was that
the shipment was destined for an unknown source expected
to be in the greater Boston area.

Thread number two was wound around an ongoing investigation initiated to detect a clandestine lab in a suburban
home north of the city.

Agent Stanley Burroughs received information from a
very reliable informant that Al Buglio, member of the Rene-
gades, a local motorcycle club known for controlling most
of the speed traffic in the Norfolk, Virginia, area, was gathering P-2-P, allegedly to ship north to a clandestine lab.
Buglio had bragged he would be the courier or delivery boy
and that he was in for some big bucks for bringing the load
north. Burroughs corroborated the information through his
own investigation and another source.

The informant seemed on target. Buglio was out to divert
some P-2-P. Stanley Burroughs obtained warrant permission from US magistrate Laurence Cohen to install a directional radio beacon for the purposes of controlling the
extralegal shipment to delivery.

Burroughs and his informant kept close tabs on Buglio in
the time left before his departure. It appeared the motorcycle gang member was doing some business with a Norfolk chemical manufacturer, one legally certified to process
P-2-P. Buglio had presented himself as a maintenance company owner, thereby legitimizing his need for certain industrial chemicals. Buglio let it be known he was also an avid
amateur photographer who did his own film developing,
which gave him another plausible reason to purchase eso-
teric chemicals.

Buglio had been ordering small amounts of chemicals for
some time to establish himself as a steady customer. Paying

promptly, he increased the size and varied the scope of his orders until he felt safe ordering what might otherwise be targeted chemicals. P-2-P purchases are always suspect.

Agent Burroughs enlisted the aid of technical officer Pat Fitzgerald. When Buglio packed for his trip, our boys secreted a bird dog, a DEA minibeeper, into the brown cardboard box containing the P-2-P. Close surveillance began as he headed north through Virginia Beach. The beeper was working.

Meanwhile, up north, Agents William Simpkins and Steven Boeri were closing in on a clandestine lab connected with known members of the Hell's Angels. One of the principal suspects was old friend Joseph Urbi, the East Boston ex-firefighter who had been involved in the North Shore pacs investigation.

Starting with a tip from an informant, the agents had begun surveillance on a house in Peabody, Massachusetts, suspected of being a clandestine lab.

Initial observance of the house revealed telltale large window fans operating full blast. These fans were pulling precious heat out of the house in energy-conservation-conscious New England—in November. Starting from there, a full-scale investigation took hold.

A check of the tax rolls revealed the undistinguished suburban Victorian house was owned by Ned Coletta, small-time hood and motorcycle gang member. Continued observation yielded some interesting visitors to the house on Overlook Avenue. First visitor was Carlo Ricci, a longtime associate of Coletta's and fellow member of the Hell's Angels. Next to visit were Urbi and then John Wicke, aka Sid Vicious, a suspect in several other drug investigations, and one Pasquale Caputo, an associate of Vicious.

Tails were established on all visitors. Most stakeouts have about the same interest level as watching grass grow. Not this one. Due to the number of visitors to the Overlook Avenue house and barn, their high level of activity and their sometimes humorous antics, there was never a dull moment.

It was interesting to see that the characters joined here to perpetrate crime upon the public weren't above trying to put the screws to one another in the process. Someone was always working a scheme, even if it was just forgetting the change from an errand. Some of the suspects were noted purchasing various materials at local hardware stores and supply houses that would be consonant with operating a clandestine lab. When a full stakeout was later established, agents close enough to the house on night watch reported strong chemical odors. Sometimes ammonia, sometimes ether.

"You get close, the friggin' dogs start yapping," one agent noted.

"S'okay. They help you stay a safe distance," his partner said. "You get *too* close, you'll probably have to throw your clothes away, the ether smells so bad. I went home this morning my wife thought I was working in a hospital." Nobody was looking forward to a prolonged stakeout.

Checking mail and express-company deliveries and then tracing backwards, it seemed the Peabody residence was using a lot of glass beakers, Pyrex dishes and rubber tubing. They had also ordered industrial amounts of ammonia, sulfuric acid and other easily obtainable chemicals. Common, but suspicious.

Simpkins ran a check of all possible suppliers of inert materials necessary in the production of tablets. There was no way he could be denied a search warrant if he could trace these materials to the Peabody house. (In addition to active ingredients, most drugs contain several inert materials, including diluents, binders, lubricants, and disintegrators. Diluents are the cutting material, the diluting substance such as lactose that is added to give the product its bulk. The average LSD tablet, for example, contains only one or two *ten-thousandths* of a gram of LSD, so it's obvious that some material must be added to make tableting possible. A binder allows the powdered material to remain intact after compressing. Holds the powders together. The most commonly used are starch, gelatin, molasses, sucrose and synthetic gum. Lubricants keep the substance from sticking to the dies and punches and other tablet machinery. A disintegrator is added to a tablet to facilitate its breakup and absorption into the blood stream, thereby speeding up the high after taking. Most disintegrators are either corn or potato starch. I always thought disintegrator the perfect name for what the drugs do to ambition, hopes and lives.)

Simpkins soon had all the accessory evidence needed to justify twenty-four hour surveillance and apply for search warrants. Evaluating his intelligence, including the known specialties of the cast of characters visiting the suspect clandestine lab, it seemed certain they were set up to cook speed. All that was needed was some refinement of intelligence in order to time the bust for maximum effect. It was imperative to present the least possible bodily risk to the enforcement personnel, while at the same time bagging the optimum number of bad guys. Timing was crucial to catch the crew while they were cooking, and equally necessary as evidence was a quantity of the finished product!

While Simpkins was intensifying his investigation of the clandestine lab, thread number two, the P-2-P, was weaving its way up the seaboard. The bird dog continued sending its steady beep out from the cardboard box in Buglio's car trunk to Fitzgerald and Burroughs and the rest of the tailing DEA team.

The northward surveillance was being conducted by a variety of surface vehicles on the road, aided by DEA aircraft out of Baltimore. Buglio was sticking to Route 95, the traditional main road up to New York and points north. When Buglio bypassed New York City and drove into Connecticut, logic and probability suggested his target was the Boston area.

Back at Overlook Avenue, surveillance agents had witnessed Sid Vicious and Pasquale Caputo at various times dismantling what appeared to be a rolling clandestine lab from the camper cab of Caputo's pickup truck. Vicious, apparently acting in this setup as assistant chemist, was an arguer. He would dispute anything, chemical formulae or the time of day—anything, with anyone, any time, for any reason. Agents observing him concluded he just liked to argue. He was also a klepto. He had been seen stealing in stores, but he wasn't limited to just commercial theft.

Agents watched as he pocketed several small articles from the camper while helping his "pal," Caputo.

Over the course of the next few days the agents watched the crew carry into the house various supplies, including Bunsen burners, a hot plate, a triple-beam scale and what looked like gas masks. The boys weren't reenacting World War I; they were really cooking.

The two separate threads began to come together just before Christmas. The P-2-P arrived in the Boston area on December 20. Burroughs had kept the Boston office DEA apprised of his controlled delivery operation since the possibility the P-2-P was headed our way.

Agent Simpkins, aware that the clandestine lab was cooking and that speed was probably on their menu, saw the possibility. When he learned that Urbi was involved, he suspected the P-2-P coming north was intended for him. Urbi had been involved in the local pacs industry with the unsavory likes of rogue pharmacist Angelo Baratto. Not the best character reference. Internationally, the Royal Canadian Mounties were still hoping to nail Urbi for a major theft of precursors in their country. They and our federal police both wanted him as well for smuggling hundreds of pounds of the finished speed product back across our northern border.

The importation of southern P-2-P and the high volume lab operation seemed to have Urbi's stamp. The Outlook Avenue location was at the top of the list of suspected P-2-P delivery points because of him. Wherever Urbi was, there was a good chance of criminal activity. Simpkins dearly wanted to nail Urbi along with the drugs, though his primary concern was to grab the lab and put it out of business.

On December 20 Simpkins's surveillance team followed Sid Vicious and Pasquale Caputo to the Squires Lounge in Revere, Massachusetts. When the two suspects were safely ensconced inside, the field men called boss agents Simpkins and Boeri.

"Looks like they got a meet set up," Pete Vinton reported from a phone outside the Squires. "They're schmoozing, having a few drinks—but acting like they're waiting for somebody. Maybe a delivery?"

"Keep a close eye on them, we'll be right there. If they move, let us know by radio."

Simpkins left to help the surveillance. They took a receiver with them tuned to the frequency band the bird dog transmitted on, just in case. It was worth a shot. Word had come in that the southern surveillance team had crossed the Massachusetts border earlier in the day. Instinct told Simpkins that if the P-2-P hadn't been delivered elsewhere by now, it was headed to the kitchen crew on Overlook Avenue.

Simpkins joined his stakeout team in the Squires parking lot. Shortly after his arrival, a car bearing Virginia license plates entered and circled the lot twice. The driver got out, went inside and joined Caputo and Vicious.

"Turn that thing on," Simpkins said, indicating the receiver. Eureka! The signal receiver lit up, blinking red in the dark of the parked stakeout vehicle.

Another car, assumed to be part of the southern surveillance team, entered the busy parking lot and drove to the back end. Simpkins confirmed the DEA-coded plates then dispatched Agent Skipper Crowe to confer and coordinate with our southern counterparts.

The newly arrived suspect was established to be Al Buglio. Buglio was observed to converse with Vicious and Caputo briefly before they all got up and departed the lounge. Outside, they separated and left the parking lot in their respective vehicles.

"You stick with Urbi and Vicious," Simpkins told Peter Vinton. "I'm going with the bird dog."

The tail was easy at first. Both vehicles took the same route to the Lynn Marsh Road, a stretch of blacktop through a tidal salt marsh, semideserted at this hour. The suspect vehicles pulled over, parking near each other. Buglio went to his trunk and took out a large cardboard box, which he transferred to the El Camino driven by Caputo and shotgunned by his partner. When the suspect vehicles parted company, the signal from the DEA directional radio beacon now emanated from the El Camino rather than the original vehicle registered in Virginia.

The Norfolk DEA team was road-weary, shivering in the December chill and more than happy to surrender the surveillance to their northern winter parts. The P-2-P had been delivered. And Buglio's part was complete.

The northern team let Buglio go for the time being and followed Caputo and Vicious, concentrating on the P-2-P. Caputo drove first to a tenement-crowded neighborhood street in Revere, where he again transferred the P-2-P, this time to a gray Chevrolet pickup with a camper cab, the same camper that had previously been observed around the premises at Overlook Avenue, a suspected clandestine lab on wheels.

Leaving the El Camino in Revere, Caputo and Vicious drove directly north toward Peabody for about a mile before initiating intricate evasion tactics designed to throw a tail. That the men instituted evasion tactics simply as a matter of routine policy showed the level of their planning and organization. Luckily, our men were experienced at bird-dogging. They hung in there undaunted as the pickup doubled back to its starting point. Careful not to let the suspects know they were in pursuit, the tails kept pace. Vicious and Caputo obviously knew the stiff penalties they faced if caught connected with clandestine lab operation. The camper pickup went through various standard evasion maneuvers, such as alternating speed from very slow to very fast, switchbacks, changing directions, and entering and exiting traffic rotaries from differing points. Massachusetts traffic rotaries should be listed in "The Getaway Guide"; they are an evasion tactic all by themselves.

"Having two cars helped the good guys, as did the beeper," Simpkins said later. "We didn't have to be right up his ass the whole time. It was obvious they were taking great pains not to lead anyone back to the lab. We assumed they were headed to Peabody, but we had to stay on them. No *guarantee* where the P-2-P was going till it got there. Wouldn't do to lose it now, not after they'd followed it all the way up the coast." Despite all the evasion, there finally came a time when Caputo was confident he'd shaken any possible tail, and he drove to his destination. His trail led to the Overlook Avenue property. They parked by the barn next to the clandestine lab. It was shortly after midnight when the cardboard box was taken in to the kitchen. The signal was steady.

Next morning, Urbi was the first to show up and go inside. Agent Allen Keaney watched Caputo drive up and carry in a box of aluminum shavings. Later in the day Caputo went out and came back with the El Camino. He and Ned Coletta then lugged a small freezer from the camper to the barn. Handy for storage of drugs. It looked like they were ready to cook up some P-2-P.

Word on the street during this period correctly reflected a somewhat loosely defined DEA policy of concentration on clandestine labs. Yet unconfirmed sources reported that despite the known risk from alert authorities, the Peabody lab was being operated because Ned Coletta needed money "very badly."

"Urbi himself owes heavy bread from a previous deal to some big people in Canada," an informant reported.

The daytime surveillance team was set up in a delivery van across the street assisted by roving car observers. Every shade in the house was drawn shut. The big window fans were working full time. Agent Boeri moved to a vacant field to the rear of the Overlook Avenue barn to observe the kitchen area of the residence. He could see Sid Vicious writing in a blue notebook next to the triple-beam scale. He also observed Sid and Urbi cutting up strips of aluminum foil.

At one point, Agents Crowe and Keaney observed Carlo Ricci and Ned Coletta load the rear of Caputo's El Camino with what looked like trash bags before driving off. Eager to find out the contents of the bags, the agents followed. Passing an empty lot the suspects stopped and flung the plastic bags into the weeds.

"I'm gonna add littering to the list of charges when we bust these bums," Keaney said.

"Stay with them," Crowe advised. "We'll come back here later."

The agents continued to follow the suspects to a local hardware store where they witnessed and later documented their purchase: a red cylinder of hydrogen chloride gas. Things were moving ahead. When the suspects were safely back inside Overlook Avenue, the agents went back to the field where the trash bags had been dumped. Grubbing through the contents they discovered empty chemical solvent bottles and ammonia containers as well as other chemical refuse consonant with the cooking of speed.

As evening approached, surveillance became a little simpler. Simpkins called in the locals, telling them he expected to move that night. Lieutenant John Moran represented the Peabody force. In the gathering dark, agents were able to move in closer to the house and monitor conversation. Urbi and Vicious were overheard arguing. Apparently Urbi was the head chemist but Vicious was experienced from earlier lab jobs and had some "suggestions."

"Should be cut only five times," Vicious argued.

"Cut it eight, and you and me'll have the difference to split between us," Urbi conned. They compromised, reluctantly.

This close to the kitchen, the agents were aware of a strong odor of ether that hung like a curtain around the house. Two of our men stalking the bushes beside the house were nearly caught when two of the men from inside came out. Our guys ducked. The suspects passed by, carrying galvanized pails from which they dumped dark sludge on the ground near the old chicken coop in the yard near the barn. The thick sludgy material was a common expendable by-product from home speed manufacturing. The volume of chemicals and the mass of waste product suggested a very sizable operation.

Simpkins busily coordinated the raid from the van. To the agents near the house, the ether odor seemed stronger than ever. Suddenly there was an explosion. Flames could be seen inside the house in the area of the kitchen where the lab was believed to be. Smoke poured out of the house from the exhaust fans.

Several voices were heard yelling inside.

"Stupid sonofabitch!" The agents waited, ready to pounce. They feared that if the fire spread or a chain of explosions started in the kitchen lab they'd lose all the evidence. Or an unsuspecting fire department could answer an alarm and blow everything away.

Simpkins and Boeri had a problem. Do they act now, with all the principals there inside and in confusion—but with the chance that the explosion and fire destroyed their evidence? Or do they take a chance, hoping the suspects bring the fire quickly under control, gamble on letting them get set up again so as to be sure to catch them actually manufacturing and in possession of the finished product? In those days, without a sample of the finished speed product for evidence it would be next to impossible to make their bust stick in court.

Fate stepped in. The gang that couldn't shoot straight managed to bring the conflagration under control. Maybe it was Urbi's training as a firefighter. The smoke thinned out. Simpkins and Boeri figured if the fire was contained that quickly, chances were that some of the speed survived. Also, the principals they most wanted to arrest were now inside. They decided it was time to act.

Simpkins already had the search warrant. A hasty conference was held near the van. Agents Skipper Crowe and Pat Doherty each took station at a rear corner of the building. Other DEA agents accompanied by state troopers were assigned positions outside the residence. Chemists Jack Fasanello and Anthony Fonseca were on hand to assist in the safe search and dismantling of the suspected methamphetamine clandestine lab. One explosion was enough.

At seven-thirty Bill Simpkins, Steven Boeri and Detective John Colella, accompanied by John Moran, approached the front door. They knocked. Immediately, the yappy racket of dogs barking started from somewhere in the house. Through a small window near the door they could see no one was coming to answer their knock.

The dogs continued to bark.

"Federal agents!" Simpkins shouted. They waited. Nothing.

"Kick it in," Simpkins ordered. Entering, they were immediately immersed in a strong chemical haze throughout the Victorian residence and an odor that would knock over a horse.

No one was in sight. They rushed down the hallway through the house toward the kitchen in the rear. In one room they spotted a Skilsaw and a large pile of partially cut rolls of aluminum foil. This was no small-scale operation.

Agent John Colella spotted suspect Ned Coletta fleeing just off the main hallway. "Freeze!" It was his pleasure to arrest Coletta and book him. Colella's fellow officers had had a lot of sport over the similarity of their names.

Simpkins, Boeri and Moran burst into the stinking, hazy kitchen, only to see their quarry taking flight. The wooden screen door slammed shut behind the fleeing back of Sid Vicious. Urbi crashed through the window to the back porch. As trained DEA men, Simpkins and Boeri had as their first concern the drug, the product, for evidence. More conventionally police-trained, Moran was out the door after the suspects in a flash.

"Halt!" he shouted. Urbi was crouched, running through the wintry gloom toward a corner of the backyard. "Halt!"

Moran let a warning round go, then fired another, catching Urbi in the right side and buttocks. He was down. Moran whirled, letting off another blast at Sid Vicious, who was scrambling over the wooden fence encircling the yard. There was no need to fire twice for Sid. Sid accepted the warning and cut his losses, dropping to the waiting arms of the officers in the yard.

The agents were in luck inside. The kitchen crew had been cooking and operating at full blast. No telling how many pounds of methamphetamine had been lost in the explosion and fire (at least ten pounds), but because they hadn't halted production for the sake of safety, the agents found not only the materials and precursors in various stages but the finished product cooking on the table—and tablets being processed.

A search warrant for the surrounding land and barn yielded several fifty-five-gallon drums of liquid chemicals. Pasquale Caputo and Carlo Ricci couldn't be found at the time of the bust but were subsequently apprehended.

Simpkins had the suspect prisoners brought into the kitchen so Urbi could receive emergency medical attention. All defendants were officially informed they were under arrest for violation of federal narcotics laws and each was advised of his rights.

It was prudent also for the prisoners to be present during the assessment and dismantling of the clandestine lab. That way if our men were about to touch anything that might be especially dangerous or apt to cause an explosion, the suspects, not wanting to get blown up too, would warn them. Needless to say, the no smoking rule was in effect. The evidence men were warned not to use flash bulbs—strobe lights only for photos. We shut off any electric motors in case of sparks, leaving only the exhaust fans going.

Once the foolish dogs stopped barking, the telephone started ringing. It seemed nonstop. Agent Crowe picked up the phone.

"Yeah? Sid here," he answered, and began taking "to go" orders for speed. Crowe invited several of the prospective buyers to come over now to pick up their purchases. In that way they also rounded up several users.

Using the bird dog for a controlled delivery had paid off handsomely.

Urbi was taken first to Salem hospital for treatment while

the others were transported to the Boston district office for photographing, prints and strip search. Pasquale Caputo was picked up at his house. Ricci turned himself in the next day.

After some unproductive phone calls to friends as he looked for bail, Sid Vicious only heard rumors that Urbi planned to sell him out, so he decided to start looking out for himself.

"Looks like you got me good," he said. "What do you want? I'm tired of people rolling over on me. I'll tell you what you want to know."

He outlined the organization. The clandestine operation had been organized from Montreal. This lab was intended to join the supply network that distributed speed through eastern branch members of the Hell's Angels motorcycle gang to points throughout Massachusetts, Pennsylvania, New York and Florida. Vicious was guaranteed financial security by the crime cartel in return for being their chemist. He explained that Urbi was, though a constant cooker for himself and others, in *this* deal on a one-time basis only to clear up some money owed.

Urbi denied this. "Don't turn me over to the IRS—that's all I ask."

We didn't. Not until we were through with him.

15 From Deutschland With Love

NUMBERED SWISS BANK ACCOUNTS, JAGUAR automobiles, speedboats and beautiful women—these are the details that fill the romanticized notion of what life is like among the jet-set elite of the drug culture. And it's true —for a few. Like Horst Dieter Wolfe. Those at the very top. While it lasts.

Unfortunately, many in our "me first" society equate richness with goodness. Some of our citizenry have grown up thinking that big bucks are an appropriate reward for naked greed regardless of the consequences. The thought process seems to go along these lines: "It's there, I want it; therefore, I should have it." Note that the process leaves out the notion of balance—that if you want something, you should earn it. Movers and shakers in the drug world fit the mold. They think the world owes them a living and they don't care how it's come by. Criminals who profit from drugs profit from the deterioration and death of human beings. Drug kingpins are scum. Rich scum, but scum nevertheless.

For racketeers especially, money is power. Even after a prison sentence, if a criminal has a money supply hidden away (real estate, legitimate business fronts, hidden accounts), he is back in business minutes after release. Or using his economic base, he may never have let go of the reins during his time in prison. The government learned that years ago, when it saw how jailed Mafiosi ran their operations from behind the security of prison walls, then returned to the streets to larger and richer businesses than they had going in. Much of that has changed.

The DEA, like the government, has learned a valuable lesson.

Grab them by the assets.

With the help of the Organized Crime Act (Racketeer Influenced and Corrupt Organizations Act, or RICO), the DEA is working to make it very expensive for those who get caught.

We're going after them where it hurts. Take away their dough, you take away their power and remove their power base.

Applying this lesson, the DEA is now totally cost effective. Through seizure of cash, property and other physical assets of the criminal scum, we're taking in more than we're spending.

Just as I seized valuable real estate, airplanes and other chattels from people like Botenkranz and Clarkey, the agency as a whole scooped in cash and property in fiscal 1988 amounting to the tune of nearly $400 million—an amount significantly higher than our annual budget. We've seized everything from log cabins and airfields in Maine to exotic antique autos and boutiques in California. The Philadelphia office DEA even seized seven million dollars stashed in sewer pipes. It is my job, but I have to admit a lot of satisfaction when we kick one of the bullies out of the sandbox. It's even more fun when we take away all his toys.

Aside from the moral value and the valuable, if temporary, blockage of illicit speed manufacturing, the assets seized during Horst Dieter's arrest will greatly enrich the nation's coffers. Because the stuff we grabbed was contraband, illegal or illegally gained, we get the value regardless of the length of Wolfe's sentence or whether or not he's deported. Some of the secondary reverberations of his arrest are already hitting the underworld, especially among the syndicate in Philadelphia.

This is the sensitive story of a man who headed a small, efficient organization allegedly involved in smuggling and distributing large amounts of cocaine from South America, including an estimated sixty tons smuggled into the US from Colombia alone. But more interesting to the DEA was his illicit importation of illegal chemicals from the Federal Republic of Germany, and elsewhere in Europe, for combination into deadly analog drugs in clandestine US laboratories. And his connections. Horst Dieter Wolfe's recent arrest ties into forty-three indictments in the Philadelphia area among organized crime families.

Wolfe was the stuff of drug fantasies. Until recently, he lived a lifestyle of the rich and famous. With his megaprofits periodically and systematically stashed safe in Swiss bank accounts, he used operational cash to acquire goods and services. Wolfe owned a luxury condo in Paris, several homes in international resorts like the West Indies, as well as homes and safe houses in several cities, including Frankfurt and Boston.

He owned many aircraft and luxury cars and enjoyed surrounding himself with beautiful young women. Very young women. His tastes were a bit kinky—or degenerate, depending on what generation you belong to.

"Cocaine. No brain—no pain." So went the oft-repeated motto of this pillar of society. Apparently enamored of his own penis, Wolfe favored photographs of himself in the buff, usually accompanied by a nubile coed from one of the great institutions of learning clustered around the Hub.

I objected mostly to the way he obtained the means to support his lifestyle. He smuggled heroin from Europe, cocaine from South America and supplied the East Coast syndicates with the chemicals to produce most of the speed for the entire country. He was smuggling P-2-P, which sells legally in Germany for twenty-three dollars per gallon. Smuggled into the US, it sells for twenty thousand dollars per gallon to the illicit clandestine manufacturers, many of whom are in Philadelphia. One gallon of P-2-P combined with other readily available legal chemicals makes eight pounds of speed, in powder form, which then sells for $120,000. A decent markup.

The manufacture of P-2-P is legal in West Germany. Importation to the US is illegal (except to a few legally designated chemical works), and its use is now strictly monitored. Until 1980, when P-2-P went on the list of controlled substances, we could only have gone after Wolfe if he was cooking the speed himself. The only known use for P-2-P is in the manufacture of amphetamines.

Philadelphia is the national center of illicit speed labs, and anyone cooking speed pays vigorish to the Philadelphia organized crime families—or they are dead. There are many subcontractors in the geometrically profitable amphetamine industry. Supplied by the old-line crime families, a new generation of dealers has emerged. Fully half of the nation's amphetamine traffic is now controlled by the major motorcycle gangs: Pagans, Outlaws, Hell's Angels and the Bandidos.

The Wolfe case took over two years to develop and was based on information originally received from the DEA in Frankfurt, Germany. Our office there reported receiving information that in 1984 Wolfe had smuggled to the US enough P-2-P to manufacture several billion dosage units of speed.

Wolfe's brother, a German national, was alleged to be his partner in crime on the continent. All this information on Wolfe came as incidental intelligence in an investigation of one of his underlings, a dealer he supplied in Rhode Island. US Customs subsequently developed a reliable confidential source of information, who implicated Wolfe. The FBI came in on the case somewhat peripherally, and our office was ably represented by my former super, Bobby Russo. About five-foot-eight, his dark hair beginning to gray, Bobby is a bulldog when he goes after a perp. He and I go way back; he was my first supervisor, and we have a relationship that includes keeping each other informed of progress of separate investigations. In his mid-forties, Bobby is a graduate of the Massachusetts College of Pharmacy and a registered pharmacist who entered the DEA through the old Bureau of Narcotics.

Though no hard, prosecutable proof against Wolfe was immediately forthcoming when Russo first heard of him, Horst was domiciled and supposedly running his smuggling operations from a base in our area. Bobby started chipping away at the case. The more he learned about Wolfe the less he liked him. By the time customs had developed a source of information, Bobby was off and running with the case.

Russo started gathering valuable intelligence. He learned that the Rhode Island Attorney General's office, in the course of a local narcotics investigation, recorded that one D. Inkster had called the same phone number in the Boston area over a hundred times. The number was traced to an answering service telephone pager leased to Wolfe. The Rhode Island authorities defined Wolfe as the probable organizer and financier of Inkster's narcotics operation, which included shiploads of South American marijuana and cocaine.

Investigators followed the string. Toll registers now on Wolfe's home phone in Cambridge, Massachusetts, revealed a series of calls to two other German nationals at a phone listed under a bogus aircraft company traced to a private home in Kingston, New Hampshire. One of the German nationals, Fred Geppert, was running socially with a Delta Airlines pilot. Any aircraft pilot connected to anyone suspected of drug activity is cause for at least a raised eyebrow. Russo figured he was on the right track.

Geppert was discovered to be an illegal alien who had been refused entry into this country twice: once when he tried to enter through Canada, driving the Delta pilot's VW. An ex-con, Geppert had done time in Dortmund, West Germany, for fraud. So Wolfe wasn't calling the boys in the choir. It looked like he had something new in the works.

Through an informant Russo learned that Geppert, a pilot himself, kept a specially adapted short take-off and landing wingtips aircraft, a Cessna 172F modified to burn gasoline, hidden at a clandestine airstrip in New Hampshire.

Another informant reported that the 1984 P-2-P deal had started when Wolfe contacted Geppert by phone while he was home with his parents in Germany. Wolfe asked Geppert to shop around for an airplane for him. He later wired five thousand dollars as a down payment on a Cessna. They subsequently met in Wiesbaden. Wolfe showed up with a male of Italian descent later identified as Vin Stefano of New York, alleged to be a member of one of the major New York Mafia families.

"We want the plane to ferry chemicals to the US . . . plastic softeners," Geppert was told.

He was given $100,000 cash to conclude the purchase. An unsuspecting commercial pilot was hired to bring the plane by way of Greenland and Newfoundland into Bangor, Maine. The pilot hit some temporary customs snags at Bangor. That was why he'd been hired of course, so that if caught, *he'd* go down, rather than someone in the organization. Also, he couldn't tell authorities much beyond who had hired him.

There were some wrinkled brows in the Wolfe organization before the innocent commercial pilot finally cleared customs and delivered the load to Massachusetts. There, the pilot was paid off and released. The "plastic softener" was taken away in a pickup truck, care of Wolfe. Geppert was given the airplane. Given.

Geppert also did occasional pilot work for Wolfe, ferrying him on drug runs from his Cape Cod island retreat to Pompano Beach, Florida. Shortly, Geppert was once again given $100,000 cash by Thomas Ledale, another associate of Wolfe's to buy a second airplane. Geppert met with people from Massachusetts, and others from overseas, looking for cocaine sales as well as airplanes, but never found the right one. High-rolling Ledale eventually gave Geppert a twenty-five-thousand-dollar commission just for trying and put the rest of the plane purchase cash into a mob-favored Oklahoma oil company.

This investigative material may sound a little ho-hum in the recitation, but these people are serious in the their intent to keep dealing. Deadly serious. Ledale maintained a sumptuous North Shore condo that had been exquisitely decorated by professionals to impress his associates, but he made no attempt to conceal the several handguns, shotguns, rifles and submachine gun he kept on hand. Ever ready. Drug agents who want to stay alive proceed on the assumption that the only reason these weapons exist is because the dealers intend to use them.

Wolfe also had numerous lethal weapons secreted at *all* his pads, including several of the infamous, bullet-spewing Israeli Uzi automatic submachine guns in his fashionable Beacon Street stash pad alone. Small wonder—he kept a tidy fortune in cash and cocaine there in a floor safe with a combination lock. Early on, Russo decided that when it was time to bring down Wolfe it would be done with extreme caution.

Utilizing the FBI, customs, foreign intelligence sources and his own informant network, Russo had gathered the above information on Wolfe by the time the key customs informant agreed to cooperate. Here was an opportunity to knock out a major supplier of marijuana, cocaine and speed, and at the same time do a big favor for the agents working the Philly labs.

Customs had the reluctant but realistic informant; DEA had the expert undercover agent in Bobby Russo. A perfect marriage to work an Organized Crime Drug Enforcement Task Force case.

The informant agreed to introduce Russo to Wolfe and to vouch for the agent as a legitimate buyer. On New Year's Day, 1987, Russo initiated his undercover phase of the case. He met with Wolfe to discuss the proposed sale of 450 liters of Phenylacetone, P-2-P, for a price of $400,000.

"To look the part, I had rented a Lincoln Towncar," Russo told me, beginning his narrative.

"We were supposed to meet Wolfe at, appropriately enough, a big foreign car import place out on Commonwealth Avenue. I guessed maybe the guy's accent isn't noticed so much there. We'd learned he did some steady drug business with some of the auto employees, especially a service manager of one of their western branches. But apparently the owner never realized what Wolfe was up to. Wolfe even made a bunch of overseas calls on their business phones without the owner's knowledge. He had bought several of his high-priced foreign cars there, so they tended to overlook some things."

Upon their arrival, the informant asked around with some of the salesmen, but no one had seen Wolfe. When he called his number, the pager beeped him from the bar across the street where he also spent a lot of time.

"As soon as he showed up, they asked me to wait in the show room while he and the informant went outside, out of my view. This was, I assume, for my man to assure him I was straight."

Wolfe appeared to be in his late forties, blue eyes, brown hair. A big guy; about six foot three, 200 pounds. He didn't look like a drug kingpin. He wore a Yankees baseball cap (reason enough to be suspect in Boston), a sleeveless vest over a turtleneck and Nike sneakers. He was ruggedly handsome even with vertical facial scars on each cheek, running from the eye to the corner of his mouth. Like duelling scars.

They were back in a few minutes. Apparently the informant had said the right things about Russo. Wolfe shook his hand.

Russo gave him the impatient bit.

"Can we talk?" he said.

Wolfe suggested they go out to the Towncar. Russo sat in the driver's seat, Wolfe behind him. Looking out the window, Russo realized he was parked practically in the shadow of the State Police headquarters. Handy.

"I think I have something you're interested in," Dieter began. "I was reluctant to meet as we didn't know each other."

"Same for me. But it's necessary for us to meet if we're going to do business. My friend here has done his job."

"Correct."

"What's the actual chemical name of P-2-P?"

"Phenylacetone. I have the chemical formula at my place. If you need it."

"Just want to make sure I'm getting the same stuff as the sample I received." DEA labs had tested the sample, delivered in a cologne bottle.

"Don't worry. What I deliver will be the same chemical, same quality as the sample."

"I understand you want $400,000. How much product does that involve?"

"I have nine fifty-liter drums: 450 liters, about 118 gallons. It's waiting at the company in Germany where it was manufactured. It will have to be relabeled before being shipped."

"I figured that. I know you can't bring P-2-P into the country legally."

"It's legal in Europe, but the company that manufactures it has to show that lot number such-and-such was used in batch so-and-so of pharmaceuticals. Strictly accounted for. Lots of documentation."

"I represent an organization in Philadelphia that distributes this stuff to lotsa laboratory operators. We do some cooking ourselves, too."

"Don't get me wrong, I like profit," Wolfe said, "but . . . why isn't Phenylacetone manufactured over here?"

Russo shrugged. "Government. The only use for P-2-P's in amphetamines or methamphetamine."

"Even in Europe it's not easy to come by," Dieter said. "The DEA has people overseas keep a close watch on it."

"Tell me about it! Would I be paying you $400,000 if I could get it myself?"

Wolfe went on to brag about what an excellent supplier he was because he was European himself and knew all the people there and the intricacies of the chemical business. He "happened to be willing to supply" Russo only because a former client had recently gone to jail.

"He wasn't too smart," Dieter said. "Tried to do business behind my back, cut me out from my contact. But the suppliers wouldn't deal with him."

"I hear you," Russo said. Wolfe looked the type who meant business.

They went over the details of the potential transaction. Wolfe showed him a two-part shipping invoice with the firm *BismarkChemie GMBH* listed as the sender. Wolfe stated this was a fictitious company so that if anything went wrong it couldn't be traced to him.

"Smart," Russo said, pulling out a color brochure for Lone Star Synthetics. Lone Star was a legitimate New England chemical company cooperating with the DEA. Russo wanted him impressed with his preparation, which would suggest a large organization behind him. "This is where to send the stuff. Here's their IRS number and my contact person at the company. He's on my payroll. They import a lot from overseas, so there's no reason for customs to inspect anything sent to them. Label the stuff under the name thioglacolic acid." He spelled out thioglacolic, named the customs broker he wanted used and gave Wolfe instructions to label the load *hold for pickup* at Logan. He had his reasons for that down the line, if the deal went that far.

"You come prepared," Wolfe granted. "This is a good plan."

"I think each drum should be individually crated for safety. Nine drums . . . Will a standard van carry nine drums?"

"Perfect, this size shipment," Wolfe said, pointing to a full-sized Ford van double-parked nearby on the heavily traveled Commonwealth Avenue. "They'll be shipped Lufthansa, out of Frankfurt." He signaled a shift of gears here by glancing at the informant before he spoke. "I still owe some money on some of the drums being stored. I'll need about ninety thousand dollars up front to get them released for shipment."

Russo was ready for him. "Out of the question. I give you ninety thou, you leave and never come back." Then he threw him a curve. "What about I go to Germany with you, inspect the merchandise?"

"Why not?"

"I'll check with my people—but I doubt the front money. Why not just sell me the part you don't owe on?"

"Look, I'm doing you a favor on this already. Usually my customers take possession of the stuff in Germany and worry about getting it in here themselves."

Russo knew he was lying, so he knew how far he could bargain.

They went over some of the same ground again; Wolfe eventually said he'd try a call to Germany but that he couldn't make the call until Monday, January 5, because the firm was closed until then. Wolfe wanted his customers to label the shipment something other than a chemical with acid in the name as it might cause attention at customs. Russo suggested butylamine.

"Okay, get me thirty of the company's shipping labels with their name on them." His request for thirty labels showed he expected to be in business for a while after this deal. "Also, I need to grease some palms in Germany as well as prepay freight forwarding and my own airfare. I'll *definitely* need between five and ten thousand up front, right away."

"My people will go for that," Russo said. "Though we figured those costs were included in the $400,000."

"No, extra. And once the shipment has cleared customs I expect immediate full payment."

"You don't want it wire-transferred?"

"Cash. To our friend here," he said, pointing to the informant.

"Once *we're* sure it's the right stuff."

So ended the first meeting. Wolfe went back into the imported car show room. Russo dropped off the informant and headed for the airport customs office, conferring en route with the surveillance agents assigned to cover him.

A week went by during which Wolfe allegedly made his calls to Germany. He had set things up by January 5.

Meeting covertly with the informant and customs agent Jim Scott the next morning, the drug agents learned that the previous night Wolfe had ordered the informant to travel with him to Germany. Wolfe also told him that he wanted the expense money from Russo before traveling, and for the informant to collect it.

Our CI feared there were too many possible screwups that could endanger his life if he accompanied Wolfe to Europe. A plausible excuse for him *not* to go to Germany was thought up for him to spring on Wolfe at the last minute. Following our instructions, around noon he called Wolfe at the Oceanside Club in Cambridge. "We'll bring the money and labels," he said. "Meet you at Lufthansa about four-thirty this afternoon. Everything's set."

DEA agents instituted surveillance in and around the Lufthansa ticket area near four o'clock. The informant parked outside the Lufthansa area and waited with Russo. Wolfe was late checking in. Wearing a full-length black leather coat, he looked like a Gestapo agent when he finally swept over to the car just minutes before boarding time. Wolfe was bullshit that the informant wasn't going but was mollified somewhat by the thirty Lone Star shipping labels. They were worth a king's ransom to him for future smuggling deals.

After listening to some more squawking about butylamide and making sure he had all the necessary papers, Russo handed him ten thousand dollars of official government funds. Wolfe fanned the bills with a thumb.

"As long as I'm going alone, why not give me the two thousand dollars you were going to give him?"

Sighing, Russo gave him another two grand. "Law says you got to declare everything over ten thousand going out of the country," he said, trying to lighten things up.

Wolfe didn't think he was so funny. He stuck it all in his zippered clutch bag. "If anything happens after the stuff lands, you still have to pay me half," he warned.

"I expect lower rates on future deals," Russo countered. Wolfe ignored him, turning to the informant.

"I have that pay phone number. Expect my call any time, night or day." He got out of the car. "Just remember to cash up once this load is past customs. No credit lag."

Our surveillance people watched him board the plane and waited until the plane took off. Wolfe did not declare the twelve thousand dollars with customs.

There was no word from Wolfe for a couple of days. With the suspect out of his reach, Russo was on pins and needles. He'd given Wolfe twelve grand of government funds, only to see Wolfe drop down a hole. It wouldn't be the first time a suspect absconded with official advance funds, but Bobby wasn't looking forward to it happening in *his* career.

Finally, late on Thursday, January 8, the informant reported getting a phone call at his home from Wolfe. We'd recorded the conversation, but as it was in German we would have to wait for an official translation. Meanwhile, the informant related the gist of the overseas call.

"Dieter called about nine. Said he was having 'trouble' with the export papers but that he had the stuff on a truck and would be delivering it to a freight forwarders, Schenkers, in Bremen on Friday, tomorrow, the 9th. Schenkers is supposed to put it on Lufthansa to transfer at Frankfurt for the flight to Boston."

"That's it?"

"That's all."

"Okay, then the stuff should be arriving here in Logan Saturday the 10th or Sunday the 11th. Keep in touch."

Nothing happened. Friday passed. Saturday. All day Sunday.

Customs agent Jim Scott was home with our informant when a call came the evening of Sunday from an obviously agitated Wolfe. Again the conversation was in German. Recorded. Below is the translation.

CI: "What's happening?"

Wolfe: "I almost fell into the shit. The, those . . . stupid fucking labels are no good—"

"What's wrong?"

Wolfe: "The chemical written on the label is *flammable*, for Godsakes. The fucking customs here confiscated the Phenyl—"

"Christ!"

"Yeah—Christ! I got it back, but . . . it took a lot of luck."

"You got it back?"

"Stop fucking repeating me. Yes, I got it, but . . . but things are very complicated here now. Totally ridiculous. Butylamine is a flammable substance so the customs are *very* interested in it. Never let a substance like that on an airplane. Pig luck I got it back. Things are not going easy over here."

"You need something, tell me. Russo and I will take care of it."

"This deal is total shit. I might have to come back to the States and then back here again. I almost went behind Swedish curtains with that stuff. Plus the weather. It's twenty-six below in this monkey store! Everything is frozen closed," Wolfe said. (That year saw the worst winter temperatures in Europe in over a hundred years.)

"Russo's been calling and calling," the informant complained. "He wants to know if the stuff is on the way yet. His people will flip out if that stuff isn't coming."

"Not for at least three more days . . . It might have to go by ship now. I have to get papers, declare it differently, somehow."

"You think you want to come back here without shipping it?"

"I don't know which pig to grease now. I have no connection," Wolfe snarled.

"I'll tell them the problem. But I wouldn't suggest coming back without shipping the product. These people think it's easy for you to get the stuff out of Germany."

"Tell that fucking Russo it was his shit flammable labels that *caused* the problem. He doesn't have to deal with the German police. You know what they can be like."

"They think it's on the way," he persisted. "You better get the shit rolling."

"I thought Russo was some kind of expert in the business. But he's a nonalphabet. *Flammable.* Can you get over here now?"

"What would that change?"

The conversation ended with Wolfe giving our man a number to call him at in Hamburg. The number traced to the Elysian Hotel.

Monday the 12th, the informant called Wolfe in Hamburg.

The smuggler was still complaining. No progress. Wednesday Wolfe called the CI in the evening. He had new labels made out but was still considering shipping by boat. On Thursday, using a phone in the customs office at Logan, the informant initiated a call to Wolfe with Russo monitoring. Russo took the phone after a while.

"What's the delay?"

"Problems. Right here where I am they just busted a guy three days ago with a ton of P-2-P. The DEA is working with the cops over here. The heat is on. They're taking X-rays and sampling all liquids being shipped. I'm working on a way around it, but I had to get new labels and a stamp. Butylamine is on the dangerous cargo list."

"The butylamine labels should've been okay. Lone Star gets it all the time."

"Once it goes into a German customs zone it's supposed to be sampled. I got to pay. I relabeled it Magnetite, for curing leather. Your guy at Lone Star is all fucked up. If it was coming out of England, no sweat—England's easy but Germany's a real cocksucker."

"Ship it to England, then," Russo said.

"Fucking river is frozen. No ships moving."

"Is the reason you can't fly it out because of the sampling?"

"Absolutely. I *told* you, they just busted a ton of the shit! They're checking all liquids . . . I got the newspaper clipping right in front of me."

"Holy shit."

"Plus, to ship such a large load . . . you need a special customs declaration once you get over a hundred kilograms. I'm trying to grease someone but it's only a week I'm over here."

It seemed like a good time for Russo to drop some fleas into his shorts. "I'm going to have to shut down our operation, you don't get that stuff here soon."

"No other supply?" Wolfe asked. Smart. He knew he had the power. If Russo had no other source, all his bitching would get him nowhere.

"I'm seeing you 'cause our regular's in jail," he said. "All this rush may cost you extra. I might have to go through another country. It's a bitch here. Palestinians. They caught that TWA hijacker and . . . unless you can get me the names of five companies to ship to? Then I could break up the load, make each one under a hundred kilos, ship each from a different city and not need the special declaration. Or they could have separate house-airway bills then consolidate it later under a master airway bill if it was all going to the same place . . ." Wolfe also told Russo there'd be no problem getting methylamine in the future and that they'd work it through England or Holland, get the stuff from a Dutch factory. He complained that "Germany was like a concentration camp" due to reaction to terrorist activity.

The next call from Wolfe came on Friday. He sounded ebullient. "I found my ace in the hole. Greased him. Finally had a decent meeting with someone receptive to a little lubrication."

"A customs agent?" Russo thought it would be nice to get the name.

"Works with customs," Wolfe said. "My guess is he owns the customs guy. By the way, the stuff won't *really* burn, will it?"

"The real stuff? The real stuff isn't flammable."

"He wanted to know. Looks like it'll cost ten grand. He said the customs guy sounds receptive but that he wants to take a peek, make sure there's nothing stupid in there. I said if it worked out there'd be a repetition every two months or so."

"What's he mean something stupid?"

"Who knows—explosives? Terrorists, you know? If everything goes right it should be out of here by end of next week.

It looks good now, but I don't eat the chicken that hasn't been hatched. But Wednesday looks like the target date," Wolfe said, hanging up. Fine with Russo. He wanted to get this case closed.

The informant called the night of Tuesday the 20th.

Wolfe had just called, saying he was "in the country where the cheese with the holes comes from."

"Switzerland," Russo said.

"Hanging around with the FBI has paid off for you," the CI said.

Russo went on as though he hadn't heard. "Must be visiting the vaults. How does that news affect the operation?"

"Don't know. Wants me to call him back at two this morning."

"Meet us at customs, we'll call from there."

Wolfe had left the number of the Crown Hotel in Schaffhausen, Switzerland, just outside Zurich. When the overseas connection was completed he said everything was set—he was leaving Zurich on Swissair for Boston the next day, the 21st.

"The stuff is stored in legitimate hands, a paint and chemical company. It should be leaving Deutschland Friday the 23rd, or absolutely by Monday the 26th."

On Thursday, January 29, 1987, nine plastic drums, individually crated in wood, containing a total of 564 kilograms of Phenylacetone arrived from Frankfurt. The shipment was seized by customs agents, who turned it over to DEA, Boston. Lab tests confirmed the substance in the drums was 96 percent pure Phenylacetone, P-2-P. It had cost Wolfe peanuts, really, but it was worth thirteen to fifteen million to the clandestine labs. We'd stopped billions of dosage units of speed from hitting the street.

Now came the sweet part. Once it had been legally established that the load was illicit, the DEA could put Horst Dieter Wolfe away.

His arrest was a combined effort. Well aware of Wolfe's predilection for firearms, particularly the murderous Israeli Uzi, the agents went well prepared. The arrest team consisted of three DEA, one FBI and four customs agents. Due again to the proliferation of illicit automatic weapons everywhere Wolfe went, they were also joined by two agents of the Bureau of Alcohol, Tobacco and Firearms. The local Cambridge police force covered the outside of the building near Harvard Square, sealing off all the exits and escape routes.

On February 3 the feds had marshaled forces at Logan International, then set out for Cambridge armed with more than just warrants. The tension was obvious as they drew near jumpoff time. Wolfe had a lot to lose if he was taken down. They were prepared for the worst. Wolfe didn't keep all those guns to exhibit. After a last check of assignments they entered the building.

Arms drawn, they gathered outside Wolfe's door. Russo took a deep breath, reviewing a mental list. Everything had been covered. Now it was up to Wolfe. Be ready to drop and roll, boys. Nodding, Russo gave the silent signal to the agent to kick in the door. He stepped back for the leg thrust. The wood splintered.

The good guys burst in, weapons poised. "Don't move!" Russo shouted, ordering him not to reach for a weapon.

It could have gone either way. There were enough weapons around for a Latin American revolution. A silencer-equipped Uzi was placed within easy reach. The silencer helps at conviction time. It would be difficult to claim in even the most liberal courts that a muzzled Israeli automatic, infamous for the number of rounds it throws per second, was kept for grouse hunting.

They were in luck. Not a shot was fired.

When they kicked in his door, Wolfe was, fortunately, in a typical pose—and unable to go for a gun. He was under the sheets with a Wellesley student.

Wolfe was arrested and charged with importation of a controlled substance and incarcerated pending posting of a $100,000 bond and $10,000 cash.

As mentioned earlier, Wolfe was a fancier of expensive foreign autos. By the time we pulled his plug he owned eight valuable cars, seven of which we've seized. I test drove one of them, a $55,000 Ferrari TestaRossa which cost another eleven grand to adapt to American EPA standards. I said expensive.

This fire-engine red hummer is specked for over 180 mph. That one car is a drop in the bucket compared to all the others, plus the real estate and other assets.

Informants have confirmed Wolfe was known to have departed Boston for Zurich on numerous occasions with large deposits for numbered accounts. Swiss authorities have been requested to freeze his accounts as illegal drug proceeds.

By the time Dieter Wolfe was led from US District Court in handcuffs to begin serving his sentence, Russo and Scott had seized over a million dollars' worth of vehicles, money, securities and property from him and then turned it around to help finance an ever-intensifying war on drugs.

16 Operation Network: The Spider's Web

I USE THE SPIDER WEB ANALOGY FOR THE FOL-
lowing globe-spanning investigation because it's the best
way to describe the tenuous overlay of connections between
established international Mafia drug syndicates and upstart
and would-be crime families on both sides of the Atlantic.
Operation Network is a recent happening, valuable as a case
study, a project to exhibit the pervasiveness of drug corruption, not just in the United States but around the world.

The web analogy also describes the intertwinings of people and product, which if followed far enough always seem
to lead back to the center. The way a web traps its prey is
also pretty good symbolism for what happens to people attracted to it. The spider feeds off his prey.

Today's drug problem is global. And local. The drug bar-
ons can get drugs from anywhere, to anybody, anywhere.
Half the illicit drugs in this country come from the Middle
East, South America or the Orient. Despite television and
mid-American misconceptions, the delivery points for all
those drugs aren't just Times Square, New York, or the Los
Angeles barrio. It's next door. Many of us would like to
believe the problem is limited to the Big Apple. It isn't; it's
in Moline, Wisconsin, and it's on the corner of your neighborhood street.

This showcase heroin investigation illustrates how the
drug travels from its natural state in the Afghan and P-

stani poppy fields, through the crude Lebanese and Cypriot refining labs, into the hands of the multinational smugglers and then along the importation and wholesale purchase process. The ongoing full-scale wars in some of those countries apparently don't disrupt the flow of the product. Back in this country the drug flows to a local major distributor, then all the way to the pound and ounce and gram dealers—and down to the end of the line, the user.

From source to importer to distributor.

The spider's web begins with the nabbing of a small-time Lebanese national mule carrying five pounds of heroin from his arrest in Boston, back to his sources: Pakistan, the island of Cyprus and war-torn Lebanon and Afghanistan. The smuggler's trail leads through London and Paris to Canada, where a Middle Eastern candyman in Ottawa imports his goodies from Lebanon and Brazil and sells it in faraway New York, Cleveland and Miami.

The circular trail eventually leads all the way to a Boston Irish-American distributor operating under the protection of the Sicilian and American Mafia. The Irishman buys his imports from local Lebanese-Americans, whose heroin comes from the original source family back in the Middle East.

DEA group supervisor Domenick Mingione got a bust call in mid-February from US Customs agent Joseph Leone at Boston's busy Logan International Airport.

"We got a live one here. Lebanese," Leone said. "He's wearing a girdle."

"You holding him for bein' a transvestite, or what?"

"A laugh a minute, you guys. No, there's white powder in the girdle. A lot of it. I don't think it's baking soda."

"Be right there." Mingione didn't need to remind Leone to detain the suspect.

Dom Mingione rounded up his colleagues. They met the customs man at the international section. The Massachusetts Transportation Authority interpreter was on sick leave, so an outside interpreter had been contracted and the suspect had been advised of his constitutional rights in his native language by the time our people got there.

Six foot three and dark-skinned, the suspect, Ghazi Wad Cairoz, had arrived on British Airways flight 277 from London. Proceeding through immigration without problem, he'd been detained in customs for a luggage and a body search. The customs officials noticed a girdle and apron tied around Cairoz's midsection. Inside the girdle was a white powdery substance, nearly ten pounds of it, which would eventually test out at 97 percent pure heroin. This mule was carrying a full load.

"What's in here?" Dom asked, gesturing to the contraband. "Cocaine . . . He says it's cocaine," the interpreter answered. Cairoz must have thought the sentence was lighter for coke than heroin. Either that or he was trying to present himself as a know-nothing who was just taken for a ride by a nasty drug smuggler.

The suspect said he had no friends in the US. But included among his personal effects was an address book with multiple US listings. The address book eventually turned out to be a gold mine of leads and information for us. Ghazi Wad Cairoz, a resident of Bechwar, Lebanon, was also in possession of a Rhode Island driver's license in his name.

At first, Cairoz agreed to cooperate; indeed, he seemed eager when asked to participate in a controlled delivery. Explaining his involvement, he stated he'd been contacted in Lebanon by Mouhammed Rouchi from Cyprus, who instructed him to enter at Boston, take a room at one of three designated hotels and await a phone call. He would receive a fifteen-thousand-dollar fee for his part.

"Why'd you do it?"

The interpreter talked to the suspect, listened, then said, "Says he owned two businesses in Jounieh, Lebanon, that were in financial turmoil due to the war. He was approached by an associate in the video game business who said he could make three grand plus expenses for running a little errand."

"Three? He just said fifteen thou," Mingione said.

"That was at first. Things . . . escalated," the interpreter said.

Cairoz then volunteered to "turn," be a double agent. He told our agents he was willing to wait as bait in the Airport Hilton for the drug payoff person to show up, and we could arrest him if we wanted.

"Lemme think it over," Mingione said. "You're also willing to do a controlled delivery?"

"Yes."

Legally, when a suspect agrees to cooperate we are bound to give a detailed explanation of what was expected of him, and the probability of risk and danger. That way we can't be accused of leading someone blindly into jeopardy. We must also restate the Miranda warning and give the suspect every opportunity to consider the situation so it doesn't look like coercion. In Cairoz's case that necessitated a rereading of his rights in front of him, even though he'd already said yes.

We did everything by the book. He and the interpreter conferred for a while. Then, suddenly, Cairoz's whole attitude changed. He changed his mind! He'd do no controlled delivery, he'd do no baiting at a hotel. He wouldn't cooperate in any way.

The suspect had spooked.

It took us a little while to figure that one out.

Cairoz was held for grand jury.

Though he'd changed his mind about cooperating, his address book was giving us plenty to work on, more threads to follow. Cairoz's book contained over twenty names that eventually were proven to belong to suspected drug dealers, known smugglers, and other convicted criminals. It also held papers relevant to the Arjay Company of Cape Cod, known to have exported arms to Lebanon and the Arab states.

Agents Joe Ritucci and Leone continued their inquiries with Interpol while others began running down the names on our own national computers and field-testing them with informants. The family names Hebbi and Mashoub seemed to come up the most often.

While Cairoz was being held in our custody, our DEA man in Nicosia, Eugene Habib, scanning the interoffice reports, had been alerted by the name El Kharim Hebbi, especially Hebbi's connection to the seizure of Cairoz and the heroin in Boston. Habib knew the Lebanese Mashoub/Hebbi families were up to their necks in every phase of heroin production and traffic. But as every lawman can attest, knowing it and catching one of them at it are two different things.

So fate stepped in right about here.

While Agent Habib was noting the coincidence of Cairoz having one of the Hebbi family names in his little black book, another coincidence was taking place on the island of Cyprus. The Cypriot police grabbed El Kharim Hebbi at the Lanarca Airport, returning from the US by way of London with seventy-five thousand dollars in his suitcase. Habib jumped on the case.

An investigation into Hebbi's trip from Lebanon to the US, and his connection to Cairoz revealed the following: the passenger list from the ship *Alisur Blanca,* sailing between Beirut and Cyprus, showed that two days before Cairoz's seizure, Hebbi, Cairoz and a certain Toni Radames all boarded the vessel together. Arriving on February 12, they were met at the teeming dockside by a US citizen with the unlikely sobriquet of Robert Krait Carnak-Ariadne. They all went to the Stavros Hotel together, Cairoz and Radames sharing a room. Hotel telephone logs revealed calls to the US from their room paid for by Radames.

During this time tickets from Lanarca via London to the United States were purchased for both Hebbi and Cairoz. At his arrest Hebbi's passport showed a US entry. Among his personal effects were found the name and phone number of Sammi Checkers and a ballpoint pen inscribed *Boston Park Plaza Hotel.*

The questioning started there.

"What's your connection to Sammi Checkers?" Habib asked the smuggler.

"A prostitute gave it to me," Hebbi said. "She said it was for to call a taxi if I ever got to Ottawa, Canada."

"Sure," Habib said, pressing on. "So what were you doing in Boston?"

Hebbi changed his story a dozen times. First he was visiting a cousin; then he wasn't in Boston at all. Next round he said his cousin gave him the money, but he couldn't remember her name or where she lived. Next story—he collected the money in the US for refugees in Lebanon after a Saudi Arabian wrote him a political fundraising letter in English. Then he said he begged for the money himself, raising it all in donations of five, ten and twenty dollars.

His final story for Habib was that his female cousin gave him forty-five thousand dollars for safekeeping just before he left the US. The other thirty thousand came while he was at a travel agency getting his ticket. At the travel agency he met three men, each of whom pressed another ten thou upon him to bring to relatives in Beirut.

"How come you returned via Miami?" Habib asked.

"I got lost getting to the airport."

Hebbi had been previously identified by CENTAC as a major source of heroin in the Lebanon/Cyprus area. He adamantly denied knowing Cairoz. Or Sammi Checkers. He was an innocent traveler. Forgetful, perhaps, but a victim. Sergeant Theodoros Hercules of the Cypriot police found records of tickets purchased for Cairoz and Hebbi, same time, same destination. Purely coincidence that he, the man with seventy-five thousand dollars, and Cairoz, the man caught with the heroin, happened to be traveling the same route at the same time.

Toni Radames was a member of the Radames crime family, generally considered the biggest family smuggling operation in the Middle East. Radames possessed falsified documents giving his identification as a member of the Cypriot police force.

He also had an Irish passport in the name of Tony Ryan.

"Just for a joke—I'd never use it."

Radames owned an Ohio driver's license and bank books

in his name in Paris, France, and Cleveland, Ohio. He was also carrying the name of a company in Houston, Texas. Radames deserved a frequent flyer discount from British Airways. He too was "coincidently" staying at the same hotel with the people who were moving heroin illicitly.

Krait Carnak-Ariadne worked for the Cape Cod arms shipping company, ARA International. ARA was also known as American Trade Promotions. Carnak-Ariadne was a fugitive from Canada. In the face of his denials, authorities found letters and other papers linking him to both Cairoz and Hebbi, as well as his personal and business checks made out to both of them.

Agent Habib sent us what he'd gathered to coordinate with our investigation of Cairoz. Held on a million dollars bail, Cairoz was eventually found guilty and sentenced to eight years.

What we found the most interesting among Habib's finds was the Canadian connection. One of our men was already developing a case on Sammi Checkers, the name given as a Canadian taxi driver. Definitely not a cabbie, Checkers was rapidly being considered the major distributor of heroin and cocaine in Ottawa. His organization has established smuggling routes from Lebanon for heroin and Brazil for cocaine, both through New York and Boston into Canada. And sometimes back again. Cairoz had led us to Hebbi; now Hebbi was heading us toward Sammi Checkers.

Special Agent Robert Allen had set up an undercover case negotiating to buy large amounts of heroin from Checkers. Two names came to light in the initial investigation: Samir Sikally, a Checkers underling connected to the Lebanese heroin source, and George Mashoub, a Mideast Airlines employee related to Sikally and various Mashoub/Hebbi family members, all tied back to Boston. Mashoub has been grabbed with several pounds of H in a false-bottom suitcase at Ottawa Airport. Sikally and Mashoub had relatives all over the greater Boston area. In addition to comprising a drug pipeline, they worked regular jobs or ran businesses as rug merchants, bakers, caterers and restaurant owners.

Agent Allen had had great difficulty, despite the in from a CI, getting close to Checkers. Checkers always sent Samir Sikally to negotiate for him. Sikally acted as though he was more interested in buying cocaine for himself than in selling heroin. Allen offered to supply coke in exchange for H. That's as far as the first two negotiation meets got. To deepen his cover, Allen supplied Checkers with a Miami phone contact to set up a subsequent meeting. Sensing Checkers's reticence to do business before he'd been thoroughly checked out, Allen had preset arrangements with Miami DEA agent Bill Yout. It must have worked. Allen was next given a phone number which turned out to be Checkers's candy store on O'Connor Street in Ottawa.

When Allen contacted Checkers at his store, Checkers was complaining about the drug business.

"It's always a worry . . . I worry about phone taps. I once drove all the way to Montreal just to make a phone call."

"I know what you mean," Allen commiserated. "They're always listening in."

"My cousin in Boston was only discussing buying a car and the cops accused him of setting up a drug deal. I'd do even more business in Boston, but the problems with the Lebanese community . . . Not all want to pay the Cosa Nostra, and then some others are cooperating with the cops against their own kind. Can you believe it?"

"No," Allen said.

"We can do this deal in Florida if you'd rather."

"Up here's good. Let's just get to it."

"Call back tomorrow."

When Allen called again, Checkers agreed to meet him day after next in the Hilton at Montreal Airport. Arriving there, Allen was instructed to call another phone number which traced to a Checkers relative on La Jeunesse. He was near the end of his patience, but Allen hung in there. They finally set a meet for a drink in the airport promenade.

Checkers arrived with a hunchbacked bodyguard. Allen, hard-pressed to talk to Checkers without the bodyguard, had to refuse to do business before Checkers had the grim henchman sit at a separate table. In the course of the negotiations Checkers assured Allen he'd get him all the H he wanted. "I'm already doing some big volume in the Boston area," Checkers bragged. "Connected under the umbrella, so to speak. You know?"

Allen nodded.

"All the H you want from Lebanon—available in three colors, any quality level that's wanted."

Allen threw a curve, saying he was interested in becoming a partner more than a buyer, that if Checkers could supply the stuff, he'd even take delivery in Europe and be responsible for it from there.

"I could deliver it in Amsterdam," Checkers mused. "But how you gonna get all that cash to Europe?"

"Not sure."

"Why me? You been doing good, you said, in coke—why H now, having trouble with the Cubans?"

"Something like that."

"The first ones would have to be cash. After that we could use regular banking channels. We control some dummy corporations that come in handy for that. I know a way. Also how to transfer funds down to the Grand Caymans."

Toward the end of their meeting, Checkers alluded to his cousin, Ghassan Mashoub—out of Boston. Allegedly, Mashoub was operational head of the Mashoub/Hebbi families' smuggling network Checkers used so successfully. Allen was elated to be gathering new intelligence on operations back in Beantown. The meeting broke up with Checkers setting Allen up with a deal with Samir Sikally to take place in Florida. Allen apologized to the hunchback of Montreal on his way out.

Allen set up a buy with agent Bill Yout and Checkers's man, Samir Sikally, at the Shooters Restaurant in Fort Lauderdale, Florida. Checkers was to receive a commission on any deal that went down.

"Why you guys dressed so . . . like that?" Sikally asked, gesturing at Yout and Allen.

"Huh?"

"If I met you in Boston wearing sport coats, I wouldn't talk to you. Have to be either wearing a wire or carrying."

"You want to search us?" Bill Yout offered, unbuttoning his jacket.

Sikally relented. "Sorry, it's just . . . some of the Lebanese around Boston are cooperatin' with the cops . . . I get nervous."

The agents were able to allay Sikally's fears about them being undercover agents. He finally relaxed, relating his success story—how he'd left Lebanon, then been in the Miami area for several years before going to Ottawa and getting connected with Checkers.

"That's been good for you?" Allen enquired, squinting in the glare of the Florida sunlight through the restaurant windows.

"I already brought in enough H to this country to fill this restaurant," Sikally bragged.

"Talents like that are valuable. Never been caught?"

Sikally shrugged cryptically. "Sammi Checkers loves me. Samir, I'm the man for the job. I got the right connections in Lebanon. I speak the language. Practically everyone in Zahle knows my face. Plus, my rep. Sammi knows I'm honest and dependable. I can even get H on consignment—no dough up front. And with my Canadian citizenship I can travel anywhere in the States, no restrictions. You want this stuff delivered? I do it."

"What's Zahle?" Yout asked, interrupting the sales pitch.

"Where, you mean. In Lebanon. That's where it's at. *The* center for all H traffic in the Middle East because that's where the labs are. They take the raw stuff from Pakistan and Afghanistan, tough now with them and the Russians but . . . hey, Zahle's the best. Would the Sicilians use them for their morphine base if they weren't the best?"

"Guess not."

"I'll get you quality. Pure. I'll get you a sample of the brown will be the purest you ever saw in your life!"

"That good, huh?"

"Lissen—if I can trust you—I'll put you onto such stuff you never dreamed of—97 percent pure. Hey, Sammi Checkers himself gave me a sample of brown for you guys, but after I tested it I told him it wasn't the best. This business . . . Everyone's out to cheat you. Nabyl."

"Huh?"

"Nabyl. My own brother in New York, even. Tucked it to me. I gotta be able to trust you or we don't do business."

"If the product's right we'll want fifteen kilos a month."

"A month?"

"We got three steady five-kilo monthly customers. Has to be quality, though," Yout said.

"Where can you take delivery—New York, Cleveland, Chicago?"

"Boston."

"Boston's pretty tight. You clear with Mr. B? He doesn't allow much free-lancing." This was an opening, information the agents were hoping for. Confirmation of the involvement of Mr. B (an alias for Larry Baione, aka Ilario Zannino) in the Boston operation intimated substantial local ties to the Mafia. Nailing Mafiosi is every agent's dream.

"We're aware of Mr. B," Allen said.

This buy ended when Sikally said he had to go to Cleveland to obtain his sample. Angry but futile telephone calls were exchanged, first with Sammi Checkers. Agents complained about the delays.

Just before Sikally left the next day for Cleveland, he inadvertently supplied us with important information. Bragging about the international operation, he let loose that they even had Lebanese interpreters registered and on standby so that if authorities were overworked they sometimes called in syndicated interpreters to help interrogate arrested syndicate suspects! It also worked as a method of learning about nonsyndicate operations and supply routes. No wonder Cairoz changed his mind about cooperating in Boston after talking with the stand-in interpreter. Allen was on temporary hold with Checkers but excited about the new organized crime intelligence and other data regarding Boston heroin distribution.

With all his efforts, and despite the varied directions of international travel, much of the focus of this complicated case seemed to be drawing Bobby Allen back toward Boston. But first he had to go to New York.

Continuing his investigation, Allen met with Special Agent Patricia Meahl and her supervisor John Costanzo regarding the trafficking of heroin amongst the Lebanese communities of New York and Boston. Agent Meahl brought a CI to the meeting.

"I was at the track and I saw Zemo betting heavy," the informant began. "Knowing he'd been broke I figured he had to have set up a buy for Jack Fayad before Fayad went to jail. I know a Zemo nephew brings in a lot of H from Lebanon.

"He goes there a lot and sells drugs out of his candy store, the Snickers on Ralph Avenue in Brooklyn. They're friends with the Sikally brothers who are right now having a big fight over a heroin payment Nabyl supposedly screwed Samir out of. Meanwhile they're still doing some deals together. Samir is working for Sammi Checkers, trading H for coke on a three to one basis." So the informant confirmed much of what Allen had learned himself. "These Sikally brothers got a great supply because their uncle Joe runs a conversion lab in Zahle, Lebanon. I met him here on a visit; he stayed at the Abington, nice old dude. Anyway, he gets the base from Afghanistan, he says, and Turkey, of course, and converts it to H in his lab. I guess he's a little old-fashioned because the only way he believes in smuggling is like Checkers, in a false-bottom suitcase. He told me he was 'amazed' when another nephew, Hebbi I think, of the Boston branch of the family came over to Zahle and took back eight hundred grams sewn into the side of a pair of leather boots . . . Revelation. Like it wasn't official if it didn't go in a false-bottom suitcase. It's like the old guy started one way, and that was it."

"Which Boston Hebbi?" Allen asked, confused by the many relations.

"Bouhanna Hebbi. He's dumping his drug profits in real estate around Lawrence. Tied in with Mashoub too," the informant said.

Mashoub/Hebbi seemed to be the general drawstring, the thing that pulled everyone together. Was it the same Mashoub, George, of Middle East Airlines? Or Ghassan, of oriental rugs and a partner in Sabra Catering? Allen soon learned it was Ghassan Mashoub, the Lebanese capo. Ghassan was tied to Sammi Checkers from his Zahle connection, though he wasn't above importing from Syria and Jordan as well as Lebanon. Whenever war conditions in one country became too tough, he switched.

Allen soon saw that the best place to enter the spider's web was in Boston, so he came full circle, joining up with fellow agents monitoring the local scene. Once he had corroborated the activities of the Checkers organization with the new data about the Mashoub/Hebbi families and with the infamous Mafioso Mr. B, he started feeding into a joint investigation being run in Boston by Agents Steve Murphy and Al Reilly. The local investigation would turn out to have international implications.

The local effort was cooperative. The Boston police had been working this a long time and now had a hot line on what looked like a major distributor. But they'd gone about as far as they could go. Their need for us coincided with our narrowing the international scope of the network down to our own backyard, where we'd started.

In addition to the hard work of Mingione and Allen, the BPD investigation had started with two federal intercepts of business phones in the South End section of Boston. Yet to be discovered by yuppies, the South End was still being enjoyed by the marginal and disenfranchised segments of society. In the neighborhood that we needed to conduct an investigation, it was almost impossible to perform standard surveillance. The area was so closely controlled by organized crime and its spotters and other hirelings that normal surveillance would be uncovered in minutes. Fortunately, just as our interest increased, the Boston department reached out to us. There was a need for special vehicles, equipment and observation posts. But even we had to request extra budget. Much of the stuff was just not in the DEA inventory or available from other agencies at this time.

It was immediately obvious we couldn't John Wayne our way around the South End. We'd have to practice unusual stealth. To assure control of the area around the bars they operate from, the suspected criminals had secured ownership of many surrounding buildings, stores and apartment houses.

A certain amount of neighborhood loyalty, stemming from rent subsidies, small handouts and a natural Robin Hood perception among the ignorant suspicious public, tends to hamper investigations in ethnic urban settings. In addition to these friendly neighbors and bar patrons, the crime organization employs a handful of people as spotters solely for the purpose of identifying undercover law enforcement vehicles. This neighborhood for years had two full-time gambling parlors adjacent to the target store. Additionally, one of the adjacent stores was the subject of a well-publicized state police intercept some months before, so the local inhabitants were very cognizant of police surveillance methods.

Numerous discreet attempts by law enforcement people to rent strategically located apartments for surveillance use had been negated, or fell through for various mysterious reasons.

Besides, any new tenants in the area would be subject to intense scrutiny and their lack of background immediately known to the targets. So we had to depend on vehicles, cameras and wire intercepts.

The major targets were distributor Robert O'Brien ("the most significant organized crime heroin trafficker in the Boston area"), Mr. B, Mafia supervisor and crime chief answerable only to Gennaro Angiulo, and the Mashoub/

Hebbi smuggling organization, which tied into the Checkers setup and back to the laboratories and source in Lebanon. And anybody else that fell into the net.

The initial Boston PD investigation had been shepherded by Detectives Robert Ryan, Frank Dewan and Charlie Fleming. Over a year earlier they'd installed a number of pen registers on phones belonging to the O'Brien organization, but the telephone repair people were destroying the lines almost weekly. Detective Fleming did yeoman service, climbing telephone poles in the dead of winter reinstalling interception gear.

Ryan's Organized Crime Detail unit was eager to continue with and cooperate in the investigation it had started. Among other investigative duties, they helped us monitor the cameras viewing the target phones because of their familiarity with the principals. Frank Dewan also helped us with the installation of room bugs as well as with his network of informants.

The target locations for the phone intercepts were the Braintree Tavern and O'Brien's Patio in the squalid South End neighborhood. The next step was to get video cameras in place which could take pictures of the locations and relay them to an observation post. Finding suitable locations and getting cameras in place is difficult work anywhere. But in hostile territory the difficulty multiplies.

One camera, transmitting its image by microwave, was installed in the bell tower of Holy Cross Cathedral, the major edifice of the Roman Catholic archdiocese of Boston. This camera, though utilizing an extremely high-powered lens, gave only a partial view of the locations. In order to meet federal legal standards for the intercept, another camera sending regular radio transmission signals was ecumenically installed in the local Greek Orthodox church—which gave a wide view of the targets. The images were beamed back to a suite rented in the 57 Hotel.

Neither church knew specifically what we were up to, only that they were eager, as good citizens, to help the forces of law and order. The 57 Hotel was chosen both for its anonymity and good reception.

Also needed was a good mix of vehicles and truck rentals that would blend in with the generally commercial nature of the area. A variety of vehicles would be vital so that the spotters wouldn't clue in on an extended surveillance. The target location was a known meeting area for organized crime figures.

We required several vehicles because we would need one posted close enough to identify new subjects by photographing. Aside from simple drive-bys in front of the places, we had also wanted ready mobility to try to check out the vehicles of any subjects new to us. We also wanted to observe any impromptu meeting taking place out of camera range.

In good weather the subjects tended to converse on the sidewalk. If we had a truck somewhere near, we could monitor those conversations. We requested a periscope as it would greatly enhance the quality of photos. Shots from inside darkened trucks don't always give a good picture.

Agent Albert Reilly wrote up a convincing operational budget request and we got most of what we needed. Our most helpful acquisition was a discarded Boston Edison step-van, which we positioned about a block and a half away. An Edison van was easily accepted in this neighborhood. Even parked in mid-street by a manhole for a week or two it would arouse no suspicion because the legit ones do it all the time. A mobile command post was set up in the van to key off other surveillance vehicles in the area.

O'Brien's Patio sat near the corners of Shawmut Avenue and Union Park Street. Kitty-corner from it, next to the Lebanese-American Social Club, was the Braintree Tavern, whose liquor license was held in the name of Doris Baione, niece of the suspected Mafia boss Mr. B. The Baiones' owned several other bars and apartment houses in the area as well.

When the intercepts became operative and the subsidiary equipment and personnel swung into full action, three things became immediately evident: As suspected, Robert

O'Brien ran a major drug distribution ring, gaming operation and loansharking setup; his prime sources for heroin included the Mashoub/Hebbi organization listed above, and the Sammi Checkers smuggling organization we had also been tracking; as big as O'Brien was, he reported to, and paid territorial tribute to, Mr B, aka Larry Baione, aka Ilario Zannino, local Mafia chief and sotto capo to Gennaro (Jerry) Angiulo.

Many of the subjects were intertwined socially and in business, and their connections with one another tended to overlap. Peeper Whiteside, for example, delivered drugs to O'Brien for the Mashoub organization but also patronized O'Brien's establishment to drink in and to contact prostitutes. Further, he did his sports betting *with* O'Brien but also subsidized some of his gambling by running messages to O'Brien's layoff men *for* him. And sometimes he bought drugs from O'Brien and acted as a conduit to certain dealers in the black community.

Bobby O'Brien constantly evinced a fear of getting caught. He worked hard at insulating himself by using mules like Peeper at one level, and couriers such as his three brothers Jim, Dick and Jackie the Junkie at the next level. But like many criminals who seem to have minds that are adept at setting up nefarious organizations with safeguards built-in to minimize the risk of arrest, they tended to disregard those safeguards when faced with a chance of losing some profit.

The investigation was yielding a ton of inside information until the Saturday we intercepted a call from a customer and neighbor, an old-timer who called O'Brien at the Patio.

"Bobby, your bar was just on TV."

"Whattaya talkin?" O'Brien said excitedly. Then he yelled for someone to turn on the television.

"Channel 83—on the cable, someone's got a camera."

"Get the picture, asshole—channel 83!" O'Brien screamed at his customer. The old timer's voice came over the line.

"Oops—now it's got a regular program on there."

"Shit, we must be bugged—get off the phone!"

Imagine the uproar in our camp! There was panic on both sides. The crooks were trying to figure why their neighborhood would be showing up on the airwaves. We were confused and angry, frustrated that so close to grabbing some seriously bad guys we could be thwarted by some quirk of nature. Nobody really knew what was happening. Yet.

It was later determined that the old-timer must have had a floppy tuner on his set and just happened to catch our radio transmission from the church steeple on a channel not normally picked up with commercial receivers.

Meanwhile we held our breath. For several days they avoided the telephones entirely. As far as we could tell, the O'Brien camp was totally paranoid. Other denizens of the Patio had reported seeing pictures of the bar on television, but no one could explain it. O'Brien's suspicions fed into his already abnormal fear of getting caught. His business establishment was not a happy place for a time.

With us also, tension reigned. We could see all that work and expenditure going out the window. Until, finally, O'Brien started answering his phone again. He was still skittish at first. He attempted, when use resumed, to let no one speak too specifically, but sometimes it was a losing battle because he was the one who would breach security.

Either he got tired explaining, forgot, or got greedy. During the first calls after the TV scare, it was as if O'Brien knew somebody had tapped his phones, and his speeches seemed calculated to make us think he was misunderstood regarding drugs. For example, if his brother Jackie called requesting some drugs in rudimentary code, O'Brien would react angrily.

"I'd never do that! You know I never touch drugs—you can get pinched for that. I'd never become a junk dealer!" He appeared to say all these things just in case of an intercept. But then, in that puzzling about-face observed in many criminal mentalities, he ended up by giving Jackie explicit instructions to call "Sam" to get the drugs he needed. It was as if his precautions only went so far, as if the person who was listening, once he had heard his righteousness speech, would be satisfied and stop monitoring.

Hanging up after stating his innocence, O'Brien then called another junkie who guarded a distribution apartment around the corner on Washington Street.

"My brother will be coming by. Give him what he wants."

As the investigation and intercepts continued we gathered evidence tying all the parties together for eventual conspiracy charges, if nothing else. We also got evidence to shut down the gaming and prostitution shops. O'Brien was also suspected of visiting violence upon competitors and compatriots alike. Calls of the type of the following from Cape Cod from someone named Charlie, last name unknown, substantiated O'Brien's ongoing criminal activities.

"I called you at the health club," the Cape Cod caller said.

"Ma kicked me out early today." Separated from his wife and living with his mother, O'Brien frequented a Waltham health club daily. "What's all the noise—you in a joint?"

"I'm calling from a bar in Hyannis. Thought you'd want to know I ran into someone down here that's going around saying you're the biggest coke dealer in the city."

"Jesus! Stop talking like that!"

"Fuck ya then, ya don't wanna hear—"

"Sorry—just so nervous lately. We were on TV." O'Brien explained to the caller the uproar caused by the mysterious signal on channel 83. The station had been instructed to answer all inquiries with a plausible but confusing story involving amateur productions and satellite images bouncing off the ionosphere. O'Brien parroted this to Charlie as if he knew what he was talking about. Charlie listened to the explanation then said his friend on the Cape also told him that O'Brien was putting together a ten-pound coke deal. O'Brien was enraged.

"Asshole, spillin' his guts—I'll take care of him," O'Brien promised. "Take care of" did not mean pay his social security.

Soon after the flap over the TV signals, it was time to pull the van. It had been too long in one location. The cooperating investigators were hoping for some conclusive evidence on the smuggling organization before moving the van.

Finally, a series of calls centered around the Mashoub/ Hebbi and Checkers organizations bringing in kilo quantities of heroin via Logan airport. In his excitement, O'Brien threw all caution to the wind. He assured callers his phones were secure. A back-and-forth series of orders and confirmation calls between O'Brien and the smugglers rang in the names of various Mashoub nephews and cousins. This helped alleviate our confusion and finally delineated which businesses they worked in or owned.

It was time to shut the operation down.

Operation Network turned out to be an excellent example of how the global and the local intertwine, and why the cooperation of law enforcement agencies from every level is essential in the drug war. The operation ended with nineteen separate arrests in Boston, Miami, Fort Lauderdale and London, England. Not counting the previous arrests in Boston and Cyprus. Robert O'Brien received a ten-year sentence for operating a continuing criminal enterprise. Evidence from this case also helped bring down the underworld's Mafia kingpins of the New England Patriarca family, Gennaro Angiulo and Ilario Zannino.

Most importantly, the combined effort stopped a good deal of 97-percent pure from destroying more lives. After all, the flies who get caught in the web are usually those with nothing to lose but their lives.

Epilogue

Although it was getting late that November night while the two men sat in a vehicle on the corner of 81st Street and 18th Avenue in Brooklyn, their work as minor organized crime figures was just beginning.

Suddenly, a blue van pulled alongside and witnesses heard multiple gun shots. Constabile "Gus" Farace was killed and his companion critically injured in what could only be described as a "mob hit."

Farace had been the subject of a massive manhunt for the brutal, unprovoked murder of DEA special agent Everett A. Hatcher nine months earlier. The murder had occurred on a lonely stretch of pavement in Staten Island, New York. Each agent from the DEA, FBI, US Marshal's Service and New York Police Department assigned to the task force pursuing the investigation of Farace would have preferred that Farace had been apprehended and brought to the criminal justice system. He would have been the first individual tried in Federal District Court under the new statute calling for the death penalty in the killing of law enforcement officers conducting drug investigations.

Instead, the concurrent program of orchestrated pressure on New York's organized crime "families" apparently had made Farace the subject of a parallel underground search that equalled in intensity the one being conducted by the law officers.

The contrast between special agent Hatcher and Gus Farace was startling. Everett Hatcher was a family man and churchgoer, active in community affairs, who left behind a loving wife and two children. He had been a Vietnam veteran and a Lieutenant Colonel in the Army Reserves. Agent Hatcher dedicated seventeen years to the DEA, was well-liked and respected by his colleagues and one of the agency's best recruiters.

Farace was a hoodlum with a lengthy prison record who was prone to violence. He abused steroids and cocaine and was a menace to society in general. Farace murdered special agent Hatcher because he felt like it!

We, as citizens, must do a better job fighting the drug problem, so that the law enforcement officers who have died helping us, have not died in vain.

Often the public appears to be overwhelmed by the scope of the problem. Every day we are confronted with the "crisis" of drugs and crime. We are barraged with news stories about violence and homicide, and drug-related youth killings. We hear about "source countries," "transit countries" and "consumer countries," and the corrupting influence of drugs on all of them. And what about the health consequences and costs, including an ever-increasing incidence of AIDS among drug abusers?

My advice is to take a step back and evaluate the situation. For now, let's not concern ourselves with the global problems as painted by the news media. Instead, we should concentrate on matters that we can control. Leave the general law enforcement strategies to the new "Drug Czar" William Bennett and the senior executives of the various enforcement agencies.

The nourishing of the American system requires a sense of responsibility, not only on the part of individual citizens, but also on the part of America's leadership. I am not just speaking of political leaders, but the leaders of all phases of society as well.

To the extent that they do not exercise their power and influence in the direction of the common good, they are undermining the very system that has given them their power and influence. In the war on drugs, I will ask no more of you than I do myself. So let's start educating our young people with the following message:

If you are not on drugs—just say no.
If you are—seek help and get the hell off.
Associate with others who don't.
Do not marry a drug or alcohol abuser.
Make sure that your spouse-to-be is clean for at least two years before marriage.
Form attachments—but not with chemically dependent people.
Love one another.

Glossary of Drugs

Controlled Substances—
Uses & Effects

DRUGS/ CSA SCHEDULES		TRADE OR OTHER NAMES	MEDICAL USES	DEPENDENCE	
				Physical	Psychological
NARCOTICS					
Opium	II III V	Dover's Powder, Paregoric Parepectolin	Analgesic, antidiarrheal	High	High
Morphine	II III	Morphine, MS-Contin, Roxanol, Roxanol-SR	Analgesic, antitussive	High	High
Codeine	II III V	Tylenol w/Codeine, Empirin w/Codeine Robitussan A-C, Fiorinal w/Codeine	Analgesic, antitussive	Moderate	Moderate
Heroin	I	Diacetylmorphine, Horse, Smack	None	High	High
Hydromorphone	II	Dilaudid	Analgesic	High	High
Meperidine (Pethidine)	II	Demerol, Mepergan	Analgesic	High	High
Methadone	II	Dolophine, Methadone, Methadose	Analgesic	High	High
Other Narcotics	I II III IV V	Numorphan, Percodan, Percocet, Tylox, Tussionex, Fentanyl, Darvon, Lomotil, Talwin[2]	Analgesic, antidiarrheal, antitussive	High-Low	High-Low

DRUGS/ CSA SCHEDULES	TOLERANCE	DURATION (Hours)	USUAL METHODS OF ADMIN.	POSSIBLE EFFECTS	EFFECTS OF OVERDOSE	WITHDRAWAL SYNDROME
NARCOTICS						
Opium	Yes	3-6	Oral, smoked	Euphoria, drowsiness, respiratory depression, constricted pupils, nausea	Slow and shallow breathing, clammy skin, convulsions, coma, possible death	Watery eyes, runny nose, yawning, loss of appetite, irritability, tremors, panic, cramps, nausea, chills and sweating
Morphine	Yes	3-6	Oral, smoked, injected			
Codeine	Yes	3-6	Oral, injected			
Heroin	Yes	3-6	Injected, sniffed, smoked			
Hydromorphone	Yes	3-6	Oral, injected			
Meperidine (Pethidine)	Yes	3-6	Oral, injected			
Methadone	Yes	12-24	Oral, injected			
Other Narcotics	Yes	Variable	Oral, injected			

1 Designated a narcotic under the CSA. 2 Not designated a narcotic under the CSA.

DEPRESSANTS

DRUGS/ CSA SCHEDULES		TRADE OR OTHER NAMES	MEDICAL USES	DEPENDENCE	
				Physical	Psychological
Chloral Hydrate	IV	Noctec	Hypnotic	Moderate	Moderate
Barbiturates	II III IV	Amytal, Butisol, Fiorinal, Lotusate, Nembutal, Seconal, Tuinal, Phenobarbital	Anesthetic, anticonvulsant, sedative, hypnotic, veterinary euthanasia agent	High-Mod.	High-Mod.
Benzodiazepines	IV	Ativan, Dalmane, Diazepam, Librium, Xanax, Serax, Valium, Tranxexe, Verstran, Versed, Halcion, Paxipam, Restoril	Antianxiety, anticonvulsant, sedative, hypnotic	Low	Low
Methaqualone	I	Quaalude	Sedative, hypnotic	High	High
Glutethimide	III	Doriden	Sedative, hypnotic	High	Moderate
Other Depressants	III IV	Equanil, Miltown, Noludar, Placidyl, Valmid	Antianxiety, sedative, hypnotic	Moderate	Moderate

DRUGS/ CSA SCHEDULES	TOLERANCE	DURATION (Hours)	USUAL METHODS OF ADMIN.	POSSIBLE EFFECTS	EFFECTS OF OVERDOSE	WITHDRAWAL SYNDROME
DEPRESSANTS						
Chloral Hydrate	Yes	5-8	Oral	Slurred speech, disorientation, drunken behavior without odor of alcohol	Shallow respiration, clammy skin, dilated pupils, weak and rapid pulse, coma, possible death	Anxiety, insomnia, tremors, delirium, convulsions, possible death
Barbiturates	Yes	1-16	Oral			
Benzodiazepines	Yes	4-8	Oral			
Methaqualone	Yes	4-8	Oral			
Glutethimide	Yes	4-8	Oral			
Other Depressants	Yes	4-8	Oral			

1 Designated a narcotic under the CSA. 2 Not designated a narcotic under the CSA.

DRUGS/ CSA SCHEDULES		TRADE OR OTHER NAMES	MEDICAL USES	DEPENDENCE Physical	DEPENDENCE Psychological
STIMULANTS					
Cocaine[1]	II	Coke, Flake, Snow, Crack	Local anesthetic	Possible	High
Amphetamines	II	Biphetamine, Delcobese, Desoxyn, Dexedrine, Obetrol	Attention deficit disorders, narcolepsy, weight control	Possible	High
Phenmetrazine	II	Preludin	Weight control	Possible	High
Methylphenidate	II	Ritalin	Attention deficit disorders, narcolepsy	Possible	Moderate
Other Stimulants	III IV	Adipex, Cylert, Didrex, Ionamin, Melfiat, Plegine, Sanorex, Tenuate, Tepanil, Prelu-2	Weight control	Possible	High

DRUGS/ CSA SCHEDULES	TOLERANCE	DURATION (Hours)	USUAL METHODS OF ADMIN.	POSSIBLE EFFECTS	EFFECTS OF OVERDOSE	WITHDRAWAL SYNDROME
STIMULANTS						
Cocaine[1]	Yes	1-2	Sniffed, smoked, injected	Increased alertness, excitation, euphoria, increased pulse rate & blood pressure, insomnia, loss of appetite	Agitation, increase in body temperature, hallucinations, convulsions, possible death	Apathy, long periods of sleep, irritability, depression, disorientation
Amphetamines	Yes	2-4	Oral, injected			
Phenmetrazine	Yes	2-4	Oral, injected			
Methylphenidate	Yes	2-4	Oral, injected			
Other Stimulants	Yes	2-4	Oral, injected			

1 Designated a narcotic under the CSA.   2 Not designated a narcotic under the CSA.

DRUGS/ CSA SCHEDULES		TRADE OR OTHER NAMES	MEDICAL USES	DEPENDENCE	
				Physical	Psychological
HALLUCINOGENS					
LSD	I	Acid, Microdot	None	None	Unknown
Mescaline and Peyote	I	Mexc, Buttons, Cactus	None	None	Unknown
Amphetamine Variants	I	2,5-DMA, PMA, STP, MDA, MDMA, TMA, DOM, DOB	None	Unknown	Unknown
Phencyclidine	II	PCP, Angel Dust, Hog	None	Unknown	High
Phencyclidine Analogues	I	PCE, PCPy, TCP	None	Unknown	High
Other Hallucinogens	I	Bufotenine, Ibogaine, DMT, DET, Psilocybin, Psilocyn	None	None	Unknown
CANNABIS					
Marijuana	I	Pot, Acapulco Gold, Grass, Reefer, Sinsemilla, Thai Sticks	None	Unknown	Moderate
Tetrahydrocannabinol	I II	THC, Marinol	Cancer chemotherapy antinauseant	Unknown	Moderate
Hashish	I	Hash	None	Unknown	Moderate
Hashish Oil	I	Hash Oil	None	Unknown	Moderate

DRUGS/ CSA SCHEDULES	TOLERANCE	DURATION (Hours)	USUAL METHODS OF ADMIN.	POSSIBLE EFFECTS	EFFECTS OF OVERDOSE	WITHDRAWAL SYNDROME
HALLUCINOGENS						
LSD	Yes	8-12	Oral	Illusions and hallucinations, poor perception of time and distance	Longer, more intense "trip" episodes, psychosis, possible death	Withdrawal syndrome not reported
Mescaline and Peyote	Yes	8-12	Oral			
Amphetamine Variants	Yes	Variable	Oral, injected			
Phencyclidine	Yes	Days	Smoked, oral, injected			
Phencyclidine Analogues	Yes	Days	Smoked, oral, injected			
Other Hallucinogens	Possible	Variable	Smoked, oral, injected, sniffed			
CANNABIS						
Marijuana	Yes	2-4	Smoked, oral	Euphoria, relaxed inhibitions, increased appetite, disoriented behavior	Fatigue, paranoia, possible psychosis	Insomnia, hyperactivity, and decreased appetite occasionally reported
Tetrahydrocannabinol	Yes	2-4	Smoked, oral			
Hashish	Yes	2-4	Smoked, oral			
Hashish Oil	Yes	2-4	Smoked, oral			

1 Designated a narcotic under the CSA.   2 Not designated a narcotic under the CSA.

About the Authors

Poet and novelist Richard Radford is an honors graduate of Boston State College and University of Massachusetts, Amherst. He is the author of several nonfiction works, including the *Golfer's Book of Trivia* and *Trooper*. A teacher and consultant in substance abuse, he formerly directed the Middlesex Shelter for the Homeless. He resides with his family in Brookline, Massachusetts where he is a deacon at St. Mary's parish. He summers in the Sebago Lake region of Maine. His novels range from romance to the upcoming mystery/suspense series starring Gavin, a Boston-based detective.

Jack Crowley is a graduate of the Carroll School of Management, Boston College where he earned a B.S. in Finance. His "graduate" work took him to the Fort Benning Infantry Officer Candidate School, where he was commissioned as a Second Lieutenant in 1969. Following his three-year stint in the Army, which included a tour of duty in Korea, he worked in private industry before joining the Bureau of Narcotics and Dangerous Drugs (DEA's predecessor agency) as an investigator in March, 1973. He is proud that his wife, Jane, is an Assistant Director of Admission at Boston College, where his daughter, Jane, is a junior, majoring in Pre-Med and English. He resides with his family in Brookline, Massachusetts.